PRAISE FOR

THE RACE FOR TIMBUKTU

"The story of the race between Laing, Clapperton, and others to reach Timbuktu makes for a gripping historical tale."   —*Wall Street Journal*

"Kryza's narration of Laing's perilous journey is electrifying."   —*Booklist*

"Frank Kryza has given those of us who still yearn for the days of romantic adventure, 'undiscovered empires,' and vast empty spaces on our maps an immense satisfaction. Kryza's tale is so well told that the reader is swept up in the African explorers' experience of heat, distance, disease, and marauding Saharan bands."
                    —Lynn Schooler, author of *The Last Shot* and *The Blue Bear*

"[Kryza is] a crafty storyteller with a sharp eye for detail. . . . He has peppered his tale with vivid portraits."   —*San Francisco Chronicle*

"Kryza, who lived in Africa for eleven years and traveled Laing's route, writes evocatively of the beauty of the African landscape and provides chilling glimpses of the barbarism of the slave trade."
                                        —*Publishers Weekly*

"With vivid insights and solid research . . . Kryza's evocations of the political infighting, the mesmerizing expanse of desert sands, and the elusive but deeply sinister Tuareg tribesmen are stunning."
                        —Pat Shipman, author of *To the Heart of the Nile*

About the Author

FRANK T. KRYZA spent eleven years in Africa and traveled much of the territory described in *The Race for Timbuktu*. Author of *The Power of Light*, he is a twenty-year veteran of the energy industry and a former newspaper reporter and editor. He lives in Dallas, Texas.

ALSO BY FRANK T. KRYZA

The Power of Light

HARPER ● PERENNIAL

A hardcover edition of this book was published in 2006 by Ecco,
an imprint of HarperCollins Publishers.

First Harper Perennial edition published 2007.

Designed by Kate Nichols

The Library of Congress has catalogued the hardcover edition as follows:
Kryza, Frank T.
The race for Timbuktu : in search of Africa's city of gold /
Frank T. Kryza.—1st ed.
p. cm.
ISBN-10: 0-06-056064-9
ISBN-13: 978-0-06-056064-5
1. Tombouctou (Mali)—History—19th century. 2. Laing, Alexander Gordon.
3. Africa, West—Discovery and exploration. 4. Explorers—Africa, West—Biography.
5. Travelers—Africa, West—Biography. 6. Explorers—Great Britain—Biography. I. Title.

DT551.9.T55K79   2006
966.23—dc22   2005049491

ISBN-10: 0-06-056065-7 (pbk.)
ISBN-13: 978-0-06-056065-2 (pbk.)

07 08 09 10 11 ❖/RRD 10 9 8 7 6 5 4 3 2 1

THE RACE FOR

TIMBUKTU

In Search of Africa's City of Gold

FRANK T. KRYZA

AN  BOOK

HARPER PERENNIAL

NEW YORK • LONDON • TORONTO • SYDNEY

IN MEMORY OF MY FATHER

E. GREGORY KRYZA
(1922–1998)

FOREIGN SERVICE OFFICER
(1950–1980)

CONTENTS

AUTHOR'S NOTE

IN WRITING THIS BOOK, I have often quoted firsthand sources dating from the early nineteenth century. In such quotations, the original and erratic spelling, punctuation, grammar, and typographical conventions (for example, the liberal use of uppercase initial letters for many words) have been retained, except in longer passages where I found them distracting. Similarly, abbreviations common in the era (RN—Royal Navy; HMB—His Majesty's Brig; RAC—Royal Africa Corps), but now unfamiliar, have been spelled out to avoid confusion.

Some proper names and names of vessels have variant spellings depending on the primary source consulted. I have employed the most commonly used form where this can be ascertained. When it was not possible to determine the most common form, I selected one and have been consistent in its use throughout the narrative.

Geographical places are referred to by their names at the time, with the modern equivalent, if different, in parentheses at first mention. My source for the modern spelling of geographical names is *Webster's New Geographical Dictionary.*

Mileage figures are given in statute miles—5,280 feet per mile. Temperatures cited are in degrees Fahrenheit. One pound sterling comprised twenty shillings; a shilling comprised twelve pence. A guinea equaled a pound plus a shilling. A sovereign was a gold coin worth a pound. When dollars are referred to, they are Spanish dollars unless otherwise stated.

Though it is difficult to attach a modern value to these figures, cost-of-living indicators for the era provide a basis for comparison. For example, in 1825, 500 pounds a year was a comfortable annual wage for a mid-level government bureaucrat living in London. The salary of 950 pounds a year paid to His Britannic Majesty's consul general to the Regency of Tripolitania, spent in Tripoli (where living costs were far lower than in London), would have accommodated a princely lifestyle.

Finally, a word about the transliteration of Arabic words. Writing Arabic words in English presents a number of difficulties, even for those familiar with both languages. In 1926, when T. E. Lawrence sent his 130,000-word manuscript of *Revolt in the Desert* to be typeset, a sharp-eyed proofreader noted that it was full of inconsistencies in the spelling of Arabic words. Among other things, the reader pointed out that "Jeddah" (the city) alternated with "Jidda" throughout the book, while a man whose name began as Sherif Abd *el Mayin* later became *el Main, el Mayein, el Muein, el Mayin,* and *le Muyein.* Lawrence refused to change the spellings. "Arabic words," he replied, "won't go into English exactly, for their consonants are not the same as ours, and their vowels, like ours, vary from district to district." So it is.

In early drafts, I found *jabal, jebel, gebel, gibel, and* gabal (meaning "mountain") appearing randomly throughout my pages, while *coffle, caffle, goffle, kaffila,* and *kafila* (meaning "caravan") also made seemingly spontaneous appearances. My first inclination was to solve this difficulty by omitting all Arabic words from the text, excluding proper names, but I soon discovered that this robbed the narrative of some of its flavor. I therefore restored some of the excluded words, settling on a single spelling throughout, trying to pick the transliteration that best captured, phonetically, the original sound as spoken by a native speaker from the southern Mediterranean. When its meaning was not obvious in the context of the sentence, I have provided a definition of the word at first mention.

INTRODUCTION

AFRICA'S GOLDEN CITY

I N THE FIRST TWO DECADES of the nineteenth century, no place burned more brightly in the imagination of European geographers—and fortune hunters—than the lost city of Timbuktu. For five centuries, legends about its wealth and culture had circulated from Venice to London. Like El Dorado in the Americas, Timbuktu assumed the quality of a mythic dream hidden in the unseen sprawl of Africa, a city paved with gold that lay just beyond the next range of mountains or a bit deeper in the unexplored African jungles.

Timbuktu, like El Dorado, held the explicit promise of riches and fame. No European explorer had been there and returned since the Middle Ages. Whoever got there first was guaranteed worldwide renown, but the journey would be bitter and hard—and could be fatal.

El Dorado, it turned out, was a city never found for the compelling reason that it did not exist. But Timbuktu was a real place. It is easily located on any modern map of Mali, near the center of the country, on the southern edge of the Sahara, about eight miles north of the river Niger.

From that moment in the 1780s when an armchair-bound coterie of

British aristocrats decided they *would* find it, along with the termination of the Niger, a determined search for Timbuktu was to occupy European explorers for the next fifty years.

Beyond its attraction as a center of great wealth, no city was more worthy of discovery for geographical and scientific reasons. Arabic texts documented that merchants from Tripoli to Morocco had gathered at Timbuktu since the late thirteenth or early fourteenth centuries, when it was incorporated into the great Malian Empire, to buy gold and slaves in exchange for prized European manufactured goods, cloth, horses, and the mined salt of the desert. Scholars reputedly made up as much as a quarter of the city's huge permanent population of 100,000, many of whom had studied in Cairo and other seats of Islamic culture, and who had themselves attracted students from an even wider ambit, stretching as far away as Mecca and Baghdad and deep into the northern reaches of sub-Saharan Africa, where Islam had made inroads unimagined in Europe.[*]

The Sahara was known mainly as a vast swath of inhospitable desert, but there was evidence in Moroccan archives that trade had been conducted across the region since early times. Evidence from the pre-Islamic era was sketchy, but it seemed likely that gold, animal skins, ivory, gemstones, perfumes, and black slaves from the Sudan states (in the terminology of the age, here, as elsewhere in this book, Sudan or "Soudan" refers to *all* those states southwest of the Sahara, not the modern nation of Sudan)[†] were exchanged for the manufactures and trinkets of the Phoenician, Roman, and Byzantine worlds. The Muslim Arab conquest of North Africa from the seventh century onward saw the establishment of a regular trans-Saharan trade in black slaves.

Having taken their empire, the Arabs sealed it off. Foreigners who dared

---

[*]Seen from space, the landmass of Africa can be divided roughly in two: a wet green central south and a dry sandy north. For centuries, the perception has been of two dissimilar regions: Africa south of the Sahara Desert, or sub-Saharan Africa; and North Africa. For some, the dividing line is more than the edge of the great sand sea visible from satellites—it is culture, language, skin tone, and more.

[†] "Sudan" is a contraction of *Bilad-as-Sudan*, Arabic for "Country of the Blacks," referring to the combined savanna and sahel stretching across Africa south of the Sahara. The word "savanna" is also derived from Arabic, meaning the grass-covered land between the sahel and tropical forests. "Sahel," also Arabic, means "coast" or "beach" and suggests terrain not quite as lifeless as a desert, yet not so grassy as savanna.

set foot in any part of it were confronted with a harrowing choice: either take a vow of abiding allegiance to Islam, forsaking all other loyalties, or face decapitation. An idea of the Arab empire's extent emerges from the documented travels of the indefatigable Berber wanderer Ibn Batuta, who spent forty years touring a score of countries from western China to modern-day Mali without once leaving the Arab hegemony.* Soon the integrated web of lands under Arab sway became a vast trading commonwealth, the principal objects of commerce at Timbuktu being salt, gold, and slaves.

Gold and slaves were paramount. The importance of the slave trade is illustrated by estimates suggesting that from the seventh to the end of the nineteenth centuries, between 9 and 13 million slaves were transported north across the Sahara. This is comparable to the numbers shipped seaward during the four centuries of the Atlantic slave trade, though the Saharan traffic has received less public discussion.

TIMBUKTU TODAY is an insignificant place, a village that festers, foul-smelling and intractable, in the heart of modern-day Mali. It has a population of less than 19,000, a fifth of the inhabitants it boasted in its golden age half a millennium ago. Though there is sporadic air service to Timbuktu, visitors to the town at the dawn of the twenty-first century can reach it reliably only by camel, Land Rover, shallow-draft riverboat, or on foot.

It is an ancient settlement, likely founded around 1100 as a seasonal camp by Tuareg nomads. Within the next hundred years, Timbuktu became an important crossroads and trading post for tribes who would otherwise have slaughtered one another in encounters outside its purlieus. Word of the goods for sale spread to the north, and it soon became a caravan destination for Arab traders from the Barbary States flanking the Mediterranean. Timbuktu was uniquely situated: although a desert town of the southern Sahara, it flourished on the banks of the Niger, in proximity to the great lakes and swamps of the upper river, thus connecting it to Africa's canopied rain forests and jungles, the place where "camel met canoe." Timbuktu was thus a nexus, a bridge—the only one

---

* His *Travels of Ibn Battuta,* in Sir Hamilton Gibb's magisterial 1958 translation for the Hakluyt Society, is as readable today as any modern travelogue.

in fact—between black Africa, a region into which even Arabs were loath to wander far, and the Sahara, a land blacks saw as off limits because of its inhospitable climate and the risk of abduction.

Timbuktu grew to become an opulent city boasting real infrastructure—markets, mosques, and important Islamic libraries and schools. The wealth to fund this cultural and intellectual development was generated from the gold mines of West Africa, worked by black slaves for their black and Arab masters, and the merchants who carried their goods on camels, oxen and asses, and men's heads, and in the canoes of tropical Africa's rivers and lakes.

This trading community was a strange hodgepodge—Arabs, Berbers, and black Africans, Muslims and pagans, the occasional Jew, and even, apparently, the rare Christian merchant from Venice or Lisbon. They gathered in sprawling covered markets to exchange salt and dates for grain from the savannas, slaves, ivory, feathers, and kola nuts from the forests beyond, and above all, gold from the far south.

By 1200, word of Timbuktu's wealth extended to the coasts of Guinea and the northern Mediterranean, where merchants bartered for gold thought to have come from Sudan. Europeans were dimly aware that the precious metal had originated far to the south. Some of this gold, in the form of a particularly fine dust packed in leather pouches, found its way to Europe, especially Venice. The gold dust was alleged to have originated in elusive Timbuktu.

The shroud clinging to the city, from the distant perspective of those merchants who traded along the Mediterranean littoral, did not lift until the fourteenth century, when Timbuktu's greatest ruler made his first appearance in the wider world. His name was Mansa* Musa, and his spectacular arrival in Cairo in 1324, accompanied by a vast and magnificent caravan, convinced medieval Europe in a way no rumor or speculation could that immense wealth lay hidden in the heart of Africa.

It was in that year, the seventeenth of his reign, that the great Mandingo emperor of ancient Mali crossed the Sahara on a pilgrimage to Mecca, passing through Egypt on his way. Cairo received the emperor

---

* *Mansa* is the word for "king" in the Mandingo language.

goggle-eyed. His procession of soldiers, courtiers, wives, and concubines "put Africa's sun to shame," in the words of one chronicler.

Surviving accounts tell us that Mansa Musa was accompanied by a caravan of sixty thousand men, including a retinue of twelve thousand slaves dressed in brocade and Persian silk. The emperor himself, on horseback, was preceded by five hundred slaves, each carrying a gold staff. A baggage train of eighty camels trailed, each carrying three hundred pounds of gold.

It is alleged that during the passage across the Sahara, the emperor's principal wife asked to have a bath. Mansa Musa put scores of slaves to work digging a ditch into which thousands of water bags were poured. The wife and concubines "swam with intense joy" in this artificial lake. The story makes no mention of the hundreds who must have died of thirst because of the loss of those water bags.

Tales of the camel trains and servants, along with the emperor's wives and women, gifts and arrogant horsemen, all the trappings of a king whose realm was as large as all of western Europe and, arguably, more civilized, lingered as familiar gossip after the ruler's departure from Egypt. The Cairenes, cynical and jaded, considered southern Africa to be inhabited by savages who were barely human, but Mansa Musa created an indelible impression to the contrary. An Arab historian who visited Cairo twelve years after the emperor's visit found the city still singing his praises. So deep had been his pockets that the flood of gold into Cairo markets had led to a persistent diminution in price from which the metal had not yet recovered. Even allowing for the exaggeration characteristic of ancient accounts of great rulers, by any standard of his time Mansa Musa was uncommonly wealthy and powerful.

Mansa Musa completed his pilgrimage and returned to his capital. Nothing more was ever heard from him, but he had left his mark. Timbuktu made its first appearance on a European map within fifty years, when Abraham Cresques, a cartographer based in Majorca, drew his famous *Catalan Atlas* for Charles V. He called the city "Tenbuch" and marked it as the capital of a huge Malian Empire ruled by a powerful Mandingo dynasty. He depicted a monarch on a throne. "This Negro lord," the inscription reads, "is called Musa Mali, Lord of the Negroes of

Guinea. So abundant is the gold which is found in his country that he is the richest and most noble king in all the land."

FOR TWO MORE CENTURIES the written record again lay blank. Then, in 1546, came the publication of *The History and Description of Africa and the Notable Things Contained Therein* by Leo Africanus (Leo the African). Leo, a Spanish Moor, had visited Timbuktu at the beginning of the century as a representative of the ruler of Fez. Still a young man, he was captured by Christian pirates and presented as an exceptionally learned slave to the Renaissance pope Leo X, who freed him, baptized him under his own name (Johannis Leo de Medici), and commissioned him to write a detailed survey of Africa. Leo's lavish portrayal of Timbuktu mesmerized European courts. It was mainly on the basis of his account that the legend of a gabled romantic city arose—a city poor men could dream of reaching to make their fortunes, magical in its remoteness yet tangible in its wealth:

> The rich king of Tombuto hath many plates and scepters of gold, some whereof weigh 1,300 poundes. He keeps a magnificent and well-furnished court. He hath always three thousand horsemen, and a great number of footmen that shoot poisoned arrows. Here are a great store of doctors, judges, priests, and other learned men that are bountifully maintained at the king's expense. And hither are brought diverse manuscripts of written books out of Barbaric, which are sold for more money than any other merchandise. The coin of Tombuto is of gold.

The Italian edition of Leo's travels was widely read, but it didn't make its real mark on European consciousness until 1600, when it reappeared in an English translation by John Pory. "As touching his exceeding Travels," wrote Pory, "I have marveled much how he should ever have escaped so many thousands of imminent dangers. How often he was in hazard to have become captive or to have his throat cut by the prancing Arabians or wild Moors? And how many times escaped he the lion's greedy mouth and the devouring jaws of the crocodile."

Leo himself was an unassuming man, a self-preserving trait in the papal court of the Medicis. "For my own part," he wrote, "when I heare evil of Africans being spoken of, I will affirme myself to be one of Granada, and when I perceive the national of Granada to be discommended, then I will professe my selfe to be an African." These two elements—the widespread distribution of the Pory edition, and Leo's engaging humanity—guaranteed that his story would have a profound impact.

For nearly three hundred years (until well into the nineteenth century), maps of the interior of Africa reflected, with hardly any change at all, the geography Leo portrayed. Leo, of course, had described Timbuktu at the peak of its power and prosperity. It was precisely the description a vulnerable Europe, depleted of humanity and wealth by the Crusades, wanted to hear. Timbuktu was a powerful *idea* as much as a place, its texture and weave to be shaped by each man who heard the tale. To popes and kings who needed money and reinforcements, it was the mythical kingdom of Prester John;* to merchants it was a great center of commerce with streets paved with precious metal and gemstones embedded in every wall; to politicians it was the capital of a great Central African Empire; and to scholars it was a place of learning whose priceless manuscripts would solve the mysteries of the age. Leo also accurately mentioned "cottages built of chalk and covered with thatch," but those hints of poverty interested no one and were ignored.

The Moorish conquest of Timbuktu in the sixteenth century cultivated the vision of wealth. Commercial correspondents in Marrakech staggered the European merchants who employed them with reports of Timbuktu's affluence. In August 1594 one of them, Laurence Madoc, told his principal in London of the arrival from Sudan of thirty mules laden with gold. A month later, Madoc wrote that "the rent of Tombucto is 60 quintals† of gold by the year, the goodness whereof you know. . . . The report is that Mahomed [the Moorish general] bringeth with him such an infinite treasure as I never heard of; it doth appear that they have more gold than any other part of the world beside. . . . This King of Morocco is like to be the greatest prince in the world for money, if he keeps this country. . . ."

---

* Prester John was a legendary medieval ruler thought to have reigned over a Christian kingdom beyond the boundaries of the Western world, perhaps in Ethiopia. Rumors about him began to circulate in Rome around the twelfth century. At the time of the Crusades, cash-strapped European monarchs sought him out to help fund conquest of the Holy Land.
† A quintal weighed anywhere from 100 to 130 modern pounds.

Five years later, Jasper Thomson, another English trader at Marrakech, advised London of the arrival of a "great store of pepper, unicorn's horns . . . and great quantity of eunuchs, dwarfs, and women and men slaves, besides fifteen virgins," together with "thirty camels laden with tibar, which is unrefined gold," and which he valued at 600,000 pounds.*

Once this trade with other countries took a firm grip of merchants on either side of the Mediterranean, the Arab monopoly in Africa was threatened. It was a time for the expansion of Europe, and in the van of the expansionists came the explorers. Western nations cast their eyes covetously on hitherto unknown lands.

In the next hundred years the Moors lost their hold on the Sudan and places south, their administration followed by anarchy. The flow of gold to Morocco dropped sharply, but it never wholly ceased, and the idea that there were huge gold mines near Timbuktu (whether they were presently productive or not) had taken deep root in the West.

Maps of Africa in the seventeenth century show fairy-tale landscapes drawn from rumor and imagination, liberally illustrated with drawings of fantastic animals and men to fill in the blank spaces. Timbuktu is pictured as a city plated with gold and precious jewels, where gold coins were used by the inhabitants as pocket change.

The European exploration of North and Central Africa, for all practical purposes, ceased with the fall of the Roman Empire, not to be reactivated for 1,400 years. For two millennia the mystery of Africa's interior had remained unsolved, despite the progress made elsewhere in the world. Remarkably, at the time of the first British undertaking to explore the southern fringe of the Sahara, planners in London knew more about the geography of the moon than they did of North and Central Africa.

By 1800, there remained few corners of the earth upon which some

---

* It is difficult, but not impossible, to estimate the value in today's money of this sum late in the reign of Elizabeth I. Tables of prices from the period show that fifteen good laying hens could be had in London for 1 pence (cost today: 20 pounds), a fledged peregrine falcon for 1 pound (4,800 pounds today), and a sword of the highest quality, suitable as a gift from the queen, for 5 pounds (24,000 pounds today). Using such tables, 600,000 pounds would be the equivalent in today's money of about 2.9 billion pounds sterling, or $5.2 billion U.S. If this parlor game has any value, it is to demonstrate that "600,000 pounds" was not the small sum (from the point of view of the financial press) that it is today.

Willem Janszoon Blaeu's 1630 Africae nova descriptio *("Africa newly described") is thought by many collectors to be the most beautiful seventeenth-century map of the continent. "Tenbuch" is shown where Leo Africanus placed it, but the topographical detail inland from coastal areas is pure fiction — especially, for example, the central lakes, which were based on legends dating to Ptolemy. To fill the remaining blank spaces, Blaeu added colorful drawings. It was in contemplation of an Irish copy of this map in 1733 that Jonathan Swift wrote:*

> *So geographers, in Afric-maps,*
> *With savage pictures fill their gaps*
> *And o'er uninhabitable downs*
> *Place elephants for want of towns*

restless European foot had not trod, but most of Africa remained a blank on the map, an empty space of eleven million square miles (an area *three times* the size of the present-day United States, including Alaska). Crossing the Sahara Desert and penetrating the Congo River basin were feats no one had lived to tell about.

Until that August day in 1826 when the first white man in three centuries is known to have walked through the gates of Timbuktu, some dozen European explorers tried to find the city. For two of these, Cap-

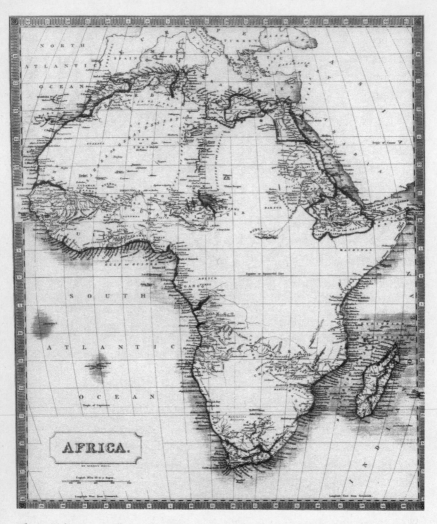

*The British cartographer Sidney Hall produced this continental map of Africa in
1829, just four years after Alexander Gordon Laing set out from Tripoli. It is considered one of the first "honest maps" of Africa, in the sense that Hall kept strictly to
known geographical facts, which meant that much of the interior of the continent
had to be left utterly blank. Note the enormous amount of white space—terra
incognita—amounting to some 80 percent of the surface area of the continent. It
was easier to map the surface of the moon with a telescope in 1829 than to produce
a detailed map of Africa.*

tain Hugh Clapperton and Major Alexander Gordon Laing, winning this prize became an intensely personal competition, crossing that thin line that separates a passionate but realizable dream from an irrational and dangerous obsession. Each man had a sense of entitlement to Timbuktu's discovery, feeling that the trophy was deservedly his, and both knew that success would be crowned with worldwide fame, a great deal of money, and a permanent niche, like that accorded to the lionized Captain James Cook, in the history of exploration.

It may be difficult to understand today how tantalizing this unsolved geographical puzzle was nearly two centuries ago, and why men would so willingly risk their lives in its solution. Every expedition into the interior returned defeated or never returned at all. And yet, the remedy seemed, at bottom, so simple: one just put one foot in front of the other. Any young man who could hike the wilds of Scotland could easily imagine himself claiming the prize.

These European explorers called themselves "African travelers," meaning they were private persons with amateur status, not trained professionals. They were sponsored (though rarely generously) by learned societies interested mainly in acquiring geographical knowledge. The purpose of early African exploration was scientific and amateur in the old sense: the search for and dissemination of learning thought to be the common property of mankind, undertaken by men who were motivated by love of the task. Of course, there were also the reinforcing motivations of treasure and fame.

But beneath the veneer of heroism and adventure, African exploration hid more sinister elements. Though Africa was a cipher to white men, caravan routes and rivers were familiar to those black Africans along the western coastline who traded in their own kingdoms, and to the Arabs who had ventured deep into the interior centuries before Europeans arrived. These men were willing to risk their lives no less than Western explorers—and thought nothing of inflicting untold suffering to secure the three commodities Africa offered in abundance: slaves, ivory, and gold.

To these Africans and Arabs, European travelers were "the devil's children" and "enemies of the Prophet," meddlesome interlopers who, with their idle talk of abolishing the slave trade and supplanting Arab caravans with British shipping, challenged the established order. European explorers by this light were self-indulgent and ignorant, though to be treated with respect for they possessed powerful technologies, especially weapons and medicines. They were men whose acts betrayed a disparagement of the indigenous peoples they encountered. Worse, they were incompetent leaders who risked caravans on ill-planned, badly organized missions.

The fulsome Victorian hagiographies and autobiographies of men like Sir Richard Burton and Henry Morton Stanley would later dismiss that perspective, if they mentioned it at all. Africans and Arabs were "savages" and "barbarians" in the European worldview (or worse, putting a religious gloss on it, pagans, infidels, and enemies of Christ). The story of African exploration, as recounted in English and French books until the middle of the twentieth century, has been fundamentally one-sided, more or less a boys' adventure story of heroism, conquest, and duty—history written black and white as a Victorian morality tale suitable for adolescents in upper-class boarding schools. That misses much of the story that is most interesting, and it distorts the truth shamefully.

The second decade of the nineteenth century marked the beginning of that period when scientific inquiry, industrial expansion, and territorial acquisitiveness coalesced to create the modern world. For Africa, it was an important and dangerous time: colonial expansion would soon put all but a fraction of the continent under a European yoke. By the 1820s, an intense rivalry had developed between France and Britain over control of the West African interior. In 1824, the French Geographical Society offered a cash prize of 10,000 francs for the first expedition from any nation to *return* from Timbuktu, sparking an international race that pitted British against French explorers to claim the trophy.

Only one British contestant would succeed in reaching the city, but death would cheat him of recognition.

His story is the story of this book.

PROLOGUE

———◆◆◆———

THE FRENCH ARMY CAPTAIN with the distinguished double-barreled name approached the Djingerebur Mosque, the oldest and largest house of worship in the fabled if decrepit city. It was here, on the steps outside, that the eighty-two-year-old city notable Mohammed Ould Mokhtar had agreed to meet him.

It was nine o'clock at night and already the streets were empty. The Frenchman walked in silence, his footsteps muffled by thick layers of sand. Even in the cool of evening, the fetid stench was unbearable—that day he had seen unburied cadavers lying in a trash heap in the city, bloated like balloons. *Des rues malades,* he thought. *Des rues mourantes et des rues mortes.** He longed for his comfortable bungalow in Algiers, where the climate was suggestive of the Côte d'Azure, far from this humid hole. He thought, too, of his family estate in the Ardennes, near the river Meuse. Anything to get his mind out and away from Timbuktu.

* "Sick streets, dying streets, dead streets."

In the street by the mosque, an orange glow came from the side of an eight-foot cube of mud bricks—the kerosene lantern in a single-roomed house. The dim light fell on Mohammed waiting on the steps, a handsome man despite his age, with a carefully trimmed gray beard, dressed in a Moroccan gown. One would not have guessed, from his appearance, how bloodthirsty his uncle had been.

Mohammed insisted on addressing his important visitor in French. He spoke it well for an Arab.

"*Bonjour, Sidi,*" said the old man.

"*Bonjour, Hajji,*" said the captain.

"*Vous allez bien?*"

"*Ça va, et vous?*"

"*Merci. Ça va.*"

And so it went on for fifteen or twenty seconds—the ritual of greeting that Arabs seemed to love as much as Frenchmen.

The old man invited his guest to follow him down a labyrinthine alley to a small teahouse a few hundred yards from the mosque. Sweat dripped from the Frenchman's brow, yet he cupped his hands politely around the glass of hot sweet tea as if to warm them. He noticed that he was trembling. He could not shake the premonition of death. It clung to his back like the entrails of dead animals he had seen rotting in the streets.

Mohammed was jabbering, something about Africans as a race lacking the sensitivity of Arabs. "They do not feel physical pain," Mohammed said. "They do not experience mental suffering. They do not feel emotions of love. They are insensate." He prattled on. What rubbish! This was the twentieth century. It was time to get down to business.

The tea drinking over, they left for the promised rendezvous with the object Mohammed had agreed to show him. They followed narrow streets winding between the walls of faded gray mud buildings, broken only by doorways and gaps where houses had crumbled into dust. Thick layers of gray-white sand carpeted everything. In every lane, houses had been destroyed by the rains or simply disintegrated from neglect. There was garbage everywhere, and that inescapable stench.

Does death bring peace? the Frenchman asked himself. Many of the local people were animists, despite their outward profession of Islam. The animist is always on the alert to find the hidden meaning of observable events, he thought, for the invisible is present and active, constantly intervening in a man's life. This is the animist's nightmare. What is the meaning of a lance plunged into a man's chest? What is the meaning of decapitation while one is still alive and can see the sword arcing toward one's neck?

Mohammed tapped gently at a wooden door. It was the custom in Timbuktu to leave your door open during the day so that visitors could walk in as they chose, without knocking. At night, doors were closed. Day or night, when one entered a building, one was blinded by darkness, stumbling on ill-lit stones. If the visitor thought his host might be at home, the caller announced his arrival halfway up the stone stairs by clapping. This is what Mohammed did. A female voice answered.

At the top of the stairs waited a buxom woman in a stained white robe. Mohammed spoke to her in Wolof, which the Frenchman did not understand. She led both men to a table, and there he saw it, gleaming with a blazing light even at night in the poorly lit room. It was certainly made of pure gold, 24 karat, for there was not the slightest sign of discoloration or tarnishing, despite its age. The jeweler had left his mark on the back—the piece was probably Maltese, though perhaps made by a local in Tripoli. He picked it up, felt its solid heft . . .

The Frenchman laughed, a soft chuckle, almost inaudible. Certainly this had been worth the trip, staying the extra day in this dank hell. Here was final, definitive proof of the identity of the partial skeleton he had dug up a few kilometers outside the city, the bones that had been languishing in a shallow grave for nearly a century. He had solved the mystery. General Clozel would be pleased.

The object, of course, was not a rooster at all, as he had been told. He should have guessed! He chuckled again, the old man and the fat woman not comprehending. The golden bird, *the golden bird!* It was not a rooster, but of course to these simple people who, in a lifetime, had likely not traveled fifty kilometers from this squalid place, it would *appear* to be a rooster, a golden rooster. . . .

THE RACE FOR TIMBUKTU

Chapter One

A SCOTSMAN AT TRIPOLI

ON MAY 9, 1825, in the silver half-light of dawn, HM Brig *Gannet* sailed at six knots into the southern Mediterranean port of Tripoli, all but her foresail furled to reduce her speed in the propelling breeze. Having navigated the rocks at the bay's seaward end, she passed the dour battlements of the "Old Castle," the crenellated fortress that served as palace and principal residence of Tripoli's bashaw or ruler, before steering for the central harbor and the deep anchorage reserved for her. Whirlpooling zephyrs kept her circling for a half hour before she could position herself to drop anchor. The British naval vessel had made the journey from Malta in a leisurely six days.

On the bridge with Captain Bruce stood the only debarking passenger, a tall, trimly built man in his thirties who carried himself with the self-assurance of a military officer, though he was dressed in civilian clothes. A Scotsman, Major Alexander Gordon Laing was en route from England.

He surveyed the harbor and coastline with alert interest as the square-rigged vessel's anchor chain rumbled from its hawsehole. The

Major Alexander Gordon Laing in
his late twenties, a year or two before
his arrival in Tripoli.

Gannet's prow swung slowly into the wind, now a soft south breeze laden with the smells of land.

On shore, a half mile from the ship, the gray stenciled silhouette of the Moorish fortress broke the center of the city's skyline. Slender minarets, flat housetops, and sturdy battlements flanked it in a crescent westward. The delicate palm fringe of an oasis dimmed to the east. Green-topped minarets caught the sun's orange-gold light in a cloudless sky. The white-walled city shimmered through the curtain of changing light.

Captain Bruce told Major Laing he could expect a warm welcome from the British consul, Colonel Warrington, "a lovable John Bull of a man, well known to half the admirals and captains in the Royal Navy." Indeed, Laing had already heard a great deal about Warrington in London.

He commented to Captain Bruce on the size of the desert city; he had expected a much smaller place. Tripoli was isolated, five hundred miles from the main highways of sea travel. He saw it now as a metropolis larger than he had imagined, though certainly a city much alone—the edges of the desert plainly visible to the east and west: Tripoli, the white-burnoused city, pulsating in its oasis on the edge of the desert.

As the *Gannet*'s hands secured the vessel, the *adan*—the Muslim call to prayer—drifted over town and harbor. The *Gannet*'s first mate reported he had ordered the vessel's longboat put alongside to take Laing ashore, but before it could be lowered, dozens of slim pirogues crowded the brig. These encircled the ship, their owners outshouting each other, naming the services and wares each was eager to hawk to the men on board—transport to shore, fresh fruit, potable water, leather goods. . . . Larger craft quickly followed, battling the pirogues to attach themselves to the *Gannet*'s hull. These were cargo lighters and flimsy dugouts manned by boatmen who wore loincloths and seemed engaged in a shrieking contest. Their job was to take cargo ashore and restock the hold. By 2 p.m., the American corvette *Cyrene,* under the command of Captain Grace, had arrived from Tunis and anchored next to the *Gannet.* By late afternoon, the bashaw himself sent a third vessel, a large flat galley manned by oarsmen, to collect Laing and his baggage and bring them to shore.

"Shaking hands with Captain Bruce and his officers," Laing confided to his diary, "I disembarked amidst the cheers of the crews of both *Gannet* and *Cyrene,* who manned the rigging on the occasion." His send-off was heady stuff for a junior officer; Laing felt he was accorded the treatment of a visiting head of state.

The port founded by the Phoenicians and later fortified by the

---

A plan of Tripoli, city and bay, as it looked in the nineteenth century. With its magnificent oval harbor, protected from storms by natural outcrops of rock, Tripoli was considered one of the safest ports in the Mediterranean. The heavily fortified "Old City," completely enclosed by walls, is on the peninsula at right, protected on three sides by water. Hanmer Warrington built his estate, "The English Garden," near the country palace of Tripoli's bashaw, or pasha, in the menshia, *or garden district, shown in the upper center of the map (marked "4").*

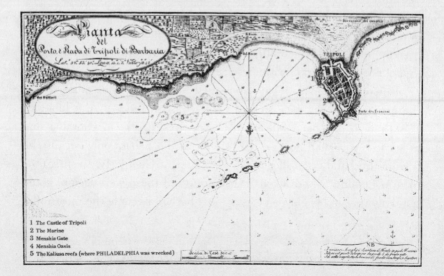

1 The Castle of Tripoli
2 The Marine
3 Menshia Gate
4 Menshia Oasis
5 The Kaliusa reefs (where PHILADELPHIA was wrecked)

Romans was now governed by a bashaw (or pasha), agent of the Sublime Porte in Constantinople.

The Regency of Tripoli was the most important of the three kingdoms on the southern Mediterranean coast (Algiers and Tunis being the two others) which owed their nominal independence to the Turkish sultan. Tripoli's bashaw was preceded by a functionary carrying his staff of "Three Horse Tails,"* a rank equivalent to the governors of the three most important provinces in the Ottoman Empire: those of Cairo, Budapest, and Baghdad. The royal yacht carrying Laing was festooned with the bashaw's flags and other symbols of office. It twisted its way through the fleet of Mediterranean sailing vessels that crammed the ancient harbor.

The distance from shore was less than fifteen hundred yards, but the bashaw's leaking vessel had nearly swamped when Laing jumped onto a flight of slime-coated stone steps leading to the wharf at the center of the mole. Here, a small mob of ragged Africans began to grapple for Laing's luggage. One man tried to make off with a sailor's duffel bag but was stopped when another man kneed him in the groin and demanded a coin for apprehending the thief. The less athletic contenders for porter were chased away and the Scotsman followed a procession of luggage bearers to the foot of the quay.

"On placing my foot on *terra firma*," Laing recalled, "(which was not until a very late hour, our progress being impeded by the freshening breeze which blew direct from the harbor) I was received by Hanmer Warrington, Esq., His Majesty's consul general, and treated with that friendly hospitality which all preceding travelers from this quarter have experienced in common with myself."

Rumors about Warrington abounded in London. Most alleged that the consul—a beefy, pear-shaped man—was no more than a bibulous Falstaff who had been released from debtors' prison in Gibraltar and exiled to his isolated post on the frontier of the Sahara only because he was the husband of an illegitimate daughter of George IV. Even so, the men in London who disliked Warrington (and these were legion) could not deny that in his eleven years at post he had become the most influ-

---

* Horse tails, a relic of the nomadic origin of the Ottoman Turks, were a mark of seniority. The sultan carried four, his senior governors three, the rest of the Barbary pashas only two.

ential of the officials posted to the Barbary States,* and that no one was more enthusiastic about England's colonization of Africa. His welcome of Laing that spring day would prove as sincere as it was effusive. The two had corresponded for months about Laing's expedition, and now at last, to Warrington's delight, the man was before him in the flesh, and the great voyage across the Sahara was about to begin.

As Laing and his host walked landward through the old city, the late afternoon revealed a perfect sky, unclouded blue, typical weather for May, Tripoli's most forgiving month. With the lowering sun the town had taken on a surreal whiteness, a brightness that was central to Tripoli's year-round loveliness. The light gave the gaps between the narrow buildings a gleaming, pulsing quality. Desert sand polished clean, and the buildings that made up Tripoli's low skyline, other than the biscuit color of the bashaw's Castle, which rose above the rest, were all a bold white. Undimmed by fog or haze, Tripoli's intense light reflected starkly on the city's smooth surfaces. The crumbling city walls were made of reddish wind-scarred sandstone. The mosque, the bashaw's harems, and the courtyards were aflame with bougainvillea. Cascading fountains blossomed everywhere.

Tripoli in 1825 was a much more important city than it is today. The flags of eight European countries and the United States snapped above their consulates overlooking the harbor. Tripoli was a place to gather intelligence, a place where information was as valuable as the tangible goods of trade; it was the commercial and diplomatic entrepôt of north-central Africa.

The city was bordered on the north by the Mediterranean Sea and on the south by the Jafara, or alluvial plain, from which rose the encircling Western Mountains. The mountains gave way in turn to the arid Hamada el Homra (the Red Plateau) and the Great Desert. A fertile coastal belt was magnificently cultivated with olives, the avenues separating them lined with fragrant eucalyptus trees.

About a mile from the southern gate and across the foreshore lay an

* That is, the four North African states of Tripolitania, Tunisia, Algeria, and Morocco. From the sixteenth century on, the first three were semiautonomous provinces of the Turkish Empire, while Morocco was independent.

oasis of palm trees, gardens, and villages, known as the *menshia*.* Within this oasis, which was the garden of Tripoli, lay a labyrinth of sandy lanes running between hedges of Indian fig and wells where oxen drew water to irrigate the plots of green peppers and alfalfa. This was the summer retreat of the Tripolitanian aristocracy, nestled in a forest of palm, fig, pomegranate, jasmine, and olive trees, where also were hidden the villages, country hous-es, the stables, mosques, and gardens of the bashaw and his large family.

Consul Warrington had acquired six acres of land in the *menshia* soon after his posting. He built a five-bedroom house there, and a garden that became famous. This estate, known as the "English Garden," was set in an unspoiled stretch of the country painted with palms, dark green bushes, square white houses, and gleaming cream-colored sand—not the high dunes of the inner desert, but soft, snowlike sheets that covered everything but the houses, vegetation, and, usually, the road.

Laing's first recorded impressions of Tripoli are revealing for their attention to detail, their insight, and their naïveté. He was both attracted and repulsed. He likened the city, on close inspection, to a prostitute:

> The Town of Tripoli, having for a background a beautiful mixture of the majestic Date, the broad leafed Fig, the wide spreading Mul-berry and Olive trees, is rather pleasantly situated on a flat promon-tory close to the water's edge; from eastward it is beheld to the best advantage, appearing from thence both gay and strongly fortified, numerous flags waving in the pliant air, with the tall spires of the various Mosques contributing materially to the former, and the lofty piles of embrasured walls to the latter effect; on landing, however, this favorable delusion is soon dispelled and Tripoli, like a Painted Beauty, loses all attraction on close inspection—gaiety vanishes and is lost to the eye as it travels amid the narrow, irregular dirty streets or lanes, and every impression of strength disappears, on an inspec-tion of the ill-constructed, misshapen, dilapidating walls.
>
> The Castle of the bashaw, an irregular Jail-looking pile, is intended (at least it would so appear) by its total detachment from the fortifications of the town, as a stronghold or place of defense

---

* Probably from the Arabic for "garden."

against enemies, either foreign or civil, who might possess themselves of the latter; but this also is delusion, for a determined foe, with pieces of artillery, battering rams, or even crow bars, might soon and with little difficulty effect an entrance, the walls though lofty, being constructed of small unhewn stones heaped irregularly one upon another, and held together by the presence of a copious incrustation of mortar. Tripoli with all its outward show, with all its pop gun parade, might be taken with greater ease than a well-stocked Mandingo town.

And yet, even to the seemingly jaded Laing, entering Tripoli's old city was to experience an odd sensation, something akin to that of a bucket dropping down a well—darkness, narrowness, coolness, surprise. The lanes were constricted. The British consulate, Laing's destination, was only a hundred yards inland, occupying a rectangular block of land adjacent to one of the most ancient Roman landmarks of the town, but negotiating narrow streets as dark as tunnels seemed to take forever.

The alley Shar'a Hara al-Kabira* cut at right angles from the quay directly into the most ancient quarter. Shar'a Hara al-Kabira was one of Tripoli's principal thoroughfares. It meandered along a dozen flat city blocks that Warrington, Laing, and their retinue now followed on foot, despite offers of conveyance from a half dozen mule-drawn *arabiya*, or gharries.

Laing caught sight of the Union Jack atop a flagpole fronting an imposing stone building. Here, Shar'a Hara al-Kabira wound upward between closely packed rows of dusty structures: warehouses, government offices, and stone residences occupied mainly by Tripoli's wealthier families. These homes stood two or three stories high. Their windows were barred and shuttered, and their arched doors—made of a rocklike black timber—were secured with ham-sized iron padlocks. From the upper end of the cramped street rose the diminutive sun-bleached minaret of one of Tripoli's minor mosques.

The narrow, twisting lane was packed with humanity, the crowd's density as arresting as its color. Lurching Berbers wore brown and orange

*"The Big Street."

cloaks. White-robed Arabs perched on bobbing Muscat donkeys smaller
than Great Danes. Strings of heavily laden camels, driven by beanpole
Africans in brilliantly hued wraparound sarongs, regularly interrupted the
journey's progress. Women's clothing seemed to shimmer in the shadows.
Black girls were swathed in flowing envelopes of Manchester cotton with
gaily printed patterns: caged lions, pineapples, horses, palm trees, monkeys on poles . . .

Women who glided by in grim black chadors, covering their bodies
from head to toe, suggested mysterious errands, tiny gold studs flashing
from nostrils, ankles, and necks. Bald heads of both sexes, shaved for
cleanliness and coolness, reflected the glare of a fading sun. The stench
of fresh excrement rose from open drains. Beggars with corkscrew limbs
and skull-like faces thrust their dirt-caked bowls from hidden crevices.

The torpid energy of the town suggested Asia more than Africa.
Enclosed by city walls, Tripoli resembled a nest of ants set in the desolate emptiness of surrounding wastelands. Tripoli reeked of the past, and
yet the city had also begun to show the ravages of the disruptive ways of
Europeans. It brought together sophistication and savagery, vitality and
languor, comfort and peril, loveliness and squalor—a blend that held all
the heady pong of romance.

Shar'a Hara al-Kabira crested a bluff forty feet above the quay. Laing
made his way with Warrington to the customs house, where he would
pass through the wringer of a tax bureaucracy that had taken root in the
farther reaches of the Sublime Porte eons before the British thought they
had invented it. The air was stifling; Laing was awash in perspiration.
The customs clerk sat behind a lectern with a forty-five-degree slope that
allowed his sweat to cascade to the ground without smearing the ink on
the forms he prepared in quadruplicate. Notwithstanding Warrington's
goading, the pair was delayed for half an hour.

Leaving the customs house, Laing walked to the consulate, a former
palace built by the ruling Karamanli dynasty and presented to the British
government in 1744. It was a large building of two stories standing in the
narrow lane behind the Gurgi Mosque in Shar'a al-Kurwash.* Bakers at

---

* "The Street of the Baker"

open-air ovens wielded wooden shovels, depositing crisp yellow loaves beside the white dough molds awaiting their turn. The baker worked below ground level so that the street itself became his countertop. The cry *"Barlik! Barlik!"* warned passersby of the emerging loaves.

The undersized doorway to the consulate was deceptive. Inside, an ample courtyard led to a staircase, and a graceful loggia looked out on the open space. Uniformed lackeys flanked the flight of steps to the door, and a bodyguard hovered near, for this was the distressed foreigner's sanctuary in Barbary.

Entering the consulate from the street, Laing passed through double doors into an arched passageway lined with stone benches where visitors waited. This passage in turn opened into the large central courtyard. Here, around a fountain and basin and small plots of earth from which grew orange trees, jasmine, and verbena, stood the dark rooms in which the consular servants lived. Here also resided the janissary dragomans, supplied for protection, translations, and spying by the bashaw. A kitchen, deep storerooms, and the consular prison surrounded a flight of broad steps that led to the more airy rooms above, built Turkish fashion to face inward.

On the first floor, the galleries overlooked a central court. The rooms within had smaller windows, protected by heavily waxed, dark wooden grilles and iron bars. These looked out on the narrow street below. From the gallery a narrow flight of stairs led to storerooms and a wide balustraded roof where, between rows of colored aromatic peppers spread to dry and hillocks of grain airing beneath the sky, the consular staff could walk and sit in the cool of the evening.

From this roof in the last hour of the day, Laing had a view of the harbor, the bashaw's Castle, the Marine Gate that led to the jetty (also entrance to the Jewish quarter, which at nightfall was shut off from the Muslim precincts of the city), the arch of the great Roman general and emperor Lucius Septimius Severus, and the whole steaming heap of resignation and decay that was Tripoli at twilight.

And yet, there was something else. Beneath the low throbbing pulse of whispered gossip and behind the flicker of candles lit in tiny ogive windows, there was, for Englishmen especially, the promise of excitement and secrets revealed, an enticing whiff of the gutter and the slum, of cheap drinks and tawny, doe-eyed women, of pleasures not easily found in England.

Tripoli was a crucible of raw emotions (as all uncompromising places are), a home to physical sensations that could scarcely be made real to anyone, like Laing, who was virgin to them. But they were *there,* he could sense it. It was hinted in those whispers and flickers of light in the darkness. Whatever you wanted, it could be had in Tripoli—for a price. History, in the Tripolitanian phrase, was a continuity of sorrows and of ecstasies. Tripoli's history was deep and penetrated to the human bone, to the core of feeling.

The calm at twilight was an illusion, for it concealed a brash hunger, a carnality that woke with the setting sun.

Chapter Two

———•◆•———

THE AFRICAN ASSOCIATION

HE BEGINNING of the age of African exploration can be dated to the day—June 9, 1788, a Monday—and almost to the hour. That evening, nine titled Londoners led by Sir Joseph Banks, the great naturalist and friend of Captain James Cook, met for dinner in an upstairs private room at St. Albans Tavern off Pall Mall.

They were members of the Saturday's Club, one of the small elitist eating clubs in the London of that epoch. This social coterie met weekly so that friends with common interests could gather informally to enjoy an excellent roast (along with a fine old port) and discuss the big ideas of the day. The Saturday's Club had a membership of twelve, of whom three were absent that night. The members were all wealthy, from the highest ranks of the British establishment, and wonderfully representative of the enlightened spirit of their times.

Sir Joseph Banks, who would emerge as their leader, was president of the Royal Society (which he ruled with an iron fist for forty-two years) as well as secretary of the Society of Dilettanti. A product of Harrow and Eton, the inheritor of a large fortune, and an accomplished botanist, he

Sir Joseph Banks, president of the Royal Society and a founder of the African Association, as he appeared about 1800, in his late fifties.

had accompanied Cook's first expedition around the world in the *Endeavour,* which he equipped with his own funds. Henry Beaufoy, M.P., a Quaker, became an abolitionist, as did the Earl of Galloway. The Bishop of Llandaff was both an abolitionist and a scientist, holding the chair of chemistry at Cambridge. Sir John Sinclair pioneered the science of statistics and later became governor-general of India. Lord Rawdon, another fellow of the Royal Society, drove American rebels from Bunker Hill outside Boston. He would later become governor of Bengal; he purchased the island of Singapore. Other members had equal claim to power, wealth, or fame; the caliber of membership in the Saturday's Club was high.

The conversation that Monday turned to what Banks felt was the great failing of the Age of Enlightenment. At a time when Captain Cook and others had proved that men could sail around the world, Britons knew less about the interior of Africa than the geographers of ancient Greece and Rome. Before they retired for the evening, Banks and his friends founded the Association for Promoting the Discovery of the Interior of Africa, an organization devoted to gathering scientific facts, though not averse to making money, through trade and conquest in Africa. Each member pledged five gold guineas* a year to the effort, and members of the committee were enjoined not to divulge any information, except to other members, that they might glean from persons sent on missions of discovery. They identified the river Niger and the legendary cities it supported, notably Timbuktu, as their first priority. No European had ever set eyes on the river.

The members resolved:

---

* The equivalent in today's currency of about $1,350. The first-year budget was thus just over $12,000, though Banks and others would soon augment it—with a certain stinginess—from their considerable private wealth.

That, as no species of information is more ardently desired, or more generally useful, than that which improves the science of Geography; and as the vast Continent of Africa, notwithstanding the efforts of the ancients, and the wishes of the moderns, is still in a great measure unexplored, the members of this club do form themselves into an Association for Promoting the Discovery of the Inland Parts of that Quarter of the World.

Though the prospect of profitable commerce with the unknown continent was certainly a motivating factor (it was probably no accident that the St. Albans worthies set their sights on Africa so soon after England lost her vast American territories, only five years before, in 1783), the group had more noble motives as well: the abolition of the slave trade and a sincere desire for knowledge.

The "African Association," as it soon became known, met at Banks's comfortable mansion at 32 Soho Square. Thanks to Banks's position as president of the Royal Society, celebrity traveler, scientific adviser to governments, friend of George III, and what one admirer called "the father of research and friend of the adventurous traveller," his library at Soho Square was open to all. Soon the African Association was entertaining visitors from overseas who had an interest in African exploration. In modern parlance, Banks was a wonderful networker.

The members discovered that little of practical value could be gleaned from documents; reconnaissance on the ground was essential. They did not waste any time. The first explorer selected was an American, John Ledyard, a thirty-seven-year-old native of Groton, Connecticut. Within a month of the dinner at St. Albans Tavern, he was on his way.

The son of a sailor, Ledyard had attended Dartmouth College in 1772. He left school to live among the Iroquois of the Six Nations near the Canadian border, whom he hoped to convert to Christianity. In 1773, he persuaded Captain Richard Deshon to take him on as a sailor bound for the Barbary Coast. At Gibraltar, he enlisted in (and quickly deserted) the British navy. He served in the British army, and later as a marine. He later reported for duty with Captain Cook, with whom he visited the Canary Islands, Cape Verde Island, the Cape of Good Hope, Tasmania, New Zealand, Tahiti, and what was later to become California and Oregon. He was a member of Cook's last expedition and saw Cook killed in Hawaii. In 1783 he published *A Journal of Captain Cook's Last Voyage to the Pacific*.

Ledyard next tried to establish a fur-exporting business, which failed. With the help of Thomas Jefferson, then United States minister to France, he planned a voyage across Russia, through Siberia, to Alaska, and across North America to Virginia. Jefferson admired the young New Englander, as he noted in his autobiography:

> In 1786, while at Paris, I became acquainted with John Ledyard, of Connecticut, a man of genius, of some science, and of fearless courage and enterprise. He had accompanied Captain Cook . . . had distinguished himself by an unrivalled intrepidity. . . . Ledyard had come to Paris in the hope of forming a company to engage in the fur trade of the Western coast of America. He was disappointed in this, and, being out of business, and of a roaming, restless character, I suggested to him the enterprise of exploring the western part of our continent, by passing through St. Petersburg to Kamchatka, and procuring a passage thence in some of the Russian vessels to Nootka Sound, whence he might make his way across the continent to the United States; and I undertook to have the permission of the Empress of Russia solicited.

Ledyard set off in 1786, after Jefferson obtained the necessary letters of transit. From Sweden, he tried to cross the frozen Gulf of Bothnia on foot, but the ice gave way. He reached St. Petersburg in precarious shape. The Portuguese ambassador to Russia saved him, loaning him twenty pounds. He traveled six thousand miles to Yakutsk in Siberia, but bad weather prevented him from crossing the straits. Russian soldiers seized him, putting him on a sled for the Polish border. If he ever returned to Russia, he was warned, he would be hanged.

Two years later, he knocked on the door of Sir Joseph's library in Soho Square, in rags, penniless, but ready to set out again on another daring emprise. Banks told him, "knowing his temper, that he could recommend him for an adventure almost as perilous as the one from which he had just returned." Banks promptly proposed Ledyard to the selection committee, whose members felt that his inability to speak Arabic was offset by his "adventurous nature." They spoke of him as a man who "from his youth had felt an invincible desire to make himself acquainted with the unknown, or imperfectly discovered regions of the globe."

Sir Joseph sent Ledyard to Henry Beaufoy, a plutocrat wine merchant and leader of the Society for the Abolition of Slaves. Beaufoy noted "the manliness of Ledyard's person, the breadth of his chest, the openness of his countenance and the inquietude of his eye." Beaufoy unrolled a map of Africa and drew a line from Cairo eastward, explaining the route he thought Ledyard should take. He asked the American when he would be ready to leave.

"Tomorrow morning," he said.

Beaufoy, surprised by this zeal, said he did not think he could write up his instructions so soon.

As it happens, Beaufoy's directives were ridiculous, revealing just how little England knew about the lands the association proposed to explore. From Cairo, Ledyard was to proceed to Mecca, where no Christian could hope to pass unnoticed, "and from thence (unless insuperable difficulties shall occur) he shall cross the Red Sea, and taking the route of Nubia shall traverse the Continent of Africa as nearly as possible in the direction of the Niger."

Ledyard left England on June 30, 1788, and arrived in Cairo on August 19. He found lodgings in a convent maintained by the Order of Recollects, advising his sponsors that Cairo in August sweltered, but that he had "seen it hotter in Philadelphia." Biding his time, Ledyard prepared for his inland journey and toured the Egyptian capital. He visited the slave market and met a minister of the bey. His eagerness to depart accelerated when he found that Christians in Cairo were insulted and badgered in the streets, especially when they tried to make converts to Christianity (as he regularly did).

Ledyard sent his impressions to Beaufoy in a series of letters, but suddenly they stopped. Weeks later, the British consul in Cairo wrote to say that Ledyard had died.

A bilious complaint [Beaufoy wrote in the proceedings], the consequence of vexatious delays in the promised departure of the caravan, had induced him to try the effect of too powerful a dose of the

acid of vitriol, and the sudden uneasiness and burning pain which
followed the uncautious draught, compelled him to seek the relief
of the strongest Tartar emetic. A continued discharge of blood discovered the danger of his situation. . . . [H]e was decently interred
in the neighborhood of such of the English as had ended their days
in the capital of Egypt.

In plain English, Ledyard had inadvertently poisoned himself with a
fatal dose of sulfuric acid.

Banks and Beaufoy did not long mourn him, for they had already
hedged their bets. While Ledyard tackled the crossing of Africa from east
to west, the African Association recruited a second explorer who would
cross it from north to south. This was Simon Lucas, whom Beaufoy probably knew as the son of a fellow wine merchant. Lucas, sent to Cadiz as a
young man to learn the sherry trade, was captured by pirates and sold as
a slave to the Moroccan bey. Released three years later, he was appointed
British vice-consul to the court of the man who held him captive.

Lucas returned to London sixteen years later, where he was appointed
Oriental interpreter at the Court of St. James. There he met members of
the African Association, many of whom had strong ties to the royal family.
On June 13, 1788, only four days after the African Association had been
formed, Banks paid a call on Lord Sydney, who had held cabinet rank and
was intensely interested in British exploration and colonization.* Banks
wanted Sydney's help in getting Lucas released from duties at court to
take part in an expedition to Africa. Sydney put the matter to George III,
who agreed to grant Lucas leave.

An undated note in Beaufoy's handwriting says, "Mr. Lucas, Oriental
interpreter, whose salary is 60 pounds per annum, offers to proceed, by
way of Gibraltar and Tripoli to Fezzan,† provided his salary is continued
during his absence." He seemed a choice recruit: not only did he speak
Arabic, but at court he had become friendly with the Tripolitanian ambassador.

The association financed the Lucas and Ledyard expeditions with

---

* Sydney, Australia, was named for him.
† Fezzan was a large desert kingdom roughly south of present-day Libya. Its southern border
was many hundreds of miles from the river Niger.

453 pounds sterling. Each explorer received an advance of 100 pounds, with the possibility of drawing further sums en route. To forestall requests for money, the selection committee made a virtue of its stinginess, "persuaded that in such an undertaking poverty is a better protection than wealth." A poor man offered less of a temptation to thieves. The tiny commissions appear not to have deterred Ledyard or Lucas, for it was not the pursuit of money that drew either man to the African wilds.

Simon Lucas left England in August 1788, reaching Tripoli in mid-October. While Ledyard lay dying in Cairo, Lucas was looking for an escort to take him across the Libyan Desert, just as Alexander Gordon Laing would do nearly forty years later. When he told the bashaw (in those days, Ali Karamanli, Yusuf's father) that he wanted to visit the Fezzan, the ruler remarked that no Christian had ever attempted such a trip and that Lucas would probably die if he tried. Lucas said his only interest lay in collecting plants and Roman antiquities. The bashaw told him, as he and his son would tell other explorers taking the Tripoli route, that, personally, he would be glad to help, but the moment was not auspicious because unnamed tribes in the south continued to defy his authority. Lucas, looking elsewhere for help, found two sheikhs from the Fezzan who offered to escort him. He left Tripoli with them in February 1789. He wore Turkish dress and let his hair grow so that, as he wrote to his sponsors, he looked "like a London Jew in deep mourning."

Carrying presents for the ruler of Fezzan (including brandy, which was that Muslim's favorite drink), Lucas traveled east along the coast of Libya to the seaside city of Misurata. As he was about to turn inland, the local governor warned him that warring tribes would bar his way. With the prudence of the civil servant he had become, Lucas decided to wait until the tribes had calmed down. The two Fezzan sheikhs grew impatient and left him, but not before he had extracted new geographical information about southern Libya. Left on his own, Lucas decided to return to England.

On June 30, 1789, he wrote to Banks that he had arrived penniless in Marseilles and drawn some cash at a local bank. He apologized for not pursuing his assigned route, but noted that his journey had produced valuable information and that he had brought back a collection of rare seeds. Privately, Lucas felt that destiny held better things for him. In

1798, named consul to Tripoli, he prospered for eight years before dying at post (to be succeeded not long after by Hanmer Warrington).

The members of the African Association were powerful men used to getting their way. The failure of the first two missions and the death of their first explorer acted as a spur, not a deterrent, to future missions. In fact, while their "African travelers" were in the field, the membership met with two North African visitors to London who claimed to have been to Timbuktu. They suggested that the Niger would be most easily reached from the river Gambia.

In all their talk of Africa, the Niger and Timbuktu captured the members' greatest interest. Timbuktu, more than anything else, embodied the unattainable. As Beaufoy wrote, its discovery, and that of the Niger, was "made doubly interesting by the consideration of its having engaged the attention, and baffled the researchers of the most inquisitive and most powerful nations of antiquity."

Recognizing now the difficulty of passing through northern deserts controlled by Muslims, Banks and Beaufoy decided to send the next expedition inward from the West African coast. The association's next traveler, an Irish major, Daniel Houghton, had served off the coast of Senegal, and was sent to the mouth of the Gambia. His instructions were to push up that river as far as possible and learn whatever he could about "the rise, the course, and the termination of the Niger, as well as of the various nations that inhabit its borders."

He began well enough and reached the rapids known as Barra Kunda Falls, the farthest navigable point on the Gambia, where he was assured by his guides that he could walk the "Timbouctoo Road" with just a stick in his hand. Experience proved otherwise. Houghton followed his instructions as best he could, but from the outset he had aroused suspicion among native traders, who robbed and killed him. Before they succeeded, Houghton penetrated farther into the African interior than any other European. Years later it transpired that he died in 1791 at a village named Simbing (in present-day Mali), about 160 miles north of the Niger and 500 miles short of Timbuktu. He had been lured into the Sahara, robbed, and left to die.

In the dispatches Houghton sent to London during his journey, carried back to the coast by pairs of tribesmen who specialized in carrying messages across the wilderness for Arab merchants, he correctly surmised that the Niger rose in the mountains south of the Gambia and that it likely flowed from west to east.

Sir Joseph next sent out Mungo Park, a young Scottish physician who had sailed in 1791 as ship's surgeon on an East India Company vessel bound for Sumatra. Park dazzled the membership of the association, Banks finding him "a young man of no mean talents . . . sufficiently instructed in the use of Hadley's quadrant to make the necessary observations; geographer enough to trace his path through the wilderness, and not unacquainted with natural history."

In May 1795, Park sailed aboard the brig *Endeavour*, bound for the Gambia for a cargo of ivory, and reached Jilifree on the river's northern bank thirty days later. From there he struck inland, following Houghton's route.

Dr. Park's mission lasted more than two and a half years, and his adventures and accomplishments rank among the greatest ever in the annals of African exploration. As in the case of Houghton, tribesmen constantly harassed him, demanding tolls for the right to pass through their lands. In the Moorish kingdom of Ludamar, where, he learned, Houghton had been robbed, he wrote that the tribesmen "hissed, shouted, and abused me, they even spit in my face, with a view to irritating me, and afford them a pretext for seizing my luggage. But finding such insults had not the desired effect, they had recourse in the final and decisive argument, that I was a Christian, and that my property was lawful plunder."

A band of Muslim horsemen took him prisoner and brought him to the camp of a local chieftain who ordered his right hand cut off, his eyes plucked out, and his life ended. Park escaped only because, at that moment, an enemy tribe attacked the camp. He pressed on, ridden with fever, bereft of supplies, tormented by thirst and sandstorms. He came out of Muslim territory and entered the country of the Bambara, who proved friendly. He followed a group from a place called Kaarta heading east toward the town of Segou. "As we approached the town," Park later wrote,

I was fortunate to overtake the Kaartans . . . and we rode together through some marshy ground, where, as I was looking round anxiously for the river, one of them called out, *"Geo affili"* (see the water); and looking forward, I saw with infinite pleasure the great object of my mission, the long-sought and majestic Niger, glittering to the morning sun, as broad as the Thames at Westminster, and flowing slowly to the eastward. I hastened to the brink, and, having drank of the water, lifted up my fervent thanks in prayer to the Great Ruler of all things for having thus crowned my endeavors with success.

The date was June 20, 1796, and Park had become the first European on record to lay eyes on the river Niger, and to record that it flowed *inland*, to the east. He vowed to follow it to Timbuktu and on to its mouth. He did not succeed. His situation swiftly deteriorated as he moved back into Muslim lands. In the unbearable heat, his horse collapsed, the tropical rains began, and on August 25 a gang of thieves jumped him, stripping him naked.

"I was now convinced," he later wrote with characteristic understatement, "that the obstacles to my further progress were insurmountable." Upon reaching Silla on the Niger, still some four hundred miles from Timbuktu, he turned back, struggling for a year to find the Atlantic. In June 1797, he reached the mouth of the Gambia and boarded an American slaving vessel which carried him as far as Antigua, where he caught a mail packet home. He landed at Falmouth just before Christmas 1797, and went straight to London.

News of Park's accomplishments thrilled the African Association (and indeed all of England). He was the first white man to penetrate the forbidding interior of Africa for the sole purpose of finding out what lay there, and to come back alive. He invented a new and glorious calling, creating an adventurous species of hero: the lone, brave African explorer: the African traveler. This beau ideal soon captured the imagination, fed the fantasies, and filled the literature of Europe.

English society lionized Mungo Park. The book he wrote, *Travels into the Interior Districts of Africa,* became an instant best-seller. His success was of great help to the African Association, whose membership soared to more than one hundred and came to include former prime ministers, the fabulously wealthy bankers Coutts and Hoare, the beer brewer

Whitbread, the famous potter Josiah Wedgwood, and the leader of the antislavery campaign William Wilberforce. James Rennell, a noted geographer and former surveyor-general of Bengal, provided illustrations and maps for Park's book.

Banks, with Park's triumph to point to, now launched a campaign to involve the British government (and money) in African exploration. When the rivalry between Britain and Napoleonic France spilled over into Africa, exploration took on a new, political dimension. While the African Association's explorers pushed up the Gambia, French traders moved up the Senegal.

In 1799, after the Napoleonic invasion of Egypt, Banks urged his government to seize control of the Niger and its trade before the French did. It was prescient advice.

———◆·◆———

Chapter Three

A WEDDING IN
THE ENGLISH GARDEN

HOUGH THE BRITISH CONSULATE near the center of town
had served as the residence of English envoys to Tripoli since 1788,
Hanmer Warrington rarely spent the night *en ville*. The building
was in a state of poor repair, its structure and trappings seeming to him
unrepresentative both of Great Britain and of his own personal prestige.
Warrington much preferred the spacious comforts, solitude, and wine cel-
lar of his well-guarded country home. One of his first official purchases had
been a stout six-oared boat to row him from the *menshia* to town and
back.

On the evening of Laing's arrival, after giving him a brief tour and
allowing the younger man to take in the sights, sounds, and smells of
Tripoli, he carried him off in his boat to the English Garden two miles
outside the city walls.

There, he introduced Laing to his wife; to Louisa, his flighty and
flirtatious youngest daughter; to Emma, the middle daughter, thin and of
medium height; to Jane, the oldest, a big, strong, strapping girl; to George,
the boy who would later plead to accompany Laing on his desert journey;

The "English Garden," Hanmer Warrington's country home outside Tripoli.

and to Frederick, the son who acted as his father's interpreter and was soon to help Laing with his mastery of Arabic.

The Warrington brood at the time of Laing's arrival consisted of the consul and his wife, seven sons, and the three daughters (a fourth daughter had died in 1815), but the whole family was rarely in one place and not all were present to welcome the visitor from London.

Warrington promised his guest a steak dinner. Rare was the European in Tripoli who served steak to his guests, since most local "beef" was butchered from camels that had collapsed, usually from disease, in the sewage-strewn streets. Even boiled vegetables presented a risk to the unacclimated. As for the steak dinner, somehow the resourceful consul had managed to obtain the real thing—aged cuts of beef brought that day from the hold of the *Gannet,* packed in salt and tarragon leaves in Malta.

In the meantime, Laing was escorted to his rooms. At the consul's residence one could at least have a good wash. In the bathroom adjoining his bedroom, Laing squeezed into a galvanized sheet-metal tub and sloshed himself down with hot water, his first soak in the week since leaving Malta. Another luxury awaited him on the porch outside: a tray bearing a choice of whiskey and beer. Laing took the Scotch, which he drank neat.

On this, their first evening together, Laing tried to get to know his corpulent host, the smiling bon vivant who was to be his sponsor, superior, and collaborator. Hanmer Warrington was an enigma, if clearly a man under some pressure. There was, Laing knew, among the European consuls in Tripoli a constant vying for influence, particularly between the British and the French. Could that explain the British consul's constant boasting? In Warrington's own estimation, with his arrival eleven years earlier, in 1814, England's fortunes had risen, for the bashaw found in him a character as strong as his own. It was sometimes said in consular circles that it was Warrington, not Yusuf Bashaw Karamanli, who sat on Tripoli's throne. The consul did nothing to gainsay this view.

FORTY-SEVEN YEARS OF AGE at the time of his first meeting with Laing, Hanmer Warrington was the son of a country parson, born in 1778 of an old Welsh family. He grew up in Denbighshire, a hilly country near Wrexham and the rivers Dee, Conway, and Clwyd in North Wales, where he earned a reputation as a horseman. He wanted to be a soldier. At sixteen, he joined the First Dragoon Guards by purchasing a cornetcy, the fifth and lowest grade of a commissioned officer in a cavalry troop, and the man who carried the colors. In 1802 he sold out with the rank of major. All of his military service, except for six months in Europe, was spent in Britain.

On November 27, 1798, at Croydon, Surrey, he married Jane Eliza Pryce from the Isle of Wight, by whom he would sire eleven children. The couple's first child, Jane Elizabeth, was born in Surrey in 1802. In 1812, after brief service in Spain during the Peninsular War, he was posted to Gibraltar as a minor official. He incurred gambling debts, but whatever court patronage he may have enjoyed, it did not extend to financial help. By 1813 he was the target of a lawsuit for collection of 500 pounds. A maneuver to return to London was rebuffed, but with official help he soon found a safe berth on the other side of the Mediterranean, installed as consul at Tripoli, a post he would hold for the next thirty-two years.

His wife Jane was rumored to be the natural daughter of George IV. No impregnable evidence has ever been found of this, but Warrington did in later years seem to be under some mysterious protective umbrella, held over him (perhaps) by members of the royal family. This may account for his long tour at Tripoli, which was often punctuated by official missteps.

Warrington made a good first impression at the bashaw's court largely because of a spectacular windfall he produced for Yusuf Karamanli—a 40,000-pound loan from the Colonial Office. His influence grew with the British shelling of Algiers in 1816, a reprisal against the enslavement of Christians by the Barbary pirates. The bashaw observed that when the Royal Navy was introduced into any military equation in the south Mediterranean, the British emerged victorious. Yusuf Bashaw freed several hundred Christian slaves in his dungeons—mainly Danes, Italians, Spaniards, and Greeks—with alacrity, before English warships sailed into *his* harbor. From then on, the bashaw maintained a healthy respect for British sea power.

By the time of Laing's visit, money and the threat of force had helped Warrington become an éminence grise in the bashaw's court, advising him on matters that had nothing to do with his official brief. Laing knew that with Warrington occupying the consulate, he would always be well received in Tripoli. In London, Warrington was considered a loose cannon, though a man useful to the Crown's interests.

The Warrington household was characterized, in a memoir by the wife of the Dutch consul, as "wild," though stern and puritanical in some things. "There was no question of discipline, order, or rules," she wrote. "Everyone did what he or she wanted, and, like the proverb, 'every horseman wanted to be Captain.'"

THAT FIRST cool May night under Warrington's roof, surrounded by a bevy of adoring women, it must have seemed to the well-read young officer that the whole Warrington clan had stepped out of the pages of Jane Austen. The second daughter, Emma, was a "delicate flowerlike girl with the clear pellucid skin of the consumptive," he recorded.

Laing fell instantly in love with her. The expression of her "haunting, shadowy eyes" made his heart "contract every time he looked at her." In the ensuing weeks, on rides over the rolling sands of the sahel and the cool green lanes of the *menshia*, in long intimate talks in the English Garden, where peach, pomegranate, lemon, almond, and jasmine trees were planted among the ruined marbles of Roman and Greek goddesses Warrington had expropriated from Leptis Magna,* Emma Warrington fell passionately in love with the handsome young Scotsman, just as he had with her. In the tiny consular community, it was rumored they were inseparable.

Warrington père was later to write to Earl Bathurst, head of the Colonial Office and his immediate chief back at Whitehall, that Laing was a "well set-up man, of fine physique, highly gifted in many ways. The girl herself is of a headstrong and tempestuous disposition, quite unable to withstand his ardent lovemaking. For one thing, she is younger than he, and is perhaps a little flattered by his attentions, for by reason of the pending mission to Timbuktu, he is already a public figure. . . ."

Mother and father watched the development of Emma and Laing's sudden attachment with misgiving. Warrington sincerely liked Laing, but to approve his daughter's hasty attachment to a man soon departing on a hazardous journey seemed to defy common sense. At the same time, and despite his fatherly concern, Warrington had reasons of his own for abetting the match.

By the time Laing arrived in Tripoli, Warrington's star had dimmed. Though he boasted to his new guest "of being able to do anything and everything in Tripoli," this was no longer true. The bashaw now ruled by playing the consuls against one another. The new French consul, Joseph-Louis, Baron Rousseau, was a distinguished Arabist who could converse with the bashaw without an interpreter. (Warrington's Arabic was appalling, though his Italian, a language the bashaw spoke fluently, was passable.) Warrington, lodged at his country villa, disliked the urbane, studious, constrained French colleague who rarely ventured outside the walls of Tripoli and who snubbed Warrington's invitations to the English

* A ruin sixty miles south of Tripoli, the site of some of the world's finest Roman architecture.

Garden. Rousseau thought Warrington drank too much and talked indiscreetly of private matters. He had said as much publicly, in the presence of other consuls.

Further inflaming Warrington's already splenetic emotions, the French consul's son—a weedy, anemic, artistic young man named Timoléon—had had the effrontery to court Emma. To the British consul, who often fell asleep with a copy of Shakespeare on his chest and an emptied bottle of "dry sack" at his side, this set of circumstances must have seemed a twisted Tripolitanian version of *Romeo and Juliet*. Indeed, in an era when the battle of Waterloo was a recent memory, to see a Warrington daughter married to a Frenchman, even a rich one, was unthinkable; the very idea made him apoplectic. He was determined to be more successful than Lord Capulet had been in safeguarding his daughter.

With hindsight, one wonders whether Warrington nudged Emma in Laing's direction to foil Timoléon's advances. If so, it was not a difficult plot to hoe. Laing had a self-professed "ardent nature." While still in his teens, he had written that "passionately fond of the fair sex, I had always in my eye some Dulcinea, on whom I used to dote, make verses, and squander away money." For her part, it appears that Emma regarded Timoléon as a neutered man, more of a helpmeet, cherished friend, and someone to talk to (in an environment where there were few, if any, eligible men). By contrast, from the day of their first dinner together, she perceived Laing as different—virile, brave, well traveled, already a person of some distinction in London and the greater world. She was swept off her feet. Warrington, blind to human emotions (other than his own), may well have overestimated Emma's attachment to Timoléon.

By the beginning of June, Laing was sending strong hints to friends back home of the direction his love life was taking: he asked his friend James Bandinel to buy him "a handsome little cabinet of mineralogical specimens, such a one as will suit a lady of taste and refinement. You must not form any conclusions from this extraordinary request. I am no more than interested, *much interested,* in the lady in question."

Though he had little else to do besides brush up on his Arabic, Laing's days in Tripoli were not spent exclusively courting Emma. He also tried to charm the bashaw into permitting him to leave the city under official protection, for bandits were prowling just beyond the city gates. The bashaw could only wonder at the bizarre English penchant for Saharan exploration, though he was astute enough to make money from it. He tested the waters regularly, for with each new explorer he seemed to be able to raise the price of security.

Of course, this had to be done diplomatically, for the bashaw's patronage could never appear to be for sale. The transaction had to be effected in a roundabout way, as part of a Gordian ritual. In the weeks after Laing's arrival, as he calculated with his advisers just how much cash he could extract, the bashaw kept making excuses for not granting an audience. Warrington wrote the Colonial Office that "sooner than suffer Major Laing to be detained for about four months, I should not hesitate to give His Highness a small sum to enable him to meet his expenses."

The bashaw would not think of accepting a trivial fee, Lord Bathurst replied, acknowledging "the folly of His Highness, who would not express his wants, and in consequence of those wants not being complied with, would detain Major Laing, thereby defeating the views of England." Warrington wrote back that "at the moment the Bashaw was professing such disinterested conduct, a glance of his eye and the rubbing together of his thumb and finger gave strong indications that he expected something more substantial between them."

He told the bashaw's chamberlain he could give him 500 pounds. The reply: "Tell the consul whatever he does, I shall be satisfied with," a lukewarm response Warrington correctly understood to mean the bashaw thought the British could be more generous. The consul then promised 2,500 pounds to be paid in stages as Laing progressed south, achieving set benchmarks, plus another 5,500 pounds that *might* be paid later during the expedition, assuming additional goals were met. Significantly, Warrington did not report the larger number to London, rightly fearing Lord Bathurst's probable opposition to committing so much money before Laing had taken the first step out of Tripoli.

Warrington also gave Laing a letter of credit, signed by himself and Yusuf Bashaw Karamanli, "the Slave of Allah," which authorized "the bearer Major Laing to draw on us for any money which he may require during his journey into the Interior of Africa." The preliminary negotiations concluded, Laing was at last invited to the Castle.

"It was not until the thirteenth day after my arrival that His Highness the Bashaw condescended to honour me with an audience," Laing wrote.

> Various are the rumors which were in circulation with regard to the cause of the Bashaw's coolness: one day it was said that His Highness never received anyone during Rhamadan, which at the time of my arrival was twenty days old; the next, it was rumored that His Highness had received a *douceur* [a gift or gratuity] from another Government [the French] to throw obstacles in the way of my accomplishing that object which they were desirous of effecting from another quarter; a third day the rebellion which had arisen in the Garian Mountains was assigned as the cause of the delay, and with every morning's sun fresh conjectures were formed. . . .

The senior government administration of Tripoli was housed entirely in the bashaw's "Castle." This mélange of buildings, surrounded by high walls rising from bedrock and resting on Byzantine and Spanish foundations, formed a rough quadrilateral at the southeastern angle of the city walls. Its four bastions overlooked Tripoli harbor from the north, covered the entrance to the town from the south, and faced the city below to the west. Castle guns controlled both sea and land approaches, and if necessary could quell a revolt originating from within Tripoli itself. Over the centuries, the bashaw's predecessors as masters of the Castle had shown that they trusted no one, a wise policy and one for which the strange physical structure of the buildings was perfectly suited.

There were only two ways to get into the Castle, both through narrow gates in high walls. The first, facing the city, led across an easily defended ramp. This was regarded as the main entrance. The other, used mainly by the bashaw and his senior aides, gave direct access to boats at a jetty. In an emergency, this would permit the bashaw to escape by sea.

Behind the unscalable walls lay an irregular maze of chambers, courtyards, covered passageways, stairs, armories, kitchens, stables, barracks, harems, and prisons. There was a small mosque for the bashaw's personal use, a hidden strong room for his holdings of gold and jewels, and even a pharmacy and infirmary. Private apartments housed the bashaw, his harem of wives and concubines, his personal guards, the treasury and secretariat staff, his garrison of janissaries, along with platoons of servants to care for all of them. Far below floor level were dungeons housing never less than hundreds of slaves.

The giant compound "had a dreary and disreputable air about it," according to Laing. European visitors wrote of the feeling of being "suffocated by a miasma of wretchedness that the Castle passageways engendered, halls that gave some the feeling of leading to some dreadful abode for the entombment of the living."

Not all of this concern was the result of a heightened pre-Victorian sense of the dramatic, for no sane person entered the Castle of Tripoli without anxiety. One never knew in advance what might be the outcome of an interview with the bashaw. Though rare by 1825, it was not unheard of for summary executions (by beheading with a scimitar) to take place on the spot in the throne room, in the bashaw's presence and at his command. As early as 1810, an American surgeon, Dr. Jonathan Cowdery, had treated the bashaw for volcanic fits of rage and a seizure condition, possibly epilepsy. The bashaw himself, in an explosion of anger, had once struck off the head of a Sicilian slave, drenching his silk clothes in a gusher of blood. He also made two recorded attempts to kill Peter Lyle, the Scotsman who served as his pirate/admiral-in-chief (later also his son-in-law).

Given this tension, an atmosphere of fear haunted the dark passages and courtyards of the Castle. The bashaw's brand of government, born in the shadow of the Grand

A view of an elaborately decorated corridor, this one bordering an atrium open to the sky, in the "Old Castle," Bashaw Yusuf Karamanli's huge fortress-like palace in Tripoli, from a photograph taken in the 1930s.

Serail in Constantinople, was one where fear was endemic, for treachery and distrust were part of the Turkish psychology of rulership. This imported atmosphere of duplicity festered nicely in Tripoli's stifling climate. Suspicions thrived in the Castle. At night, though iron doors separating interior parts of the compound were bolted, massive entrance gates were locked and the keys handed ceremoniously to the bashaw, who slept with them under his pillow. He also kept the key to his treasury.

As an official visitor accompanied by his consul and making a ceremonial call upon the bashaw in the official *divan* (privy council), Laing's visit, like all consular visits, was choreographed days in advance. At the appointed hour, Laing headed toward the narrow causeway leading from the city into the maze of buildings. He was in full uniform, with the rank of major. Warrington wore his own spectacular consular dress, which he had designed himself: the plumed hat of a field marshal, the red and blue coat of an ambassador, the epaulets of an admiral, and the trousers, boots, and spurs of a cavalry officer. The two Englishmen and their retainers passed across the drawbridge over a dry moat and into a wide courtyard filled with soldiers, passing the stables of the bashaw's famous gray horses. At the end of this yard, in his habitual chair, sat the striking figure of the Grand Kehya (chamberlain), an expatriate Russian renegade dressed in colored silks and a vast turban.

The Grand Kehya rose, the guard presented arms, and the party marched slowly into a labyrinth of dark passages. Laing stumbled along these ill-kept, gloomy tunnels, their floors crumbling, their twists and turns blocked by shadowy figures of guards. The retinue passed through a series of solid doors lapped with iron plates, emerging at intervals into miniature courtyards open to the sky but barred with iron gratings and surrounded by galleries supported on carved arches bright with tiles. Eventually, the lilting sounds of the bashaw's *nubar,* or band of timbrel, drum, and reeds, could be heard, and the party arrived in a large courtyard outside the throne room. Though the time of his appointment had been set, the exterior chamber was congested with palace officials, bedraggled Christian slaves, suppliants for justice, and criminals awaiting judgment. These persons circled and dodged like hyperactive children. From here, a small flight of steps led to the audience chamber itself, its doors guarded by two fearsomely large men armed with matchlocks and scimitars.

Beyond the double doors, Laing occasionally glimpsed a scene of splendor. The walls of the outsized room were lined with bright Chinese tiles along which were ranged towering *hampas* (black slaves) armed to the teeth with blunderbusses, forming a background to the assembled members of the bashaw's *divan*—religious dignitaries, and sheikhs, all in colorful clothes and uniforms who were standing at a safe distance from a raised dais at the far end of the room.

In spite of falling revenues, Yusuf Karamanli indulged in rebuilding parts of his palace, and these contrasted with the comparative squalor of the Castle as a whole. Contingents of Italian workmen, both slaves and free, brought their skills in masonry, stucco carving, and colored marbles to the state apartments and the public rooms.

The audience chamber often startled foreign visitors. An American consul reported that the bashaw received his guests with a pomp that far exceeded that of Algiers, which was wrongly considered the richest and most sophisticated of the regencies by Westerners. Bright carpets and cushions from Constantinople and gilt chairs from France were thrown about the room. Innumerable gilt-framed mirrors (some still bearing the labels of their manufacturer in Marseilles) reflected the deferential circle of the bashaw's courtiers. On a throne of plush carpets and tasseled cushions sat the bashaw himself, a tiny plumlike figure on this huge stage, his personal guard surrounding him, a water pipe close at hand. He wore sumptuous silks of psychedelic coloring—refulgent blues, reds, pinks, violets, greens.

The British delegation was eventually shepherded into the throne room by the Grand Kehya, where Laing spent more than an hour with the bashaw and his court exchanging formalities and pleasantries and discussing the proposed expedition. This was succeeded by a grand meal in a neighboring hall, where the bashaw demonstrated his fondness for food and alcohol, as well as his considerable skill as a negotiator.

Laing later wrote Lord Bathurst: "His Highness informed me in the most unequivocal language that the door was shut to me unless I opened it with money, that without some pecuniary *douceur* he would continue to detain me in Tripoli for months upon the most frivolous pretences." When he received this message, Bathurst was furious at the mission's mounting cost and delay. He sent Warrington a chastening letter urging him to prod Tripoli's ruler more vigorously.

Consul Warrington, skilled at mediating precisely these kinds of troubles, quickly arranged that Laing should leave Tripoli with a Ghadames (Ghadamis) merchant named Sheikh Babani. It was always wise to pay someone in a caravan, preferably a substantial merchant, to see that one came to no mischief at the hands of fellow travelers. Sheikh Babani would play this role. They would head southwest through Ghadames and In Salah (Insalah) to Timbuktu, where Babani claimed to have good connections. Laing now had to wait only until Sheikh Babani was ready to leave. In the meantime, as often happened in Tripoli, tactical problems with the bashaw were speedily sorted out, roadblocks that had appeared as insurmountable as boulders now melted away like a morning fog. Tripoli's ruler was satisfied at last with the sums he had extorted from England.

And in the midst of all these official goings-on, Laing proposed to Emma. Though Warrington may have supported the match in private, in his role as protective father he overtly tried to prevent it. He pointed out that Laing should at least inform his parents. Laing replied that by the time a reply came from Edinburgh, he would be halfway to Timbuktu. Warrington asked how Laing proposed to support his wife on army pay. Laing replied that once he had reached Timbuktu, his fortune would be assured (an assertion the consul surely could not doubt). Warrington asked what would happen if he failed to reach the city. Laing's reply is telling of the role history held for him: "It is my destiny," he said, "to do so." The lovers were insistent on marriage and in the end the bemused parents relented.

On July 14, 1825, Alexander Gordon Laing married Emma Warrington amid the blossoms and perfumes of the English Garden. He was like a serviceman about to go overseas who marries a girl he has just met and may never see again, but with Warrington looking over his shoulder and in control of the villa, Laing (so far as we know) was not allowed to consummate the marriage. The consul made a point of telling Lord Bathurst so. His odd blend of Oriental intrigue and Victorian hypocrisy fairly oozes from the letter he sent to Earl Bathurst on the day of the wedding.

Tripoli, 14th July 1825

My Lord,

    I have the honor to Inform your Lordship that Major Laing was this morning married to my Second Daughter.

    Although I am aware that Major Laing is a very gentlemanly, honorable and good man still I must allow a more wild, enthusiastic and romantic attachment never before existed and consequently every remonstrance, every argument, & every feeling of disapprobation was resorted to by me to prevent even an engagement under the existing circumstance the disadvantages so evidently appearing to attach to my daughter.

    After a voluminous correspondence, I found my wishes, exertions, entreaties, and displeasure, quite futile & of no avail, & under all circumstances, both for the public good, as well as their mutual happiness, I was obliged to consent to perform the ceremony, under the most sacred, & most solemn obligation that they are not to cohabit till the marriage is duly performed by a clergyman of the established Church of England, and as my honor is so much involved, that I shall take due care they never be one Second from under the observation of myself or Mrs. Warrington.

    Now my Lord I do not conceive a father can possibly be placed in a more delicate situation, as long as doubts may arise as to the power and legality invested in me as His Majesty's Consul General to unite two of His Majesty's Subjects, as Man and Wife, & till that doubt is completely removed I will take good care my daughter remains as pure & chaste as snow.

    I have the honor to submit to your Lordship's consideration the Certificate I gave of the ceremony having been performed by me, in my official capacity, and as it is a question of great importance I wish to know whether a marriage so performed is equally binding as if duly solemnized by a clergyman of the established Church of England.

    At various times under various circumstances, various marriages have taken place at Algiers and Tunis, but I am not satisfied as to their legality. May I therefore beg and pray your Lordship's opinion on this most important & interesting question.

Hanmer Warrington

To the Right Honble
The Earl Bathurst K.G.
His Majesty's Secretary of State
Colonial Department

The wedding certificate was witnessed by Warrington, his wife and other daughters, and the consuls of the United States and Spain. A handwritten note on the letter, added in London, reads, "copy sent to the King." No doubt it was sent to amuse him. George IV was not one to take marriage—his own or anyone else's—very seriously.

This letter shows Warrington at his most duplicitous, and it was likely written more for Laing's benefit than for Lord Bathurst's. The wily consul fails to mention that over the years he had performed *scores* of marriages in Tripoli, all of them perfectly legal. (He was, in fact, the chief British magistrate in Tripoli, where he held autarchic powers—he routinely sentenced British subjects from Malta to stiff prison terms in a jail he wholly controlled, and could, theoretically, have hanged any of them. Performing marriages was among the least of his prerogatives.) The truth is that he wanted to preserve Emma's chastity, to ensure her future prospects should Laing perish, which must have appeared to him an alarming and very real contingency.

The groom consoled his bride by promising to be back in four or five months, certainly in time to celebrate Christmas.

ON JULY 17 Laing paid a farewell visit to the bashaw, who advised him that on the route he was taking "you must open the doors with a silver key," and gave him an escort of 150 horsemen out of Tripoli.

In the predawn half-light of the following day, veiled by a cold, silvery mist, the Englishman and his entourage met Sheikh Babani and his followers outside the walls of the white city. Babani was ready. Laing went up to the sheikh and embraced him. Could he trust this man? The old merchant laid the palms of his hands on Laing's head, as nomad fathers do when they greet their sons, and pronounced the words of welcome:

"*Salam alaikum.*" (Peace be with you.)

"Alaikum wa sàlam," responded Laing. (Peace to you too.)

"Yak, la bas." (No evil to you.)

"La bas." (No evil.)

"La bas, Hamdullah." (No evil, thanks be to God.)

And so it went for several minutes: the stylized exchange of ritual courtesies and veiled allusions that were (and still are) the formal and traditional openings of conversation among Saharan nomads, each line echoed by the other like the chorus of a beloved old song. Laing soon lost the drift, but Babani was impressed. This was no ordinary *nasrani.*[*]

As he departed with Sheikh Babani's caravan on the road to Ghadames, Laing must have felt a mixture of disappointment and exhilaration—disappointment at leaving behind his virgin bride and exhilaration at starting on a route that had not been visited by Europeans since Roman times. To reach Timbuktu, the golden city of the Sudan, he would have to cross two thousand miles of the harshest desert in Africa, territories where the bashaw's jurisdiction did not extend. Conditions could be unimaginably harsh in these lands, where human life was held more cheaply than a good pair of boots. Lawless Tuareg[†] bands made their living off the plunder of caravans.

Laing imagined he would be in Timbuktu in weeks, months at most, though deep in his heart he must have known that if his mission were that easy, it would likely already have been accomplished.

Others, certainly, including Dr. Mungo Park, had tried before and failed.

---

[*] That is, a Nazarene: a man from Nazareth, Christ's village, a term that loosely meant "Christian" or "white man" but was less offensive than the abusive name usually reserved for non-Muslims: *kafir* (infidel).

[†] "Tuareg" is a word derived from the Arabic phrase "the abandoned of God," because many of these Bedouin people did not embrace Islam as fervently as other peoples conquered during the Arab invasion. In modern usage, "Tuareg" refers both to the plural and singular, though in some nineteenth- and twentieth-century English texts readers will find the singular of "Tuareg" shown as "Targui."

Chapter Four

————◆◆◆————

WHITE MAN'S GRAVE

IN 1797, when Mungo Park returned from his first expedition, Timbuktu still beckoned and the puzzle of the Niger's course and the location of its mouth remained unsolved. No one knew this better than Dr. Park himself. As soon as he was back in Britain, he began making plans for a second mission. This would have to wait nearly six years, for Park married and began raising a family.

Considering the meager wages the African Association paid its explorers (Park received ten shillings a day), his new domestic responsibilities meant settling down and earning a living, which his training as a physician allowed him to do.

While practicing medicine in Scotland, Park had plenty of time to sort out what he had learned and develop his own theory of the Niger, especially concerning the location of its mouth. Three mutually exclusive hypotheses about the river's outlet prevailed. The oldest and most venerated supposed, as a geographer of the period wrote, "that the Niger has an inland termination somewhere in the eastern part of Africa . . . and that it is partly discharged into inland lakes, which have no communication with the sea, and partly spread over a wide extent of level country, and lost in sands or evaporated by the heat of the sun."

Detractors claimed that "to account for such a phenomenon, a great inland sea, bearing some resemblance to the Caspian or the Aral, appears to be necessary. But besides that the existence of so vast a body of water without any outlet into the ocean, is in itself an improbable circumstance . . . such a sea, if it really existed, could hardly have remained a secret to the ancients, and entirely unknown at the present day."*

Another argument asserted that the Niger flowed into the Nile. Most geographers of the period tended to dismiss this idea as popular conjecture rather than as an opinion deduced from reasoning, "since nothing appears to be alleged in its support, except the mere circumstance of the course of the river being in the direction of the Nile."

The third hypothesis held that the Niger, after reaching Wangara (Ouangara, in present-day Mali), "takes a direction towards the south, and being joined by other rivers from that part of Africa, makes a great turn from thence towards the southwest, and pursues its course till it approaches . . . the gulf of Guinea, when it divides and discharges itself by different channels into the Atlantic; after having formed a great Delta."

This turned out to be a remarkably accurate description of the river's course and termination, though at the time the reasoning supporting it seemed "hazardous and uncertain." Geographical objections to it arose, resulting in the widely held view, as one geographer of the period put it, that "the data on which it is grounded are all of them wholly gratuitous."

Park came to adopt and champion a fourth conjecture. This held that the Niger took the turn to the south after Wangara or Timbuktu, as previously proposed, but persisted in that direction rather than turning southwest, and flowed into the estuary of the Congo. The two rivers, in this novel construction, converged.

This idea was put forward by George Maxwell, another Scotsman fascinated by Africa who made his living trading on the Congo River. For

---

* A patent nonsense. Lake Victoria, exceeded in size only by North America's Lake Superior, remained hidden from European eyes until 1858, when John Hanning Speke stumbled upon it. Lake Chad was also undiscovered.

years he had championed the river's importance, pointing out little-known facts about the Congo's powerful currents and flow. The river's discharge* pushed fresh water out to sea so forcefully and in such quantities that ships approaching its mouth encountered it before they sighted land—the lowered buoyancy caused ships to sink a foot or two, alarming the crew. Deducing its immense size from that, Maxwell accurately ranked the Congo as second only to the Amazon in its freshwater outflow, and argued that it offered a natural way for the exploration of and trade with the African interior. But only after the question of the Niger's geography became a lively subject of inquiry—in the wake of Park's first expedition—did Maxwell succeed in getting the right people in London to pay attention.

Park, according to one of his biographers, "adopted Mr. Maxwell's sentiments relative to the termination of the Niger in their utmost extent, and persevered in that opinion to the end of his life." Though well aware of the geographical objections that could be raised against this theory, he found solutions to overcome each.

If the Niger was a tributary of the Congo, the combined length of the two rivers would be well over 4,000 miles (thus making it the world's longest). To this, Park answered, why not? After all, the Amazon was then accepted to be more than 3,500 miles long. Of the objection that the river would have to flow through a great mountain chain through the middle of the continent, he dismissed this on the ground no real evidence supported the existence of such mountains. To get around the difficulty that changes in the Niger's elevation did not correspond to those of the Congo and its placid flow, Park supposed that the Niger passed through a series of seventeen or eighteen lakes, buffering its discharge. He wrote Earl Camden, then the British colonial secretary, "[T]he quantity of water discharged into the Atlantic by the Congo cannot be accounted for on any other known principle but that it is the termination of the Niger."

By 1802 Park had tired of his sedentary family life as a country doctor in Peebles, Scotland, and was suffering from wanderlust. Married life was boring, and ambition was a stronger pull than a growing practice, a wife, and three children. He told his friend the novelist Sir Walter Scott that he

---

*The Congo's outflow would late be calculated to be two million cubic feet per second. At 2,900 miles in length, it is the world's sixth longest river.

The debonair and handsome Scottish physician Mungo Park, as he appeared in the frontispiece of his book, published in England after his first expedition, making him an overnight celebrity. By then, Park had lost his good looks, appearing to friends to have aged thirty years, in part because tropical disease and stress had caused all of his hair to fall out.

would "rather brave Africa and all its horrors than wear out his life in long and toilsome rides over the hills of Scotland." He wrote to Banks about the lack of satisfaction he found as a country doctor and of his wish for a more exciting career. Banks replied that he would be happy to recommend him, but that the British government was now taking an interest in African exploration, slowing down the process of outfitting new expeditions. In due course, Park was called to London and offered command of a military unit to explore that part of the Niger beyond where he had gone before, and to determine where it emptied—whether into Saharan sands in an inland sea, or the ocean.

In 1804, Park, Banks, and Lord Camden proposed a second Niger expedition, this one on a larger scale. The British government had already sent a consul to Senegambia, saw huge potential in African colonization, and was easily persuaded to provide Park with whatever military support he needed to negotiate trade treaties and discover the Niger's course. England and France had begun their competition for African colonies.

Though persuaded of the truth of Maxwell's hypotheses, Park chose not to follow the trader's plan of exploration up the Congo estuary. More familiar with the route he had taken on his first expedition, he wanted to start once more from the Gambia, strike overland to the Niger, and then sail down the river to its mouth.

If the river did terminate in a great lake in Wangara, he would return across the desert to the coast at the Bight of Benin. But, convinced that he would wind up in the Congo's estuary, he planned to sail from there to the West Indies. If his theory proved right, he told Camden, the expedition, "though attended with extreme danger, promises to be productive of the utmost advantages to Great Britain. Considered in a commercial point of view, it is second only to the discovery of the Cape of Good Hope, and in a geographical point of view is certainly the greatest discovery that remains to be made in the world." (Most geographers of the time would have disagreed: they considered the origin of the Nile an even greater mystery, though less important commercially.)

A number of Britons regarded Park's thinking as fallacious and tried to discourage him from embarking on another dangerous journey. Banks, however, backed him with complete confidence.

I am aware that Mr. Park's expedition is one of the most hazardous a man can undertake, but I cannot agree with those who think it is too hazardous to be attempted; it is by similar hazards of human life alone that we can hope to penetrate the obscurity of the internal face of Africa; we are wholly ignorant of the country between the Niger and the Congo and can explore it only by incurring the most frightful hazards.

Park set off at the end of January 1805 aboard the troopship HMS *Crescent* and arrived at Goree at the mouth of the Gambia two months later. He brought with him five navy carpenters, convicts in Portsmouth who received pardons in exchange for volunteering to build boats to navigate the river. In Goree, he recruited thirty-two soldiers and two sailors from the Royal Africa Corps garrison, also convicts; service in Africa was their punishment. They joined the party with the promise of double pay and discharge from the corps upon completion of the expedition. Park, commissioned a brevet captain, also had an army lieutenant, his brother-in-law, and a friend from Scotland. Though granted authority to hire up to twenty African porters, Park discovered that "no inducement could prevail on a single Negro to accompany me," so his party consisted wholly of white men. They sailed up the Gambia aboard the *Crescent* to the town of Kayee, where he hired an English-speaking Mandingo guide named Isaaco. In April, he struck out overland toward the Niger.

Park reckoned on reaching the Niger by the end of June. He didn't get there until August 19, having lost three-quarters of his party. The long rains had come and fever and dysentery (*shigella*) proved even more lethal than the Muslim tribesmen who attacked the caravan. The ghastly journey left no time to bury the dead; the ailing fell behind only to be stripped and butchered by bandits who followed the expedition like hyenas. Park's own health deteriorated; soon he had only ten men left. But when he saw the Niger again, "rolling its immense stream along the plain," a strange ebullience overcame him. Against all common sense, he resolved to press forward.

Park hired canoes to take the remnants of his shrinking caravan downriver as far as Segou, where the party arrived in September. He waited weeks while suspicious tribesmen squabbled about providing canoes. More members of the party died, including Park's brother-in-law. By the time he secured two vessels, illness had whittled his escort down to the army lieutenant, three soldiers, and the guide Isaaco. Park was determined to go on. He sent Isaaco back to the coast with letters to his wife and to Banks, telling Banks he intended "to keep to the middle of the river and make the best use I can of winds and currents till I reach the termination of this mysterious stream." To his wife: "I think it is not unlikely that I shall be in England before you receive this. . . . [T]he sails are now hoisting for our departure to the coast." Dated November 20, 1805, that was the last anyone ever heard from Mungo Park.

NO ONE KNOWS precisely what happened to Park, what fate he met, or how far he got before he met it, but years later, in 1810, the Mandingo guide Isaaco volunteered to return to Segou to find out, and the stories he heard generated clues. Apparently realizing that he had crossed into lands controlled by Muslim tribes and remembering their hostility from his previous expedition, Park expected trouble. He took fifteen muskets and plenty of ammunition aboard the two canoes, which were provisioned to take him safely beyond Muslim territory.

Park and his men came under frequent attack from the shore and had to shoot their way downriver. According to Isaaco's account, they managed to reach Timbuktu, but because of the hostility of its inhabitants, visiting the city was out of the question. Park pushed on. He managed to navigate 1,500 miles of the Niger's total course of 2,600 miles and reach a point barely 600 miles from its outlet to the sea. Here, at a place called Bussa Falls (where the Kainji Dam in present-day Nigeria now stands), all were killed in an ambush.

Questions persisted about Isaaco's version of events, and it wasn't until 1819 that the London *Times* finally acknowledged "the death of this intrepid traveller is now placed beyond any doubt." However it occurred, Park's death only fueled curiosity about the Niger's true debouchment.

Park sent his last reports from Segou convinced more than ever of the accuracy of his theory. He had learned that the eastward-flowing river would soon turn to the south (not yet aware that it would later turn again to the southwest, making a beeline for the Atlantic). In a letter to Banks, which Isaaco brought back, Park wrote, "I have hired a guide. . . . [H]e is one of the greatest travellers in this part of Africa: he says that the Niger, after it passes Kashna (presumably near Timbuktu), runs directly to the right hand, or to the south," and in his last letters to his wife and Lord Camden he repeated his conviction that he would return to England via the West Indies from the Congo's mouth.

If Park did get as far as Isaaco reported, he would have been forced to abandon his theory of the Niger as a tributary of the Congo. Having turned south after Timbuktu, the great river arced again soon after (at Gao) to the southwest and flowed in a direction even he must have realized could not take him to the Congo's estuary. Yet if Park revised his theory of the Niger's course, no testament to this has ever appeared.

NEVER ONE TO PIN all his hopes on a lone explorer, Sir Joseph Banks recruited yet another intrepid young man, Friedrich Hornemann, the German son of a Lutheran pastor, to launch another expedition before Park returned from his first journey. Hornemann was a student at the University of Göttingen, where one of his professors was J. F. Blumenbach, an ethnologist working on a classification of human races based on skeletal features. Blumenbach was a friend of Banks (by this time, a large and eclectic group) and referred his student to Soho Square, citing his good mind and robust constitution. Hornemann was offered 200 pounds a year, and his mother was promised an annuity if the young man died (a first for the stingy armchair explorers), as he was her sole source of support.

The route chosen for Hornemann was the previously unsuccessful one from Cairo across the Sahara. He left London for the Mediterranean and Alexandria just as Napoleon was moving the Grande Armée into Egypt in the summer of 1797. Arriving ahead of the French, he met a fellow German, Joseph Frendenburgh, who was living in Egypt as a converted Muslim. Hornemann hired him as an assistant and began learning Arabic. The pair was delayed by an outbreak of bubonic plague, and Hornemann's funds were cut off when the French defeated the mameluks at the Battle of the Pyramids. Determined and resourceful, he made friends with scientists Napoleon brought to Egypt, and through them, he met Bonaparte himself. The general was impressed with the young man and provided him with a visa and the money to launch his trek, offering to forward his letters to London.

In September 1798, Hornemann and Frendenburgh headed west in a caravan bound for the Fezzan. By now, Hornemann spoke fluent Arabic, calling himself "Yusuf," but for all his preparation he was an unconvincing mock-Muslim. He was unmasked when he was observed making sketches of ancient ruins. Confronted, he read from the Koran so convincingly that he was accepted as a *nasrani* striving to learn the true faith. After passing through the oasis at Siwa, the caravan reached Murzuk (Murzuch). Hornemann remained there seven months, preparing extensive notes that eventually found their way back to Sir Joseph. In one package of documents, he attached a bizarre instruction that no one try to find him for at least three years after news of him ceased. Hornemann did not elaborate on this request.

Frendenburgh died at Murzuk, which even then had a well-earned reputation as an unhealthy place (because of the hordes of mosquitoes infesting its oasis). Alone now and with no caravans heading south, Hornemann turned north to Tripoli, where he was taken in by none other than Simon Lucas, the resident British consul. From Tripoli he wrote to Banks, telling him, "[P]ray sir, do not look upon me as a European but as a real African and a Muslim."

He was back in Murzuk in the spring of 1800 and from there joined a caravan heading south—destined, he hoped, for the Niger and Timbuktu. He was never heard from again.

Sir Joseph respected the wish he expressed in his earlier letter, and for three years no inquiries about him were made. The association published his journals, as relayed from Tripoli, and presented a leather-bound copy to Napoleon, while still at war, as a token of thanks for his help.

Nearly twenty years later, other explorers tracking the same paths spoke with people who had accompanied Hornemann. He apparently reached the Niger and died there of dysentery. He had fully transformed himself into a Muslim and shown such compassion and caring for others that he was looked upon as a marabout (a holy man), still in his twenties.

Hornemann's faith in his disguise may have been less than total, thus explaining his entreaty that no inquiries about him be made for three years. A search for him, which would surely have included a physical description, might have compromised his disguise and served as his death warrant.

BETWEEN 1809 AND 1817, the African Association placed its hopes on a Swiss, Jean Louis Burckhardt, who was again sent to cross the Sahara from Cairo to the Niger. Sir Joseph was now convinced that his men would be safe only if disguised as Muslims, and Burckhardt perfected his disguise by traveling for years in Syria. Burckhardt became the first European since the Crusaders to see Petra in Jordan. In Cairo, he learned that no caravan was soon departing for the interior, so he began a series of excursions that led him to discover the spectacular statues at Abu Simbel, to travel farther up the Nile in Sudan than any other European, and to make the pilgrimage to Mecca—each of them a remarkable accomplishment. In 1817, just as a caravan was at last assembled by Arab merchants bound for the interior, Burckhardt contracted dysentery and died at Cairo.

The stalwart African Association took a collective deep breath, but soon sent out another explorer, Henry Nicholls. Having failed in assaults from the north (Tripoli), the east (Cairo), and the west (Gambia), the membership now proposed that an effort be made from the south. The site chosen from which to strike inland was a British trading post in the Gulf of Guinea. It was not known at the time that the Niger River emptied into the Gulf of Guinea (through the mysterious Oil Rivers delta), and so, in a cruel irony, the starting point of the expedition was in fact its destination. Nicholls sailed from Liverpool on November 1, 1804, bound for Calabar. Park was still alive at the time and planning his final, fatal descent of the Niger. In February 1805, Nicholls described his health and prospects as good. By April he was dead, probably the victim of malaria.

Meanwhile, in England, a discernible transition was taking place in the temper of African exploration. The driving force of the African Association, Sir Joseph Banks, had become ill and was confined to a wheelchair, although he continued to work. Spurred by the wars in Europe and Britain's rivalry with France, the Colonial Office and the Admiralty chose to take a larger role in Africa. The torch was passed from the private to the public sector, although the African Association continued to be involved until it was absorbed into the Royal Geographical Society in 1831.

Though the Napoleonic Wars diverted resources from Africa, interest in the questions of Timbuktu and the Niger were so heightened by the drama and mystery of Mungo Park's disappearance and the widely publicized adventures of Hornemann and Burckhardt that in 1815 an ambitious, two-pronged attack was launched. One expedition, under the sponsorship of the Colonial Office, set out to follow Park's course down the Niger. A second, under the direction of the Admiralty, was to start at the Congo estuary and follow the river upstream. The hope was that the two expeditions would meet somewhere in the middle of the continent.

In 1815, the Colonial Office sent Major John Peddie to head the first enterprise and further map the course of the Niger. He arrived in Senegal in November with the expectation of recruiting volunteers from the Royal Africa Corps, but promptly died of coastal fever. Peddie was replaced by Captain Thomas Campbell, but the struggle to move inland was hampered, oddly, by attacks of huge swarms of bees, and the expedition made little progress before turning back. Campbell died. He was replaced by Dr. William Gray and Dr. John Dochard, the military surgeons of the group. With a hundred men and two hundred pack animals, they turned inland. The journey was a nightmare, with most of the men dying, Gray

Sir John Barrow, secretary of the Admiralty from 1804 to 1845, and the man who insisted Dixon Denham give due credit to Clapperton and Oudney. Barrow began his long public service career as private secretary to the British ambassador to China in the 1790s, later serving as private secretary to the governor of the Cape of Good Hope. He was a founder of the Royal Geographical Society in 1830, where he tirelessly promoted exploration of the Arctic. Point Barrow, Alaska; Cape Barrow; and Barrow Strait are all named for him.

captured (later released), and Dochard and seven men barely reaching the Niger before turning back.

While Burckhardt was traveling in northeastern Africa, another of Banks's protégés, Sir John Barrow, was committing the British Admiralty to the second part of the exploration strategy, searching for the Niger and Timbuktu by moving in from the mouth of the river Congo—a venture soon turned into a race by the newly formed French Société Géographique, which in 1824 offered a 10,000-franc prize to the first man to reach Timbuktu and return to tell the tale.

Barrow, in his capacity as secretary of the Admiralty, selected Captain James Kingston Tuckey to go up the Congo and ascertain whether the Congo and the Niger entered the ocean together (the truth was that their estuaries are nearly 900 miles apart). Tuckey's team of fifty-four included a Norwegian botanist and a gardener from Kew. Their boats could not navigate the mouth of the Congo because of swift currents. Changing to smaller vessels, they made it to Yallala Falls and then overland for 200 miles until the weakened porters refused to go farther, at which point they turned back.

When the group reached the coast, thirty-five of the men were dead. Captain Tuckey soon joined them, expiring on October 4, 1816, on the deck of his flagship, still at anchor in the Congo estuary. The expedition added little to the store of knowledge about Africa, despite its horrendous toll.

The reaction in England to these disasters was not unlike the shock Americans would experience after the *Challenger* space shuttle tragedy 170 years later. With the very public failure of these efforts, at horrific cost in British lives and treasure, the government's interest in Africa cooled. Trying to go in from the fever-ridden coast had proved to be a poor strategy. Government ministers in London were stunned that England's best and brightest had been wiped out in both of the expeditions (65 percent of the British contingent of 117 men died in Africa, while many of the rest were terminally ill when they landed in England).

Time would need to pass before any senior member of government would again be willing to see his name associated with a British assault on Africa.

Chapter Five

THE "AFRICAN TRAVELER"

O**N THE DAWN** of that July morning in 1825 when he left Tripoli, Alexander Gordon Laing found himself taking part at last in the dream he believed would make him, as he began the fourth decade of his life, a man to be reckoned with in the wider world.

When the camels were loaded and their head ropes attached, the caravan stood waiting in the moonlight. Then Laing heard the call of their leader, Sheikh Babani, *"Nemchou Y'Allah!"* (Depart, by the grace of God!). The camels began to move forward, and Laing felt his spine come alive with a surprising serpentine motion, gently swaying backward and forward. Six feet off the ground, Laing felt like a lord of creation. He was now part of a trans-Saharan caravan, part of the backbone of an enormous snakelike procession that moved sinuously, determinedly, and unstoppably through the sand beyond the oasis of Tripoli and across the Great Desert to the humid jungles of Central Africa.

The setting moon loomed over the horizon as twilight passed into day. A night dew had cooled the morning and the caravan soon found its easy gait. A gaggle of children followed the camels for a mile or two, their white robes and black cloaks contrasting with the unearthly rose light of the desert. They called out to one another in their harsh, aspirate dialect and went off at a run, noiselessly, barefoot, with burnouses[*] flying, like bats fleeing the dawn.

The shadows of date palms stretched across the track, dwarfing the great dun-colored camels and their loads, the trudging donkeys, goats, and sheep, the swarthy figures of men, some heavily covered in their gray or white *baracans*,[†] some half naked but confident of the power vested in their crooked knives, knobbed clubs, and those flintlocks whose silvered trimmings caught the glint of the rising sun. From a distance, the weapons scintillated like scattered fireflies.

As he started across the desert, Laing's past came to a sharp focus, as though his life thus far had been merely a rehearsal for the expedition now begun. There was a calm within him, an awe of this new world into which he was pentrating at last. It was a world where all seemed dignified, silent, undefined, infinite, and suffused with that mysterious rose light.

ALEXANDER GORDON LAING was born on December 27, 1794,[‡] in Edinburgh, the eldest son of William Laing, a popular schoolmaster who ran his own private school. Laing's mother was the daughter of William Gordon of Glasgow Academy. With an academic background on both sides of the family, he studied for a career in teaching. At thirteen, he was sent to Edinburgh College, where his tutors regarded him as "brilliant."

As the first son of a prominent local educator, Laing was accorded special treatment. "I lived under little restraint from my professors while attending the seminary," he later wrote, "though I had some slight check upon my conduct from occasionally being under the eye of my father." His family connections gave Laing status within the elite schools he attended, and the latitude to assume the role of "young gentleman." Yet

---

[*] A burnous, or *burnus,* from the Arabic, is a hooded cloak made of wool or a mixture of wool and camel hair.

[†] A thick, strong, coarse outer garment, often made of camel hair. Probably from the Arabic, *barak,* a gown.

[‡] The date of Laing's birth is often given as 1793, but in an autobiographical note he says it was 1794.

the sensitive boy must gradually have become conscious of the contrast between this role and his true social status, a cruel reality in the Great Britain of that era that would carry wider implications as he grew older. By fifteen, he had completed his education at Edinburgh University and was hired for a teaching post at Bruce's Classical Academy. Six months later he returned home to become assistant to his father.

"The reading of voyages and travels occupied all my leisure moments," he recorded. "*The History of Robinson Crusoe,* in particular, inflamed my young imagination. I was impatient to encounter adventures like this—nay, I already felt an ambition to signalize myself by some important discovery springing up in my heart."

Travel books like those of Captain James Cook were the equivalent in those days of the science fiction of a later century. In rainy Edinburgh, Laing thought up long, complex possible journeys, drawing faint pencil marks on maps, planning timetables, budgets, and logistics. He entertained visions of distant beaches and jungles, of lines of blue-green breakers bursting into foam on deserted shores. He heard the wave music and tasted briny sea breezes.

As a young man in grimy Edinburgh, Laing's vivid imagination enabled him to construct an altogether different future for himself than the one his parents intended. He was glad to feel the cold rain beating upon his face and took a childish pleasure in ducking his head suddenly to watch the jet of water spouting from his hat brim. Sailors returning from distant ports looked so healthy, these Italian dockhands, Jewish tailors, nondescript young men from all over the world who had been privileged to see the sun directly overhead at the equator. To leave gray, murky Scotland and become one of their number—would that not be a glorious thing?

Laing was in a hurry. His youth, constrained by social and geographical blinders, seemed to stretch out before him with no end. Scotland was walled in, the least likely place where an ambitious young man could profitably spend these important years. Indeed, Scotland in those days was a grim place. Like so many young Scots before him, Laing sought to find some way to get out of the country as quickly as possible.

The small number of Englishmen who journeyed to "North Britain," as Scotland was sometimes called, from a spirit of adventure or on business, braved the trip with a brand of courage other travelers might bring to an expedition up the river Congo. The bleak landscape was bare, destitute of trees, a countryside of heather and morass and barren hills; its agriculture was sparse—dirty patches of crops surrounded by brush and swamps. The inhabitants of some counties appeared barely human, troglodytes with bunioned feet and coarse, hairy legs, poor creatures who spoke incomprehensible dialects, dressed in rags, living in hovels, feeding themselves on grains so poor that in England they would be reserved for livestock. When night fell, the voyager was likely to find himself in a town of dirty thatched huts. If he was lucky, he might find a shack that passed for an inn, only to get a verminous bed he could not sleep in and food he could not eat. His disgust after such a trip would be total. One English visitor of the period, returning south, summed up his impressions: "I passed at last to English ground and hope to God that I may never go to such a country [Scotland] again."

This was not the place to captivate someone of Laing's far-reaching worldly interests. After he'd returned to Edinburgh to help his father, it took him a year to flee his natal city. Dissatisfied with the staid life of a schoolteacher, Laing was roiled by an internal tumult as he tried to find a more substantial role for himself without aggrieving his parents. A poor, well-educated man is an unlovely thing. Laing had only unsatisfactory choices available to him.

Alexander Gordon Laing joined the army at seventeen in Scotland, enlisting with the Prince of Wales Edinburgh Volunteers. In 1811 his parents reluctantly agreed to let him leave the country. He sailed for Barbados, where his mother's brother, General Gabriel Gordon, was serving. His uncle got him an ensign's commission in the York Light Infantry, a West Indian regiment he joined at Antigua. Two years later he exchanged into the 2nd West India Regiment at the same rank and sailed for Jamaica. He was attached in Jamaica to the British consul's office and served as a staff aide to senior officers of the regiment.

Jamaica was an agreeable place. The largest and the most famous of the colonies that made up the British Antilles, it was a land of stately lawns and magnificent houses. On the flat, well-tended greensward of Government House, peacocks, white and blue, spread resplendent tail feathers as they circled the colossal flagstaff displaying a Union Jack the size of a bedsheet. Officers lived in thick-walled stone houses where polished tables in paneled dining rooms gleamed with old silver and cut glass—elegant rooms that spoke of a stylish and extravagant colonial prosperity. Planters' dinners were served up nightly by armies of servants: a Creole soup, roast chicken with local vegetables, boiled yam, fried plantains, sweet potatoes, tarts and cakes, all washed down with the *vin du pays,* so called, of the country (a well-aged mellow yellow rum).

The West Indies were among Great Britain's first colonial possessions, and for two centuries they had been the most prosperous, though that was changing as the slave and sugar economies shrank. Still, the Antilles showed Laing the good things life could offer a man willing to muster some ambition and put himself forward. His superiors lived well, and Laing had every expectation that his own lot in life would rise as he followed their path. In the meantime, there were sunlit skies to enjoy, green spears of the young sugarcane, yellow sands, and the ocean, turquoise and green, in this land of warmth and perfume.

Looking down from Hardware Gap at Kingston through an avenue of hills glittering in the plain, Laing had put Scotland behind him. He moved easily in his role as military attaché in these colonial and diplomatic circles, receiving guests at official functions on behalf of the consul and the military commandant with the perfect gentility and aplomb they required. He was good-looking and well liked; he had the air (if not the pedigree) of a gentleman. He may have briefly considered a diplomatic career, though he knew he lacked the social credentials and the right ancestors, and that these factors would likely bar access to the highest levels of the Foreign Office.

While Laing was ensconced in this new world, another side of his personality emerged. Beneath the smiling and complaisant exterior, Laing sometimes displayed a mocking contempt for rank and social hierarchies. In modern terms, he had an "attitude," a barely concealed surliness that would sometimes poke through his cultivated reserve. Now and then he would whisper in a friend's ear some sarcastic remark on social conventions. There was a sharp pleasure in it that he could not resist, a complex blending of outward respect for society with ridicule of its vanities. Laing knew the rules of the game and wanted to play, but he was a man apart and could not resist laughing, when it suited him, at the foibles of rulebound, rank-conscious British society.

In time, the easy life at Kingston and Montego Bay took its toll. Laing developed a "tiresome liver complaint" which led to his transfer as an invalid first to Honduras and from there back home to Scotland, where he recuperated for eighteen months at half pay. By then he had earned the respect of his senior officers—he had "friends at court," so to speak, in London and in the Antilles who made sure he was not forgotten. At the end of 1819 he was promoted to lieutenant and sent to rejoin his regiment, which was then serving in West Africa. Laing was thrilled, for West Africa was a place where an ambitious British officer could truly make his mark, an opportunity not possible in the country-club atmosphere of the Caribbean.

Africa was a rougher place. In Sierra Leone, as in all the other European settlements along the western coast, the activities of the expatriate whites—whether traders, officials, or army officers—were restricted to villages easily accessible from the ocean, if not to the narrow confines of the trading beaches where they could escape to their ships or forts at night to avoid the pestilential diseases that were thought to come with the setting sun.*

This isolation by the sea was only partly due to health concerns and the difficulty of travel through tropical rain forests. It was also the result of the slave trade, the middlemen of which had seen to it that their European customers were denied access to the hinterlands, the source of their own supply of new slaves. Though officially abolished, the "traffick" continued.

As Laing was to learn, the indigenous peoples of West Africa were loath to let white men know too much about the geography and riches of their interior lands for all sorts of commercial and political reasons. Arab traders, too, had a vested commercial interest in keeping Europeans out. They helped sow distrust by relating stories of the British colonization of India, tales not lost on local African kings.

By 1821, fifteen years after the abolition of the slave trade in Brit-

---

*Before the germ theory of disease emerged decades later, Europeans thought that fevers in West Africa were caused by nocturnal "miasmic vapors" and "exhalations" from swamps. Sailors believed they were safe from these if they stayed aboard ship, even if anchored only hundreds of yards from shore. (They were right, because mosquitoes cannot easily cross open ocean.)

ish colonies, it had become clear in London that there was much to be gained commercially, and also sometimes politically, by creating links with some of the powerful tribes of the interior instead of conducting all business through intermediaries on the coast. At the end of that year, Sir Charles MacCarthy, the British governor of Sierra Leone, decided to send a mission into the hinterland to Gambia and the Mandingo country "to ascertain the state of the country, the disposition of the inhabitants to trade and industry; and to know their sentiments and conduct as to the abolition of the Slave Trade."

Lieutenant Laing, who had shown great eagerness to explore the interior, was chosen to lead that party. He had been vying for a mission for months, and he told his friends since arriving in Africa that he wanted to find Timbuktu and the Niger's termination. "I have had for many years a strong desire to penetrate into the interior of Africa," he wrote, "and that desire has been greatly increased by my arrival on the Coast."

This expedition and two others that followed took Laing 200 miles inland through unexplored country to Falaba, the capital of the powerful Soolima tribe, and to the source of the Rokelle River. He ended the year a seasoned traveler, demonstrating that he had all the qualities the English sought in an explorer: he was brave, resolute, observant, and showed diplomatic talent in dealing with the chiefs of the interior tribes, whose confidence he won. These adventures also gave Laing his first opportunity to show his skill as a writer. *Travels in the Timanee, Kooranko, and Soolima Countries in Western Africa* was published in 1825 by the distinguished publisher John Murray in London, the first of a shelf of travel books Laing hoped to write. He reported in this account that at Falaba he had come within three days' journey (about sixty miles) of the source of the Niger, at Mount Soma. To his lasting regret, he had been unable to visit it.

> Regarding a river of such importance as the Niger, which is looked upon in the Negro world as the largest river in the universe, [he wrote] there are naturally to be found . . . many extraordinary traditions; it is said, that although not more than half a yard in diameter at its source, if anyone was to attempt to leap over it, he would fall into the spring, and be instantly swallowed up, but that a person may step over it quietly, without apprehension or danger.

The following year (1823), Laing, who had been promoted to command a company in the Royal Africa Corps, was ordered to the Gold Coast, where war had erupted between the British and the Ashanti. Exploration was temporarily set aside. In the ensuing twelve months, Laing saw constant action and was frequent witness to the horrors of ferocious jungle warfare. According to his officers, he lived up fully to the high standards expected. They remembered him especially for having volunteered to rescue a sergeant captured by the Ashanti and held prisoner at Kunmassi. His offer was rejected because it was considered too dangerous; the sergeant was later killed.

The Ashanti overwhelmed a British force led by MacCarthy in early 1824. The governor was captured and slain. Soon after, Laing was chosen by MacCarthy's successor, Colonel James Chisholm, to go back to England to report personally to the secretary of state for war and the colonies, Earl Bathurst, on the turn for the worse that events on the Gold Coast had taken.

This was an important assignment and a rare opportunity for Laing to bask in the limelight, for Bathurst was the real creator of the Colonial Office (which he ruled from 1812 to 1827). Short of discussing the catastrophic Ashanti victory with the king or the prime minister, Chisholm could not have sent him to anyone in London with more influence on the application of British power in Africa. Laing also knew that it was within Bathurst's brief to assign him anywhere in Africa, on any mission Bathurst chose. Laing was determined not to let this important contact pass without personal benefit.

In the event, he put on a good show for the boss, who was impressed by his command of the facts, the acuity of his intellect, his courage, and his poise. He did not know it, but Laing's active military career was over. Though always an ambitious man, in West Africa he was well liked, almost loved, by most of his fellow officers. His behavior in the next months would reveal a darker, self-serving side.

Back in London, he felt his services in West Africa had entitled him to the rank of major, but he realized that this promotion was now less likely because MacCarthy (his patron) had died. So, without clearing it first with his commanding officer, he petitioned the commander-in-chief of the Royal Africa Corps (no less than the Duke of York, a member of the royal family) for promotion. If his appeal could not be granted, he wrote, he hoped anyway to be given the "Rank of Major in Africa only."

At first this request was refused, but some months later, after a vacation in Scotland, he succeeded in getting the coveted promotion (though, as proposed, it was "effective in Africa only"). Lord Bathurst had probably intervened, granting him also a few months' leave to write his book.

In the meantime, on July 1, Major General Charles Turner succeeded the fallen MacCarthy as colonel-in-chief of the Royal Africa Corps and as governor of Sierra Leone. Turner, who had never served in Africa and was still in London, learned about Laing's petition for promotion only after it had been granted. It is likely that he never met Laing and had formed no assessment of him, but it cannot have made a good impression that this young captain appealed directly to a royal duke over his commanding officer. The incident likely became the subject of barracks gossip. Probably the first indication Laing received of the rising resentment in his outfit was the following note from the general's aide-de-camp:

No. 7 Penton Square
3rd November, 1824

Sir,

    I am directed by Major General Turner to acknowledge the receipt of your Letter addressed to Lieutenant Glover, extra Aide de Camp, wherein you state that His Royal Highness the Commander in Chief has been pleased to grant you leave of Absence during the period of your prosecuting some scientific researches in the Interior of Africa.

    The Major General desires that you will furnish him with your Authority for this communication as he is wholly unacquainted with the circumstances set forth by you and as they are of a Nature which under existing circumstances he could not have expected or approved of.

    I have the honour to be
    Sir
    Your most obedient humble servant,

Wm. Ross,
Capt. R. A. Corps &
Aide de Camp.

Around the same time, news of the death of another of Laing's supporters reached London: Colonel Chisholm, who had entrusted Laing with the consequential and delicate task of personally briefing Lord Bathurst. Chisholm was still field commander in the Gold Coast when he died. To the ambitious Laing, despite the ominous tone of the letter from Captain Ross, Chisholm's death seemed to suggest the possibility of another shot at promotion. He wrote an appeal to his new friend, Earl Bathurst, asking him to intervene with General Turner in support both of a promotion and of orders to conduct an expedition in West Africa to explore the river Niger.

To this letter, which is dated January 12, 1825, he added a brief résumé of his qualifications as an "African traveler." It is an interesting self-assessment by the thirty-one-year-old Laing:

> In the year 1822 Memorialist [i.e., Laing] performed a Journey of Seven Months into the interior of Africa at the request of the late Sir Charles MacCarthy; established friendly relations with many powerful inland Chiefs, and greatly increased the Gold and Ivory trade of Sierra Leone—For this service Memorialist received a letter of thanks and a piece of plate from the Merchants of the Colony.
>
> On the 2nd December 1822, Memorialist commanded the advance guard of the British army at Donquah and with it alone, defeated a large body of Ashantees and Fantees—
>
> After the above affair, Memorialist succeeded partly by negotiation, partly by determined military movement in making allies of the Fantees, among whom he remained for four months, organising them into a force, with which alone, he overthrew and expelled from their country, a large Ashantee Army which invaded it in August 1823.
>
> After the unfortunate defeat of Sir Charles MacCarthy Memorialist collected the scattered Fantees, and successfully opposed the Ashantees as long as his health permitted him to keep the field; preventing them from crossing the Boosoompra, and isolating them from the towns of the waterside—
>
> A. Gordon Laing
> Capt. R.A.C. Corps
> And Major in Africa

A comparison of what Laing wrote about his part in the Ashanti campaign with a report made by the brigade major of the British force shows that Laing's is a fair, concise, and restrained record of his performance. An anonymous critic in Africa caviled that Laing had sustained "considerable loss on his side." But he clearly had MacCarthy's and Chisholm's support and goodwill. Their letters in 1821 and 1822 reflect this, indicating that young Captain Laing was a gallant and thoroughly competent officer in the field.

Nonetheless, when a copy of Laing's package of documents to Lord Bathurst reached General Turner, now installed at his headquarters in West Africa, he attacked Laing with a ferocity that must have astonished Bathurst, to whom his dispatch, dated April 9, 1825, was addressed. This is what General Turner wrote, effectively ending Laing's career as a field officer:

> I would not fulfil my duty either to your Lordship or to the service, were I not to characterize as unwise, unofficerlike, and unmanly, the conduct of Captain Gordon Laing in this Country. In place of attending to the health and discipline of his Company, his time was occupied in editing a contemptible Newspaper (which I now possess) the columns of which are filled with the most fulsome panegyrics upon himself in prose and rhyme, in magnifying into Armies, a few Wild Negroes in the Woods, deceiving Sir Charles both as to their numbers and quality, also in inflaming the Chiefs of the Ashantees, by foul abuse against the English—Such were his Newspaper proceedings—His military exploits were worse than his poetry, for appalled at the storm he mainly helped to raise, he abandoned and left to their fate, those whom he had brought within its influence.
>
> Of his Armies nothing more was heard: and I humbly beg your Lordship, in the name of the Regiment, that he may be removed from it—and that we may not be subject to the mortification of his calling us *Brother* Officers.

No officer's career could survive such a letter, and Laing's did not. What could have incited such venom? As Laing had left West Africa months before General Turner arrived there, someone unknown is likely to have provoked this harangue—someone who resented Laing's relationship with Sir Charles or Major Chisholm. Laing was good at maintaining relations with superiors who could help him, but he was less adept at cultivating friendly relations with those peers who (correctly) viewed him as a rival.

General Turner, from other accounts, was an amiable man, well liked by his troops. Presumably, he was fair-minded and would not have signed an attack so vitriolic had he not thought it fully justified. Irritation at Laing's repeated end runs probably had much to do with it, predisposing him to lend an ear to criticisms of an ambitious and slightly insubordinate officer.

Laing, to be sure, also had that trait that armies seldom abide: he was not (and never would be) a team player.

Yet Laing still had admirers in West Africa, including Captain Edward Sabine of the Royal Artillery, another young officer with a brilliant career ahead of him. Already a respected scientist and an authority on the Arctic, Sabine was pursuing "scientific investigations" along the tropical coast. Later, he would become president of the Royal Society. It was Sabine who would edit Laing's only book and loyally see it published while its author was wandering in the Sahara in search of Timbuktu.

In the years ahead, Sabine would become one of Laing's main correspondents. Had there been any substance to General Turner's commination, it is unlikely that someone of Sabine's character would have maintained his friendship, or that Laing would have been chosen by Colonel Chisholm to report to Lord Bathurst on the troubled Gold Coast. Though we may never know the details, the circumstances suggest that Laing got caught up in a power play in Sierra Leone, running afoul of a rival who held General Turner's ear.

In the end, Laing had the full confidence of the one person who mattered: Henry Bathurst, one of the dozen most powerful men in the kingdom. Though Laing would never again fight in battle as an army officer (though he kept his commission, rank, and pay at Bathurst's insistence), his true vocation as an explorer could now begin.

As his evolving status became clear, and notwithstanding the protracted contretemps with General Turner, Laing continued to cultivate the people in London who could smooth his way. He realized how important it would be to make an ally of Henry Goulbourn, Lord Bathurst's undersecretary. Goulbourn was regarded by critics in Whitehall as a man of pedestrian talents. But he was also a man of phenomenal energy, and therefore the ideal subordinate for Lord Bathurst. Of Bathurst, it was said politely that while he did not shirk his responsibilities, he "was not one to do himself what he could depend upon others to do for him." So it was helpful in cultivating Bathurst's support to have Goulbourn's goodwill.

As well as holding Bathurst's confidence, Goulbourn had an independent source of personal power: he was a close friend of Robert Peel, the rising young star of the Tory Party and a future prime minister. Goulbourn, at this stage in his career, was happy to work in Bathurst's shadow, and it was clear that he was far more involved in the day-to-day details of colonial rule than his nominal boss. "In-letters" for Bathurst's review from all parts of the empire had Goulbourn's concise analyses on their turned-up corners. Other letters had details of the proposed reply to be made or were marked "put-by" for later consideration. Goulbourn kept all these files in his own desk, advised Bathurst on what required his attention, and directed the clerks in the Colonial Office. Bathurst himself preferred to take the long view, spending weeks at a time at his ancestral seat, Cirencester Park, though there is no doubt that in some matters, as in the Laing expedition to Timbuktu, he focused personally on, and directed, the details.

HENRY BATHURST CAME from an ancient line of intelligent and wealthy aristocrats who made government service their avocation. Unlike some of his fellow peers, who took after the playboy George IV, Bathurst was hardworking, well read, virtuous, modest, and committed to the principle of noblesse oblige: that great privilege demanded responsibility and service. He was the third earl, born in 1762, the elder son of a prominent Tory. The younger Bathurst soon developed a distinguished résumé of his own. He was elected to Parliament for Cirencester, Gloucestershire, from 1783 until he succeeded to the earldom in 1794.

In 1812 he become secretary of state for war and the colonies (a cabinet post he invented) under the Earl of Liverpool, who was prime minister. In this post, Bathurst became spellbound by Africa, and a staunch

Laing's powerful mentor and protector, Henry, 3rd Earl Bathurst, Baron of Battlesden, Baron of Apsley, Knight Companion of the Garter, and confidant of both George III and George IV. A protégé of William Pitt, he was a lord of the Admiralty and a Treasury lord from 1783 to 1791. It was Bathurst who founded the Colonial Office, where he pursued anti-slavery policies with a grim moral determination as secretary of state for colonies. He became the principal architect of England's Africa policy, launching the scramble for those vast colonial territories Britain eventually came to control.

enemy of the slave trade. He was made a Knight Companion of the Garter in 1817, thus cementing his personal relationship with the prince regent and future king.* That year, too, Bathurst was tapped to inform the Prince of Wales of the death of his only legitimate child, Princess Caroline. The news Bathurst bore to the palace was doubly tragic, for Caroline had died only hours after giving birth to a stillborn son. Few men in England had a closer personal relationship with her eccentric sovereign in 1825, for whom he served as an intellectual and moral foil. No man in George IV's court resembled the king less in temperament and character than Bathurst, or was trusted by the king more, perhaps just for that reason. Laing could not have picked a more powerful patron.

Given his abiding interest in African exploration, Lord Bathurst was a proponent of finding Timbuktu and tracing the definitive course of the Niger, though he had developed unusual ideas about how to undertake

*Founded in 1348, the Order of the Garter is England's highest order of chivalry. It is composed today, as it has been for centuries, of the sovereign, the Prince of Wales, and a few other select members of the queen's immediate family, plus twenty-four elected Knights Companion who are replaced only upon death (or disgrace—over the centuries thirty-six have been beheaded, six of them by Henry VIII alone, and many others have been expelled for displeasing their sovereign). For Bathurst to have received this accolade meant that he had been officially welcomed into the innermost circle of palace life and that thereafter he would have access to the prince regent (later George IV) whenever he needed it. On the political side, he had already established himself as a force in both Houses of Parliament. In his lifetime, he served successively in the House of Commons and the House of Lords.

the mission. He revived the old idea that explorers should penetrate from north to south rather than try the typical ingress from the West African coast, where so many had succumbed to disease. To come in from the north, you had to cross the Sahara. Crossing the desert involved traveling much greater distances than taking the coastal route.*

The shortest way to Timbuktu, he knew, was the caravan road south from Marrakech, about 1,000 miles in a straight line, twice that given the winding nature of the track (these were rough estimates, since nobody knew exactly where Timbuktu was). Farther east, it was known that another road ran through Touggourt, Wargla, and Tuat. Bathurst saw great logic in departing still farther east, from Tripoli, as Laing had now been ordered to do.

As the northern terminus of the easiest road to the Sudan, Tripoli had, since Roman times, been the main gateway to the interior from the north, and the main maritime outlet for the produce of the south. There was an old road running southwest through Ghadames and Djanet. Traversing the Sahara diagonally, it was not much used, and this was one of the reasons Sheikh Babani had selected it when he was organizing his slaving caravan In the summer of 1825—he was concerned about bandits and thought the road less traveled might provide better cover for himself, for his merchandise and servants, and for his protégé, the Englishman. The total distance involved was enormous—probably some 3,000 miles across some of the most demanding terrain in the world, six times the distance then thought to separate Timbuktu from the Atlantic.

IN THE MORNING of that first day out of Tripoli, the desert seemed lit by some sad dawning of the end of the world. The sand was painted a ruddy ocher, the color of bister and mummies, tinting the desert a half dozen shades of yellow and brown, peppered with squalls of dust. The caravan began moving south, where the great range of the Atlas ran to sand and the mighty desert met the sea. Wild nomadic tribes controlled these unbounded wastes, but Laing trusted Babani, and the caravan was a large one.

---

* Timbuktu was thought at the time to lie about 500 miles inland, traveling due east from the Atlantic. It is actually almost 900 miles from the ocean, as the crow flies, 1,500 miles on foot.

At the outset of such a journey, when camels were healthy and properly watered and fed, their heads tended to strain forward and low to reduce the pull of the ropes on their nose rings. To Laing, they looked like large angry geese as they padded quietly along. Soon they were exhausted, their heads held high on curving necks, trying to resist the awful weight of their bodies even when their nostrils were nearly pulled out, the pain of the one seeming much greater than the other. As the day grew long, Laing learned to belabor his camel from behind with his riding stick, further inciting the beast forward.

Laing quickly perceived that there seemed to be nothing but pain in the desert, for human beings and animals alike. Life was pain, Babani told him. Only in death was there relief. Yet there was such a light in the sky, and in the distance such an extraordinary clearness, that death seemed very far away, a tribute to the insidious charm of this land of sand and silence. Laing felt his resolution firm, unwavering, unyielding.

He was a traveler now, he believed, on the high road to fortune. There was romance enough in adventure, in danger. Other rewards—money and fame—would come later. As he left on his historic journey, Laing believed that much in his past and all of his recent efforts destined him for precisely this adventure and the success that would surely cap it.

Night fell quickly in the Tripolitanian desert. The sky overhead became rusty; the setting sun dimmed. As the light failed, the sky passed from copper to bronze but remained metallic as the sun's embers were overtaken by the moon's milky shimmer. In the distance, desert mountains edged their sharp outlines with a stroke of burnt sienna. A chill wind blew; the ember tint faded. All things in the ghostly light took on a translucent, weightless quality as the moon rose and became more silvery in the increasing chilliness of night. In the desert, the night was kind when it was not too cold.

Distant horizons subsided. The moon washed the land with a clean, soft light. And then there was nothing but the sand and the moon, those strange men of imposing gravity lying nearby in the camp, instantly asleep and snoring loudly, and the deep blue-black of the vault above, a transparent emptiness studded by diamonds.

Chapter Six

———◆———

THE TRIPOLI ROUTE

ORE THAN THIRTY YEARS had passed since the fateful dinner at St. Albans Tavern that gave birth to the African Association, but the time had not yet come for Alexander Gordon Laing to move toward the strange rose light of the Sahara.

By 1820 *none* of the big questions raised by Sir Joseph Banks had been answered. The origin and outlet of the great river Niger, whether it evaporated in a salt lake somewhere in the desert or flowed as a tributary of the Nile; the location of the various African kingdoms; and most of all, the size and importance of Timbuktu—all these remained profound mysteries.

The members of the association, reposing in cozy armchairs in London, now recognized, along with their collaborators in government, what had been obvious to travelers for a thousand years: Islamic fanaticism, disease, hostile tribes, territorial *coffles,** parched deserts, unnavigable rivers, and the sheer distances involved made the penetration of the interior of Africa hugely difficult.

The British decided to try a new approach, one that might co-opt Arab foes and defeat disease in one stroke: to send explorers in from the northern fringes of the continent, along the clean, dry Mediterranean

---

* A caravan, usually a slave caravan, from the Arabic *qafila*.

coast. Traveling south, the explorers would traverse the vast Sahara into black Africa, possibly succeeding even in enlisting Muslim merchants as guides, in return for a reward.

Four factors made Tripoli attractive as the point of departure. First, the dynamic English consul there, Colonel Hanmer Warrington, pushed the cause of exploration with all his disorganized but considerable energy. Second, the bashaw, Yusuf Karamanli, upon whom Warrington exerted influence, agreed to help explorers traveling through his kingdom and would (for a fee) provide protection. Third, the dry desert climate had advantages over the humid West African littoral, where unnamed diseases debilitated explorers before they could even begin their travels. And finally, the cosmopolitan atmosphere of Tripoli itself, with its odd mixture of refinement and corruption and its melting pot of a population, appealed to the English sensibility.

Commander William Henry Smyth, a twenty-eight-year-old hero of the Napoleonic Wars, planted the seed for the new British strategy. In the spring of 1816 a letter from Smyth strongly recommending Tripoli as "an open gate into the interior of Africa" landed on the desk of Sir Charles Penrose at the British Admiralty. Admiral Penrose had dispatched Smyth to Tripoli to retrieve broken columns and twenty cases of statues (probably from the Roman temple at Leptis Magna) which Yusuf Karamanli had graciously donated to the Duke of York. The warm relations between the bashaw and Warrington impressed Smyth, and he developed an exaggerated idea of the bashaw's influence in the interior of Africa. His letter asserted that "by striking due South of Tripoli, a traveller will reach Bornu [a vast plain in what is now northeastern Nigeria, sloping toward Lake Chad] before he is out of Yusuf's influence; and wherever his Power reaches, the protecting virtues of the British Flag are well known. In fact, looking to the unavoidable causes of death along the malarious banks of the Rivers of the Western coast, I think this ought to be the chosen route, because [it is] practicable into the very Heart of the most benighted quarter of the globe."

Smyth's* letter could not have been more timely. Admiral Penrose

---

* Smyth went on to a long and distinguished career, becoming, successively, an admiral, a fellow of the Royal Society, a founder of the Royal Geographical Society, and president of the Royal Astronomical Society. His charts of the Mediterranean were so accurate they were used well into the twentieth century. He died in 1865.

passed it on to Sir John Barrow, who agreed wholeheartedly with Smyth's analysis and forwarded it with his recommendation to Lord Bathurst. After the disasters on the west coast, the Colonial Office, which was now the department responsible for government missions to Africa, quickly saw the advantages of the northern route. In 1818, the first government-sponsored mission to the river Niger via Tripoli set out. All important British missions to Africa would use this route until 1829.

Tripoli was already prosperous, a Mediterranean center of commerce, one of the few ports in North Africa where European merchants traded. European seafaring powers posted consuls there, and their ships lay at anchor in its superb natural harbor, a bay fringed with date palms, waiting to transport goods and slaves from the African interior. Tripoli was an open city: the bashaw permitted *any* profitable activity as long as he received his share of the swag. Corsairs freely used the harbor to divide the spoils in the ships they had captured.

Though the British strategy may have seemed novel in London, it was hardly a new one. Tripoli had been a gateway to the African interior since pre-Christian Garamantes tribesmen sold precious stones to the Carthaginians. The way through the Fezzan to Murzuk and on to Bornu—the shortest, safest, and oldest of the caravan routes—had been trod by Roman, and later by Arab, invaders.

Whoever ruled Tripoli tried to keep the caravan routes open, but all soon learned that desert nomads could not be brought under control more than a few score miles from the city walls. As a repercussion of their raids, running caravans south was a hazardous business best undertaken by large convoys of armed men. The city itself had had many masters, including the sultan of Morocco, the bey of Tunis, Ferdinand the Catholic of Spain, and the Knights of St. John (of Malta)—and now, a strange man called Yusuf Bashaw Karamanli.

IN THE SIXTEENTH CENTURY, Tripoli was invaded by the Turks. They governed, backed by a garrison of Janissaries. A Janissary was a soldier in an elite corps of Turkish troops drawn exclusively from abducted Christian boys trained to fight and brought up as Muslims. The Janissaries in Tripoli intermarried with Arab and Berber women, and their sons were called Cologhis. The Cologhis, inevitably, grew more powerful until a fateful day in 1711 when one of them, Ahmad Karamanli, invited the officers of the Turkish garrison to a sumptuous banquet—and promptly slaughtered all of them as they ate. Calling himself the "bashaw" or "pasha" and continuing to give fealty to the Sublime Porte, he founded a Tripolitanian dynasty that would rule for the next 125 years.

At the time English explorers began using Tripoli as a point of departure for black Africa, Yusuf Karamanli (Ahmad's great-grandson) held Tripoli's throne. To become bashaw, Yusuf, the youngest of three brothers, had murdered his oldest brother, deposed his father, and exiled his remaining brother. He ruled Tripoli from 1795 to 1835, extending his authority southward with bloody wars against nomadic tribes.

One explorer, watching Yusuf Bashaw's army returning after a campaign in the hinterlands, counted two thousand human heads on the tips of Cologhi spears. These grisly trophies belonged to rebellious Tuareg whose decapitated bodies were burned in the desert. But the nomads, tough and resilient, never permitted the bashaw's power to extend much beyond Tripoli and its environs. While he did exercise some authority over the caravan routes, the bashaw's assertion that he could guarantee the safety of any traveler bound for Bornu was a fantasy.

Hanmer Warrington, a fanatical patriot convinced of English superiority (he ended one report of a disagreement with a fellow consul with the words: "I am an Englishman, thank God! He is not!"), blustering and insufferable to all who crossed him, administered British affairs in Tripoli like a despot himself. Whitehall understood his shortcomings only too well, but these were, in a sense, the *right* shortcomings—to defend British interests in a city where pirates and slavers not only had legal protection but still accounted for a substantial fraction of the bashaw's income, and where a thousand Maltese still numbered among the British subjects under the consul's care. A more diplomatic consul could not have succeeded. Warrington was brutal, but he was also effective.

Yusuf Bashaw, who had secured his throne through years of bloodthirsty machinations, appreciated Warrington's connivery. Warrington constantly tripped up the other consuls, using whatever skulduggery suited him. Far from earning a reprimand, he got high marks at the Castle, where the bashaw appreciated the achievements of a schemer as resourceful as himself. Warrington's favor at court could also be attributed to his unabashed groveling. An English soldier who visited Tripoli in 1845 (when, admittedly, the consul was elderly, partially blind, and reaching the end of his career) described Warrington watching troops marching on the beach below the bashaw's Castle:

"Tell Ali Bashaw [Yusuf's son, who had succeeded him] I never saw such splendid maneuvering in all the course of my life!" Warrington informed the interpreter.

"Tell the bashaw that as long as he has such troops as these, he will be invincible!"

"Tell the bashaw I myself should not like to command English troops against these fine fellows!"

The English visitor smiled inwardly, he reported, for the Cologhi soldiers' antics were comically inept.

In his earlier years, by whatever means, Warrington usually got his way. One morning in 1817 a corsair and its prize arrived in Tripoli harbor, the flag of the captured ship flying on the vessel's forestay. The consul recognized "with horror and amazement" the Union Jack and ran to the bashaw for justice. Within the hour the prisoners were freed, the flag delivered to Warrington, and the pirate captain hung from his mast. (This in spite of appeals from the bashaw's advisers to spare the pirate so that Tripoli's reputation as a haven for criminals would not be tarnished.)

The bashaw realized that the age of piracy was ending. Under his reign, piratical practices had already been the cause of war in 1805 between Tripolitania and the United States.* In 1819, a combined Anglo-French squadron appeared off the shores of Tripoli. The bashaw and the other Barbary rulers were ordered to give up attacks on Mediterranean shipping or face grim consequences from the world's two greatest navies. That was the death knell for the buccaneers who for nearly five hundred years had stalked the Mediterranean. It was also a huge financial blow to the bashaw. No longer could his treasury be supported by ransoms and the sale of stolen ships and booty. Though Yusuf Bashaw made halfhearted efforts to plunder the shipping of smaller nations, the threat of Anglo-French retaliation was great, even in protecting vessels that were neither English nor French. Those two powers, policemen of the Mediterranean, were themselves at

---

* Thus adding a memorable line to the U.S. Marine Corps hymn.

peace. By 1825, the bashaw found that all sources of revenue from the old trade of piracy and Christian slavery had dried up.

With a large part of his revenues cut, the bashaw had to turn else-where for money. One source of income he thought he could exploit was the sale of black slaves. With this in mind, he started to organize slave caravans to strike deeper into Central Africa than Arabs had before. This strategy, ironically, coincided with the arrival of the first British explor-ers, who came in part to *abolish* the slave trade. The bashaw discovered that these travelers could themselves become additional sources of cash, though he failed to anticipate that it was the British who would be responsible for bringing slavery to an end.

APPROVAL FOR THE FIRST BRITISH EXPEDITION originating from Tripoli reached Warrington in February 1818. He replied enthusias-tically in a letter to Barrow dated March 7: "The plan is fraught with innu-merable advantages to Geographical Science, to the Commercial interests of the civilized world, and, ultimately, I hope, it may rescue millions of our fellow-creatures from an Abyss of Ignorance and Superstition."

In October 1818, a frail and introverted twenty-seven-year-old sur-geon named Joseph Ritchie arrived in Tripoli with a twenty-three-year-old naval officer, George Lyon, and a shipwright from the Malta dockyards, John Belford (who was there to build a boat should the trio ever reach the Niger). Ritchie, a Scotsman like Mungo Park, carried with him 2,000 pounds sterling and instructions from Lord Bathurst to "proceed under proper protection to Timbuktoo . . . and collect all possible Information as to the further Course of the Niger, and of the probability of your being able to trace the stream of that river with safety to its termination or to any given distance towards that point."

The emphasis in London had shifted subtly from the days when Sir Joseph Banks and the African Association were in charge. The British still wanted to find the Niger River and the mysterious city at its northern bend, but increasingly the raison d'être for sending young men to these inhospitable regions was the possibility of commerce and the extirpa-tion of the slave trade. The government had an agenda. Warrington, his jingoism ignited by the prospect of seeing the Union Jack hoisted deep in tropical Africa, promised the Colonial Office that "when Mr. Ritchie arrives everything shall be done for the best—the full extent of this Regency is within our grasp . . . though I should suppose overtures of a specific nature must be made, and accompanied by presents." In the British consul, the bashaw had a man who, though for different reasons, thought much like himself.

The two senior members of the new expedition could not have been more different. Dr. Joseph Ritchie was a quiet, uncommunicative loner. George Lyon was a hardworking, extroverted young naval officer of considerable charm who made friends easily. Ritchie, unfortunately, was unsuited for African exploration, as soon became clear. He immediately fell ill and never recovered. Distracted and morose, he took no interest in Africa or its people, failed to record his observations, and probably caused the mission's failure through a ridiculous oversight—he left Tripoli on a journey that might easily take over a year with only 300 Spanish dollars in his pocket, money he had borrowed from Lyon. He squandered the 2,000 pounds the Colonial Office had given him on a small warehouse of useless equipment, including a load of corkboard to preserve insects, two large chests of arsenic, brown paper for keeping plants, and six hundred pounds of lead (intended use: unknown).

What little is recorded of the Ritchie mission we owe to George Lyon, a fine writer who published his classic *Travels in Northern Africa* in 1821, just before Laing set off on his own journey. "He [Ritchie] relied too much on a singularly retentive memory," Lyon graciously observed. For a time, the Ritchie party stayed in Warrington's villa in the *menshia* outside Tripoli. Later they moved into the empty Portuguese consulate in town (Warrington was briefly acting consul for Portugal) and settled down to study the manner and customs of the Muslims. It may have been on the bad advice of the bashaw that they decided to disguise themselves as Moors. Lyon hired a *fighi* (a holy man, or religious scholar) to teach them Arabic. The trio went so far to have themselves circumcised (without anesthetics!) to pass close inspection as believers. Warrington, with the practical common sense that never left him where English travelers were concerned, regarded this strategy as ridiculous.

"If we send a vice-consul to Fezzan," he wrote to a friend in Malta, "let him go in his Real Character, which is more respectable, and more to be Respected, than the adoption of the Moorish costume, or disfiguring the Person by circumcision. The result will prove whether it is a childish game and whether the lookers-on are imposed on. . . ." This was sound advice, and accepted as such by subsequent travelers.

To complete the imposture, which probably deceived no one (news of their intended trip, by the time they left Tripoli, had spread far and wide), Ritchie assumed the name "Yusuf el Ritchie," the dockyard worker Belford became "Ali," and Lyon was "Said bin Abdulla." They further announced that they would travel as mameluks (that is, as mercenary Muslim soldiers from Cairo), an additional folly.

As the weeks passed, they prepared their Arab disguises, shaving their heads, growing beards, and buying caftans, turbans, and Moroccan leather riding boots.* While Ritchie stayed indoors studying mathematics, Lyon attended clandestine meetings of the local marabouts to test his Arab costume and his facility with the language. He wrote of "marabouts in trances with nails through their faces and blood gushing from their bitten tongues whirling half-naked until they fell exhausted."

On March 18, 1819, the bashaw received Ritchie and Lyon at an official audience with their consul, telling them they could head south with his ally, the newly appointed bey of Fezzan, Mohammed El Mukni, who was soon to leave Tripoli on a slave-raiding campaign. El Mukni, who had helped Hornemann years earlier, was collecting a force of armed Arabs to attack African villages. By accompanying the bey, Ritchie and Lyon would have protection for their journey and a guarantee of further help when they reached Murzuk. They bought twenty-two camels and some *guerbas* (waterskins) and left four days later as part of a caravan made up of two hundred men and as many camels.

In the company of Sheikh El Mukni and a strong guard of Tripoli soldiers, they made the journey across the sahel, the mountains of Gharian, the stony elevated surface of the Hamada el Homra, the great basalt hills of the Jebel es Sawda, the sand slopes of the Idehan Fezzan, and at last, the flat plain leading to Murzuk. Lyon found it difficult to adapt to

*So-called Turkish boots, which have an upturned toe.

his Moorish disguise. "As I sat in our tent writing a letter," he said, "some Arabs came in and seemed to find much amusement in seeing me write from left to right; but when I told them my letter was addressed to a female, their astonishment knew no bounds; and they laughed heartily at the idea that a woman was capable of reading. . . . When I told them that Englishwomen were allowed to have money in their own power and that some of them had immense fortunes, they seemed hardly to credit me."

The British could expect a certain amount of deference in the desert, oddly enough, because they had defeated Napoleon, the only European most Arabs had heard of. "Bono Barto, as the Arabs call him," Lyon wrote, "is in great estimation amongst them, not on account of his military achievements, but because they have heard that he has 200,000 dollars an hour and he sits on a golden throne."

On May 4, thirty-nine days after leaving Tripoli, the caravan reached the outskirts of Murzuk, capital of the Fezzan, a walled date-palm oasis of 2,500 inhabitants with seven guarded gates. According to custom, the party made a ceremonial entrance. Lyon describes the scene:

Having shaved, washed and adorned ourselves in the finest clothes which we had at hand, we started. Mukni, however, unwilling that his new Mamelukes should be less fine than his own people, sent for two splendid boxes, which he lent to Mr. Ritchie and myself, for this grand occasion, making us ride on the right and left of him . . .

In this manner, preceded by drummers, pipers, and dancers, they entered Murzuk, a town built on a flat plain around a central castle and surrounded by mud walls twenty feet high, crumbling with age. The houses, too, were built of mud, since it never rained—all compact single-story dwellings with courtyards, except for the bey's palace in the middle of town, a labyrinth of turrets and connected rooms. One main street divided the town, and this wide-open space served as marketplace, storehouse, and *mukef,* or tethering place for slaves and animals. Tuareg regularly came to trade with the black population.

Beyond the city gates lay oases of date palms crowded around pools of brackish water. From these pools, at nightfall, arose clouds of voracious anopheles mosquitoes, vectors of malaria.* Murzuk had a deserved reputation for its unhealthy climate. In the town itself were pools of briny water fed by canals. Lyon correctly guessed that these "promote the advance of summer fevers and agues." It was from such a fever that Hornemann's German companion had died twenty years earlier.

The Englishmen were barely settled in the house provided for them by the bey when Lyon became ill with dysentery, confining him to bed for twenty-two days and, as he wrote, "reducing me to the last extremity." He had no sooner begun to recover when "Mr. Ritchie fell ill, and was interned to his bed with an attack of bilious fever accompanied with delirium and great pain in his back and kidneys, for which he required constant cupping.† . . . When a little recovered, he got up for two days, but his disorder soon returned with redoubled and alarming violence. He rejected everything but water and, excepting for about three hours in the afternoon, remained either constantly asleep or in a delirious state."

Nightmarish episodes filled the next six months as the lack of preparation that marked the expedition now began to exact its price. The three men went broke, reducing them to beggary. Ritchie, with maniacal stubbornness, would not let Lyon sell anything to raise cash, "lest it should lower us in the eyes of the natives." When Lyon tried to sell supplies anyway, he learned that the bey, the once-friendly El Mukni, had forbidden the locals to trade. A young Muslim told Lyon privately: "Mukni hopes you may die so that he may secure to himself all your goods." They could not borrow, for El Mukni, who had expected gifts, deserted them when he realized none would be forthcoming. They barely survived.

"For six weeks entire," wrote Lyon, "we were without animal food, subsisting on a very scanty portion of corn and dates. Our horses were mere skeletons, added to which, Belford became totally deaf, and so emaciated as to be unable to walk."

---

* The association between swampy or marshy areas and disease had long been recognized, but the roles of the mosquito and of the malarial parasites of the genus *Plasmodium* were not identified until the beginning of the twentieth century.

† An archaic medical technique employed for drawing blood to the surface of the body by application of a glass vessel from which air had been evacuated by heat, forming a partial vacuum.

Dr. Ritchie became zombielike, possibly a symptom of his illness. He "almost constantly remained secluded in his own apartment, silent, unoccupied, and averse to any kind of society."

El Mukni continued outwardly to pretend friendship. When Lyon again tried to borrow money, he apologized for not having any. In the end, he said he could let him have eight Spanish dollars, a pittance that would hardly supply the camp with food for a week. In July, El Mukni's great slave-raiding party left for the south without them. As the months passed and Ritchie showed no sign of improvement, the simple rigors of day-to-day survival absorbed them. In September, Lyon took advantage of a caravan's departure for Tripoli to send Warrington a plea for more funds, in the meantime selling one of their horses. Ritchie, though bedridden and weaker, continued to oppose giving up any of their property. "Mr. Ritchie being attacked again by illness," Lyon wrote, "I much wished him to allow of my selling some of our powder to procure him a few comforts; but to this he would not consent."

The cooler weather brought relief; Lyon was able to move around and make notes on the language and customs of the country. Food now became available, for El Mukni, who had returned, began to fear that reports of his penurious behavior would reach the ears of Yusuf Bashaw in Tripoli.

Lyon and John Belford were frequently down with fever, but Dr. Ritchie by now was slowly dying. He grew delirious, could eat no food, and sometimes drank vinegar and water. On November 17, he felt better and asked for a cup of coffee. He looked at himself in the mirror and told Lyon: "I was frightened at the blackness of my tongue, but now recollect I have been drinking coffee; had I observed that appearance without knowing the cause, I should have said I had bilious fever, and should bid you goodbye."

By November 20, 1819, it was clear he was critically ill, and his two emaciated companions scrambled to keep him alive. Lyon wrote:

> On the 20th, we got a fowl, of which we made a little soup for him. The broth which Mr. Ritchie drank was the first nourishment he had taken for ten days, though we used all our endeavours to prevail on him to eat. He said he felt much revived by it, and turned round to go to sleep. I placed my bed at the entrance of the room and

remained watching him. He seemed to breathe with difficulty; but as I had often observed this during his former maladies, I was not so much alarmed as I should otherwise have been. At about 9 o'clock, Belford, on looking at him, exclaimed in a loud voice, "He is dying!" I begged him to be more cautious, lest he should be overheard, and immediately examined Mr. Ritchie, who appeared to be still in a sound sleep; I therefore lay down on my bed and continued listening. At 10, I rose again, and found him lying in an easy posture and breathing more freely; five minutes, however, had scarcely elapsed before his respiration appeared entirely to cease; and on examination I found that he had actually expired, without a pang or groan, in the same position in which he had fallen asleep.

Ritchie died as he had lived—silent, withdrawn, uncommunicative.

Belford used his carpentry skills to make a coffin. That night, Lyon and Belford, who still posed as mameluks, secretly read the Church of England burial service over Ritchie's body. The next morning, he was given a Muslim burial in the graveyard outside town, where the bey's imam read the first chapter of the Koran over his grave. As the last spadefuls of sand were smoothed over, a messenger arrived from Warrington saying that the British government would allow disbursement of another thousand Spanish dollars.

Regrettably, Lyon was unable to lay a hand on these funds, which were in Ritchie's name, and since Warrington had never been informed by Ritchie how moneys received for the expedition were to be forwarded, there was no means anyway of collecting the fresh cash (which lay untouched at Malta). Warrington had offered Ritchie a letter of credit for use in Murzuk when he arrived in Tripoli, but the secretive doctor told the consul bluntly that he had made his own arrangements. Whatever these were, he took them to his grave.

Lyon now assumed charge. Penniless and sick with malaria, he was determined not to return to Tripoli without *some* information on the wholly unknown country to the south of Murzuk. He managed, by selling Ritchie's horse and other personal effects, to pay off the expedition's debts and buy enough supplies for a journey lasting a few weeks. Fever struck again before he and Belford could get going, and for ten days both lay in bed, tended with devotion by one little Arab girl. Then, armed with a *teskera*, or official pass from El Mukni, they set out on horseback accompanied by a diminutive camel boy who knew the route.

"We more resembled two men going to the grave than fit persons to travel over strange countries," wrote Lyon.

Weakened, they reached Tegheri, a town about 100 miles south of Murzuk. Here they saw members of the fierce Tebu tribe, parties of whom occasionally descended from the Tibesti Mountains to plunder passing caravans. These tall and handsome people, veiled like the Tuareg and wary of strangers, were black Africans, not Berbers, the northernmost part of a larger group of Tebu people whose territory extended to what we know today as northern Chad, Niger, and Sudan.

The Tebu captivated Lyon, who summoned all his dazzling social skills to overcome their chilly reserve. He became so friendly with some that they let him make portraits of them and compile a rough vocabulary of their language. He drew their dark African features, their tightly combed hair; the men wearing a cloth about the face, the women unveiled. These were tough, solitary mountain people. They had to be, for they were pitted against the Tuareg, the ferocious "blue men"* who were the dominant nomads of the central and western Sahara.

Though the Tuareg and the Tebu nominally espoused Islam, they were fiercely independent and deviated from accepted Muslim norms when it suited them. (A Tebu man might ask a prospective bride, "Whom do you love more, me or Allah?" a question even the nondevout would consider blasphemous.)

At Tegheri, Belford became too sick to continue. The party turned back. Freed from Ritchie's standoffishness, Lyon won friends in Murzuk, and the journey to Tripoli was lightened by gifts. Among his new benefactors was a high-ranking Tuareg, Hatita ag Khuden, from the Ghat region of the southern Sahara, who was later to become a supporter of Laing. Lyon promised this man an English sword.

---

* So called because the blue dye used in their veils and clothing frequently transferred more or less permanently to the skin.

*Black slaves being driven across the Sahara by their Arab captors for sale in Tripoli, in
a koffila like that encountered by George Lyon on his return to the coast.*

On February 9, 1820, Lyon and Belford, joining company with a
slaving caravan, set out on the journey back to Tripoli. Day after day, as
Lyon rode with the caravan, he watched twelve hundred slaves, most of
them women and children, shepherded painfully across the hilly wastes.
Mounted overseers battered this mass of wretched humanity with whips
and sticks; sick slaves were thrown by the road and left to die. Nauseated
by the spectacle, Lyon took notes:

> These poor, oppressed beings were, many of them, so exhausted as
> to be scarcely able to walk; their legs and feet were much swelled
> and by their enormous size formed a striking contrast with their
> emaciated bodies. They were all borne down with loads of firewood;
> and even poor little children, worn to skeletons by fatigue and

hardship, were obliged to bear their burthen, while many of their inhuman masters rode on camels, with the dreaded whip suspended from their wrists. . . .

On Friday, March 24, after more than a year of travel, the caravan had its first glimpse of the Mediterranean. That day, Lyon and Belford met Warrington and his family riding out from Tajura. The explorers' appearance was so changed by disease and starvation that Warrington at first did not recognize them. The consul and a newly arrived naval surgeon, Dr. John Dickson, took the weary travelers back to the consulate's sick bay.

Exhausted by his own hardships, Lyon was haunted by memories of the brutalized slaves. He went to the slave market to say good-bye to them. Recognizing him, they greeted him with smiles, some with tears. He later wrote:

> Notwithstanding my happiness at once more rejoining my English friends, I really felt no small regret at taking leave of our poor fellow travellers, many of whom, I knew, were destined to proceed to Tunis and Turkey. Their good humoured gaiety and songs had lightened to me many hours of pain and fatigue, and their gratitude for any little benefits I had it in my power to confer, quite warmed my heart towards them.

Lyon paid a last visit to the bashaw, who delighted in his mastery of Arabic and proficiency in the Fezzanese dialect.

On May 14, 1820, Lyon and Belford sailed for England, their work in Africa completed. Sadly, in exchange for the life of its leader, the Ritchie mission produced little accurate information. The most important claim Lyon made, based on stories collected from traders in Murzuk, proved to be wrong: that the Niger "runs into a lake called the Tsaad. . . . [T]hus far are we able to trace the Niger, and all other accounts are merely conjectural. All agree, however, that by one route or another, these waters join the great Nile of Egypt."

Lyon duly reported to London that the Niger flowed into Lake Chad and from there to the Nile, as some geographers in England had predicted. Besides this misinformation, Lyon brought back to England the only tangible product of the expedition: a *mehari* camel, which he presented as a gift to George IV,* who exiled it to the stables at Windsor Castle after it spat on him.

Lyon's account of his journey between Tripoli and Murzuk was pored over with enthusiasm at the Colonial Office and at the Admiralty, the more so as it was in harmony with all the geographical speculations (mostly wrong) then popular at Whitehall. Although he had gotten no farther south than Tegheri, Lyon encountered no insuperable difficulties. It seemed that Consul Warrington's statement about the prestige of the bashaw running far into the Sahara might be true.

Now that Lyon had convinced Downing Street that the Niger ran into Lake Chad, the new destination for exploration charted by the British became the old African kingdom of Bornu, south of the lake. No one promoted this new route to the interior with greater ardor than Hanmer Warrington. With characteristic bombast, he wrote the Colonial Office that it was as easy to get from Tripoli to Bornu (a region so far south that it is now part of Nigeria) as "from London to Edinburgh, and I should not hesitate to go myself, knowing as I do there is neither danger nor difficulty attending it."

Needless to say, at no time in the third of a century he lived in Tripoli did Warrington ever travel more than a few miles outside the city, and then only for a picnic lunch accompanied by an army of servants.

While Lyon was on his way home, Sir John Barrow of the Admiralty underwrote the financial support needed for another expedition. Lyon, in making his report, had expressed the hope that he would be allowed to lead it, which would establish a base camp for future exploration along the Niger on its supposed eastern course.

Barrow would have done well to stick with Lyon, a man who will be remembered among the half dozen most competent English explorers. Unfortunately, the secretary of the Admiralty had already picked another man for the job by the time Lyon reached London.

---

*The prince regent succeeded his father on January 29, 1820, though he had already been ruling as de facto king since 1811.

———•◆•———

Chapter Seven

HUGH CLAPPERTON

S IR JOHN BARROW selected Dr. Walter Oudney, a Lowland Scot and a physician like Mungo Park, to lead the next foray into the African interior. Oudney, thirty-one, practiced medicine in Edinburgh, having served as a naval surgeon earlier in his career. An undersized man with a pale, solemn face, he seemed to some at the Admiralty better suited to the sick wards of Scotland than the jungles of Africa.

When Consul Warrington's offer to go on the expedition himself was seen as the hyperbole that it was, Dr. Oudney recruited his friend and neighbor Hugh Clapperton, thirty-three, the tenth son of a Dumfrieshire doctor (who would go on to sire another seventeen offspring after Hugh), to go with him. "My friend Lieutenant Clapperton is a gentleman of excellent disposition, strong constitution, and temperate habits," wrote Oudney to London, "who is exceedingly desirous of accompanying the expedition. *He wishes no salary* [emphasis added]." Clapperton was an adventurer, if a low-key one. Barrow wrote to Goulbourn, Bathurst's aide, that Clapperton was "possessed of resources of superior kind." By the time he joined Oudney, he had already sailed around the world. In 1822

Captain Hugh Clapperton of His Majesty's Royal Navy, in full dress blues.

the mission to the interior via the "Tripoli route," as it soon came to be known, was duly organized.

Hugh Clapperton, who was soon destined to become Alexander Gordon Laing's rival, had first gone to sea as a thirteen-year-old cabin boy on a merchant schooner plying between the Baltic States and North America. He showed an independence of mind early—by refusing to shine the captain's shoes. At seventeen, he was press-ganged (kidnapped) into the Royal Navy, reaching the rank of lieutenant—a remarkable achievement in an era when officers were drawn from the upper classes. He sailed the Mediterranean and the South China Sea after an initial voyage that took him to South Africa and South America. He participated in the capture of Réunion from the French and spent two years patrolling the East Indies. At the battle of Mauritius in 1814, he was first in the breach and personally hauled down the French flag.

He saw service in the Canadian Great Lakes, fighting in the War of 1812 against the United States before gaining his commission and the command of a schooner in 1815. At a blockhouse on Lake Huron, he lost half a thumb carrying an exhausted youngster across the frozen lake while escaping the attack of an American schooner. Said to have become engaged to a Huron princess, in 1817 he was demobilized on half pay and returned to Scotland, a victim of the peace. With his experiences in far-off places, robust constitution, and proven military courage, Clapperton made a welcome addition to the mission. Moreover, he looked the part: he was six feet tall in an age of shorter men, with a high brow, piercing eyes, and fine symmetrical features.

The plan was that this pair, Scotsmen and friends, would form the mission to Bornu. But, through outside influence, another member was added, Lieutenant Dixon Denham, an instructor at the military college at

Sandhurst. He met Captain Lyon socially just after the latter's return to London and seemed bent on joining the new expedition.

Denham, thirty-five, was "an adventurer with the temperament of a man which drove him always to look beyond the next hill," according to a friend. Though he had never served in Africa (or undertaken exploration of any kind), he was said to be a brave soldier. At the battle of Toulouse against Napoleon, he had carried his wounded commander out of the line of fire.

Denham was also the officer-gentleman, equally poised at a diplomatic reception as on the battlefield. He told friends he had been drawn to African travel on an impulse, much as he "might have swum the Thames in winter on a bet." He had patrons in high circles, including the Duke of Wellington, with whom he corresponded regularly, and this may have been a factor in securing his appointment. Buoyant and indomitable, he had been placed at half pay in 1818 and was bored—and like Clapperton, unemployed and available. "He was the kind of man who must have adventure, or he rots," a friend recorded.

Notwithstanding his intelligence and courage, his good record in the Peninsular War, and his skill as a writer and artist, Dixon Denham was also a snob, domineering, insecure, jealous, and burdened with a devious streak of real meanness. He assumed from the outset, because of his superior social connections, that he was the mission's leader. He wrote to Barrow that his instructions should place him "independent of the Governor of Malta and the consul at Tripoli, except as concerns my interviews with the Bashaw." Whether as a result of Denham's aggressive personality or because of the actions of some shadowy backer in high places, plans for the expedition were revised. Oudney was to accompany the mission to Bornu, where, like Ritchie at Murzuk, he was to set up a vice-consulate and study prospects for trade. Denham, meanwhile, accompanied by Clapperton, was to carry out the main work: exploration of the Niger to its mouth.

Though he could not have known it at the time, Barrow had succeeded in recruiting a team that would prove even more dysfunctional than the one headed by Ritchie. If the Ritchie expedition was an example of a man defeating himself through a bizarre inability to cope with practical problems, the Denham-Clapperton-Oudney mission became a

melodrama of personality conflict. Denham, under stress, was puritanical and a martinet, while Clapperton was inflexible and swore a lot—and
poor Oudney was overwhelmed by them both. The enmity that built up
between Denham and his two coexplorers overshadowed the whole voyage, which turned into a study of the deterioration of civilized values under
the strain of traveling in the wilderness, a nonfiction *Heart of Darkness.*

Oudney and Clapperton, who may have had some qualms about the
new organization but had no idea of what they were really in for, left
England in September 1821. Denham wasn't ready to leave and stayed
behind. On October 20, Oudney and Clapperton landed in Tripoli aboard
a Sicilian fishing boat. Warrington welcomed them warmly, as he did all
visitors from his homeland. It was still not clear from Colonial Office
instructions who was leader of the party, and Oudney wisely induced
Warrington to set out in writing the fact that he, Oudney, was in general
charge. This document contained the phrase "You are charged by His
Majesty's Government to conduct this interesting and important mission
into the interior of Africa."

At Tripoli, John Tyrwhitt, the apple-cheeked son of a friend of
Warrington's in Malta, joined the two travelers. Tyrwhitt was the black
sheep of his family. He had joined the navy too young and led a dissi-
pated life. His father wrote bitterly to Warrington that his son had been
"wild," hiding for a time in Italy, where he had a torrid love affair. "I wish
him to have the least possible pocket money as he has a great propensity
for extravagance, women, and alcohol," his father wrote, hoping that his
friend the British consul would "pack him off to the most remote part of
Africa." Warrington complied, selecting Tyrwhitt to replace the deceased
Ritchie as his vice-consul at Murzuk.

Contemplating this trio round his dinner table, Warrington enthusi-
astically wrote the colonial secretary: "I never saw men better calculated
for the undertaking." It was another of his blowhard exaggerations; of his
three guests at dinner that evening, only one would survive more than
a year.

Denham arrived in Tripoli on November 19 aboard the schooner
Express carrying a copy of his own instructions from the Colonial Office.
After stating that Oudney was to remain at Bornu, where he was nomi-
nated "His Majesty's Vice-Consul to the Sultan of Bornu," the instruc-

tions directed Denham and Clapperton to "explore the Country to the Southward and Eastward of Bornu, principally with a view of tracing the course of the Niger and ascertaining its Embouchure."

Oudney was aggrieved that, instead of exploring, he would be tied up in Bornu doing paperwork. Further complicating matters, although Clapperton was to travel with Denham as his subordinate, it was to be "without any reference to his Relative Rank in His Majesty's Service," suggesting in some sense that they were equals. Finally, Oudney was to make all arrangements, hold all funds, and be responsible for obtaining the permission of the sultan of Bornu for the journeys in his territory. Thus a clear leader for the expedition was not designated, the wellspring of endless acrimony in the weeks ahead.

Denham had already vexed Oudney by setting out in writing an "Order of March" for the travelers, presumably based on rules then used in the British army. It contained such irrelevancies for African travelers as guard duties, ration issues, the posting of sentries, and punishments for dereliction of duty. He handed out copies. Oudney rejected the document as an insult, which, in the circumstances, it probably was; Clapperton simply ignored it.

Denham revealed his true opinion of his fellow travelers in a letter he sent to his brother Charles, then in London, on April 11:

> In the choice of my companions, I do not think His Majesty's gov-
> ernment have shewn their usual Sagacity; we are not well classed,
> and I have scarcely a fair chance. They are both Scotchmen and
> friends, and as one of them is under my orders, and the Consul Dr.
> Oudney, and myself, independent of each other, no small jealousy
> exists on their part, and to push me off the stage altogether would
> be exactly what they wish. [Of Clapperton he wrote,] [S]o vulgar,
> conceited and quarrelsome a person I scarcely ever met with, [and
> of Oudney he said,] [T]his son of war or rather of bluster completely
> rules, therefore any proposition from me is generally negatived by
> a Majority.

To depart, they needed the bashaw's permission. By now, Yusuf Karamanli realized that easy money could be made by "guaranteeing" the safety of English explorers, though he knew this pledge had no value south of Murzuk. Receiving Oudney and Warrington, he offered to provide an escort of a thousand armed men to Bornu and back in exchange for 5,000 pounds sterling. Warrington forwarded this proposal to the Colonial Office.

Apart from the expense, reliance on the bashaw also meant the usual inestimable delays. There were more visits to the bashaw. The Colonial Office approved Warrington's request for funds, but the consul handed over only a part of the sum, in the hope that the bashaw would use it to collect a party of soldiers to escort the mission to Bornu. Weeks passed with renewed but empty promises, and it became obvious that Yusuf Bashaw had no intention of recruiting escorts for the Englishmen.

The bashaw said he was awaiting the annual visit of the bey of Fezzan, with whom, on his return, the explorers might go free of charge. But the new bey, El Ahmar, never showed up. Feeling that they were wasting their time in Tripoli while their funds were drying up, the explorers decided to take the risk of traveling to Murzuk without escort. Besides, as Oudney pointed out, an armed escort could be a mixed blessing, since it might create the impression of a mission of conquest. And undisciplined troops were as likely to invent trouble as prevent it.

The meetings with the bashaw concluded, Oudney and Clapperton gathered their belongings and prepared to set out. They would go ahead of Denham, who had undisclosed private business to attend to in Tripoli. Traveling as Christians in their own clothes, and bearing a *teskera* from the bashaw, they took a new addition to the team: William Hillman, a shipwright from Malta. Hillman was hired by Denham to construct the boat in which to navigate the Niger, and to serve as his personal servant.

The rest of the party, which totaled the unlucky thirteen, was made up of oddly assorted characters. There was a native of St. Vincent in the West Indies, Adolphus Sympkins. Nobody could cope with a name like that and he was known simply as "Columbus" from his having been a merchant seaman and, if his own accounts could be believed, having visited most of the countries of the globe. He was "a shifty gentleman" but useful in that he spoke Arabic fluently, as well as three European languages. Then there was Jacob, a Gibraltar Jew, who appears at odd moments in all three of the journals that were kept of the voyage, but with no explanation of what he was doing. Presumably he just wanted to go to Bornu. Three bearers and four camel men completed the party. Equipment, even by the modest standards of the day, was meager, but Oudney had a good supply of trinkets to hand out as gifts to the potentates they expected to meet. Denham would follow the main party later.

A PALE, rinsed dawn broke along the seawall and a breeze brought the smell of tar and the sticky dampness of salt as the party set out from Tripoli on February 23, 1822, heading due south nine hundred miles through the great sand sea. The first part of the journey, to the Fezzan, was pleasant, even beautiful. Day after day, the sun shone out of a cloudless sky; night after night, moon and stars brooded over the scented darkness of the fertile desert. There were valleys of bright green, tangled masses of fruits and flowers, and by day the mountains were dazzling with the clear sunshine of North Africa. The restlessness and irritability of Tripoli faded in the timelessness of the desert.

Yet even the journey to Murzuk, not considered more than a preliminary to the actual march, turned out to be a test of endurance. The real desert began at Sockna (Suknah), halfway between Murzuk and Tripoli. Oudney's party got a rude initiation; travel in the Sahara, especially for a European, could be difficult. The distances were vast, the terrain brutal, and the weather pitiless. Heat was the major enemy in a land where 100 degrees Fahrenheit was considered a cool winter's day. In summer, temperatures of 150 degrees and above were not unknown, especially as one got farther from the coast. In such remorseless heat, living things became not so much paralyzed as comatose. Caravans halted, the Arabs covered themselves with burnouses on the burning sands like so many dancing pebbles of water on the well-greased surface of a frying pan.

The dry air and sandy soil of the Sahara quickly lost its heat after sunset; in the hottest regions of the planet, night cold was a significant danger. The mercury plunged visibly within the space of minutes. It sometimes fell below freezing at night, but a frost at dawn quickly gave way to temperatures hovering well above 100 degrees by ten o'clock.

To the discomfort caused by extremes of temperature was added, this trip, the ordeal of a sandstorm—called a "hurricane" by the Tripolitanian Arabs. A lurid yellow light on the horizon and a sound like

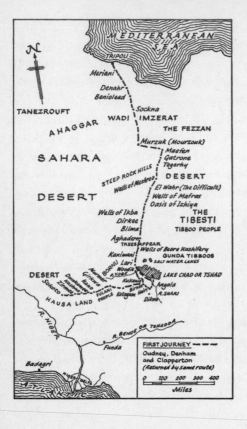

The "Tripoli Route" taken by Denham, Oudney, and Clapperton to discover Lake Chad, West Africa's great inland sea, and the Bornu Empire, thus validating Lord Bathurst's contention that it was safer (though it involved traveling much greater distances) to penetrate the heart of black Africa by coming in from the southern Mediterranean across the Sahara.

dull thunder announced its coming. The dry air crackled with electricity; touching the canvas of the tents gave a nasty shock. The heart of the storm itself descended on the Englishmen with impetuous violence. Some of these tempests had engulfed and smothered whole caravans. Men were lost in a cloud of driving sand particles, helpless against the lash of tens of millions of flying grains of razor-sharp silica. The sun was obscured and a feeling of claustrophobia, the crushing weight of immense and unpredictable forces, burdened the caravan. Tents pitched to give protection whirled away on the flaying winds. The noise was overwhelming, the curses of men and the anguished bellowing of animals piercing through the roar of the storm.

The next morning, the air was still, the sun rose and the violence was only a memory, but the camp was in disarray. Everyone in the caravan was put to searching and digging in the sand for lost objects. After an hour they simply moved on.

At Murzuk, friendly cries of "Inglesi! Inglesi!" greeted them, the people of the town crowding around the white visitors, kissing their hands, laughing and showing affection and geniality foreign to Tripoli. The women of the town inspected the explorers "with rather more curiosity than modesty." Good nature was the prevailing mood. The new bey of Fezzan, El Ahmar, successor to the one who had refused to help Ritchie, was a colorful and unpredictable character who called himself by the nom de guerre Mustafa the Red. He was a renegade who had earned the bashaw's support by marrying one of his daughters. Mustafa the Red, the bashaw had promised, would escort them to Bornu with a thousand troops. When the explorers arrived in Murzuk, the bey told them he was indeed about to leave—but for Tripoli, not Bornu. He needed to gather an armed force for the slaving expedition south. This was bad news, for Lyon had stressed the dangers to health of an extended stay in Murzuk, with its noxious pools of stagnant water.

Denham left Tripoli on March 5, 1822, soon joining his colleagues at Wadi Mimum on March 8. Denham, who had a greater fear of illness than the others, didn't like the squalor of Murzuk, and proposed that he should immediately return to Tripoli alone to see if could pressure the bashaw to provide the needed escort. He also hoped to extract more funds from Warrington. The need for the bashaw's help became more urgent when the bey announced that the Englishmen were forbidden to leave the Fezzan during his absence. To make sure they complied, he withdrew all means of traveling, including camels.

Oudney and Clapperton supported Denham's idea of returning to Tripoli. They may even have encouraged him, hoping that his fear of illness and his generally nasty disposition would dispose him never to come back. "His absence," wrote Clapperton to his mentor Sir John Barrow, "will be no loss to the Mission, and a saving to his country, for Major Denham could not read his sextant, knew not a star in the heavens, and could not take the altitude of the sun." By June 13, 1822, Dixon Denham was back with Warrington in Tripoli.

AFTER DENHAM'S DEPARTURE, Oudney and Clapperton took cursory trips to explore the desert, mainly to the west. These jaunts were dangerous, for the country around Ghat, 240 miles west of Murzuk, was the territory of the ferocious Ajjer Tuareg, through whose lands no passport of the bashaw carried prerogative. A bit of luck helped smooth the way for them. Lyon, in his last days in Murzuk, had been befriended by the Ajjer Tuareg Hatita ag Khuden, and had promised this man an English sword.

"Hateeta, a Tuarick of the tribe of Benghrasata of Ghaat," Lyon had written of his departure from Murzuk in 1820, "came to take leave of me. He now pressed me very much to promise him, that on my return to Africa, I would pass through his country, of which he is chief, and take him with me to the Negro Land, adding, that if I would bring him a sword like the one I wore, he should be perfectly content. He is the only Tuarick I ever saw who was not an impudent beggar, or who made presents without expecting a return."

Lyon had not forgotten his promise and had purchased a good Sheffield sword in London and given the weapon to Denham. Just before leaving for Tripoli, with the ragged desert molded into satin dunes by the soft spring rains, Denham had observed a tall man veiled like a Tuareg watching the mud hovel in which the British party was housed. Though he stood at some distance, Denham could see that the stranger had "large, brilliant eyes" and that he was watching him intently. Denham called out to him and discovered that he was none other than Hatita. Denham gave him the promised sword.

"It would be difficult to describe his delight," Denham wrote. "It was shortly reported all over the whole town that Hateeta had received a present from *Said* (Lyon's travelling name), worth one hundred Dollars."

It was Hatita's role as *dalil* (guide and protector) that made it possible for Oudney and Clapperton to travel safely outside Murzuk. During the next three months, the Bornu mission pretty much incorporated Hatita into its company as a full-fledged member of the expedition, at least while the explorers were in and around Murzuk and in Ghat. Beyond arranging for the hire of camels, he was determined to make his patrons a social success among the locals, and he seemed to enjoy teaching them the etiquette of the desert—a thorny jungle of human impulses even in the best of times.

"Our friend Hateeta was anxious we should shine," wrote Oudney, "and read a number of lectures to Clapperton." To have come across a Tuareg so ready, even eager, to help and advise on social behavior was a delightful experience in a land where strange manners usually excited ridicule, or worse. The engaging Hatita endeared himself to Clapperton, as he would to all English explorers. Dr. Oudney showed his gratitude by treating him for malaria, which was endemic.

This was new territory, not seen by a European in modern times. The wells amid the chaotic rocks of the desert were choked with sand that took hours to dig out. The track took them through monotonous regions where the hours and days became apparent chiefly through the variations in the wonderful light, converting it into an antilandscape. The desert floor practically disappeared and the explorers were conscious only of light and color, of pinkish yellow spreading over the lower half of their field of vision and pale blue flooding the upper—both all-enveloping and blindingly brilliant. Between the two, no clear division existed, just a perpetual watery image shivering the horizon like a shattered windowpane. Then the light would change again, reflecting distant rocks in the mirages, causing them to appear twice their real height and dangerously top-heavy, like gigantic bowling pins. At twilight, the horizon would reemerge. Clapperton and Oudney would come down to earth again, watching the sand sea change its nighttime shades from yellow to ocher to purple to gray.

On June 16, they visited the Roman mausoleum of Garama, the ancient capital of the Garamantes, which loomed abruptly over the desert like a medieval castle. They saw dunes 400 feet high. On July 8 they discovered in the heart of the mountains a forgotten community able to survive on next to nothing, a band of forlorn humans in a permanent settlement by the shores of a salt lake, Bahir Mandia. They lived on tiny shrimplike creatures (the Tuareg called them "worm-eaters"), catching them with closely woven nets.

They visited the headquarters of the Ajjer Tuareg at the oasis of Ghat. The friendly welcome of the notoriously dangerous Tuareg seemed further proof they did not need a military escort.

In the meantime, Denham in Tripoli found the bashaw as obdurate as Murzuk's bey. He insisted that the mission not leave Murzuk without Mustafa the Red and his men. The bey himself had still not reached the coast, and once he got there, would need at least six months to gather the required troops for his slaving expedition. Warrington had already paid

*Mondra Lake, also known as Bahir Mandia, the tiny salt-water body Oudney
and Clapperton discovered shimmering like a blue jewel ringed by date palms in the
pristine desert west of Murzuk. Denham would never forgive his coexplorers for
making this side-trip without him.*

the bashaw 2,000 of the promised 5,000 pounds. To ensure that he collected the rest, the bashaw was intent on maintaining the conditions of
the original deal. This meant that no move could be made from Murzuk
for months, perhaps a year.

This news outraged Denham, convincing him that Warrington was
incompetent and that he needed help from officials back home. He
decided to consult Lord Bathurst personally, ostensibly to report on the
deteriorating situation to the Colonial Office, but also, as a letter to his
brother shows, to get his own military rank raised to lieutenant colonel
and to obtain a new commission clearly appointing him commander-in-
chief. He found a French ship soon to weigh anchor for Marseilles, and in
this vessel, in spite of Warrington's protests, he sailed, commenting to one
of the bashaw's lieutenants that his government would have something to
say when they heard of the casual treatment (which he termed "duplicity") meted out to an official British expedition.

It was a move Dixon Denham would live to regret.

Chapter Eight

THE JOURNEY TO BORNU

YUSUF KARAMANLI did not like news of his ill treatment of Englishmen finding its way to London. He now concocted an alternative plan to satisfy the impatient British. A wealthy Fezzanese merchant, Abu Bakr Bhu Khallum (a man invariably referred to by Warrington in his letters by the Gilbert and Sullivanesque "Buckaloom"), with an escort of three hundred men, was about to return to the Fezzan and from there proceed to Bornu. He was leaving Tripoli, and agreed for a fee (to be shared with the bashaw) to escort the Englishmen beyond Murzuk.

Warrington, who was more than ready to pay the required sum, wrote to Denham, then in quarantine at Marseilles, hoping to forestall him:

> This morning the Bashaw has offered to send Buckaloom, with One hundred Horse and One hundred Infantry to convey the travellers to Bornou etc., provided we give Him ten thousand Dollars. The escort to leave Tripoli in fifteen days after the payment of the money, and Mourzouk in two months from the same date. It is a

most material and certainly most important point gained. . . . Therefore, the moment you receive this, I suppose you will return from
Marseilles immediately, and with your usual activity and zeal, will
join them at Mourzouk.

Denham got no farther than Marseilles, where he was overtaken by
no fewer than three letters from Yusuf Bashaw addressed to him at Leghorn, Malta, and Marseilles, as well as Warrington's letter. He realized
the consul had outfoxed him, and that he must return to Tripoli at once.
He was still so angry he fired off a furious letter to Bathurst. He wrote
of Oudney:

Never was a man so ill qualified for such a duty [as leading the
mission]. Except by water, I think, he has never travelled 80 miles
from Edinbro'. Still everything would he arrange and on we went,
blundering in misery, although at a considerable expense. Not one
word of any language could he speak except his own, yet he did
undauntedly harangue those around him who bowed, walked off,
and of course cheated him.

He should have slept on this letter before launching it in the next
packet boat for England, for if he had hoped to denigrate Oudney and
Clapperton in the eyes of Lord Bathurst, and so to command the expedition with a promotion, he failed utterly. Robert Wilmot was tapped to
send back a reprimand expressing Lord Bathurst's tart surprise

that you should have felt yourself warranted in leaving Tripoli at a
time when you could most usefully have assisted H.M.'s Consul
General in completing the final arrangements for your departure
into the interior of Africa; nor can his Lordship understand the
grounds upon which you seem to have imagined that your presence
in this country would have advanced the interests confided to your
charge. . . . [As to Denham's unpleasant remarks about his companions,] Lord Bathurst has felt considerable regret at the general tone
of your observations; and, although his Lordship will be willing to
make some allowance for the feeling of irritation which prompted

you to leave Tripoli, and for the haste in which your letter was written, yet he feels himself called upon to caution you most earnestly
in future not to allow yourself to yield to angry feelings and impressions which, if not restrained, must have the effect of disturbing the
harmony of your party and of extinguishing the mutual disposition
to amicable cooperation, without which the wishes and expectations of H.M.'s Government must be frustrated.

This rebuke was waiting for him when he landed at Tripoli. Meanwhile, news of his bid to go to England reached his companions back in
Murzuk. Both Oudney and Clapperton (and even Hillman, the carpenter)
were dumbfounded.

What [inquired Oudney in reply to Warrington's news] has taken
Major Denham to England? He has not written a word on the subject to [us]. . . . I do not know how he can exculpate himself, or look
us in the face, for leaving the Mission at a time when its objects
were so near being accomplished. . . . My countrymen [i e , the
Scots] are famed for caution, but he far surpasses them. And I am
sure he would take nothing on his shoulders. . . . I really believe he
would not go his body's length without it was insured. His conduct
has been all along what has tended to alienate affection. . . . For my
part, I have never borne so much from any man as from him, and all
for the sake of peace—it is not my disposition to be quarrelsome, on
the contrary, to live in harmony with all men, and thank God, I have
always been able in a great degree to do it, except with him. Had I
known the man, I would have refused my appointment. . . . Destroy
this, it may he considered spleen, envy, or some of the evil passions
proceeding from a mind weakened by weakness. Take no notice of
it, I beg, but always have in mind that *a Snake often lies concealed
under the Grass.*

Regrettably, Warrington not only kept this letter but shared it with
Denham, further souring relations all around. By the end of September, his chastisement from London taken to heart, Denham was on his
way back to Murzuk with Abu Bakr Bhu Khallum. Warrington watched

Denham's departure with a misgiving that he shared with the Colonial Office:

> The Hostile disposition existing in the Southern Mission, [he explained,] was due to the jealousy existing between Oudney and Denham. Probably the breach has been widened by various paragraphs in the news papers, saying that the Mission is under the immediate direction and auspices of the latter. [He added, gloomily,] Impossible to reconcile these gentlemen, and I should strongly recommend that Lt. Clapperton should be attached to Dr. Oudney. They are countrymen, very old friends, and Dr. Oudney has undoubtedly the most commanding influence over Lieut. Clapperton. Major Denham is of a difficult cast of character, and is more a Man of the World.

In a further letter in December, he commented about what he had come to call the "Great Bone of Contention":

> The Great Bone of Contention appears to me a jealousy as to whom the Mission is confided to. I think the orders and instructions speak for themselves, which clearly shew that Oudney and Denham are distinct and separate, it being the duty of the Former from his Official Appointment to afford every facility and to give every assistance to the latter. . . .

The Colonial Office, torn between Oudney's prior claim to leadership, in point of time, and Denham's, in point of influence, now suggested that a change be made in the expedition. Clapperton was to come under Oudney, and his place, as Denham's aide, was to be taken by young Tyrwhitt. Warrington wrote to Denham in March 1823 to say that the Colonial Office had made these changes, authorizing Tyrwhitt to join him. Typically of Denham, he speculated Tyrwhitt was Warrington's spy.

Denham's first journey to Murzuk had been bad, but the second was worse. The caravan spent three days passing the desolate chain of hills known as the Jebel es Sawda (Black Mountains), marching all day over glaring basalt, saved from tormenting thirst by a burst of providential rain.

At Zeghren (Az Zighan) they rested a day, everybody, including a party of slaves, enjoying as much pure water as they could drink. They rested again at a date grove, but it was an exhausted and scarecrow crew that made its entry, with all the pomp and ceremony that could be mustered, into Murzuk.

Abu Bakr Bhu Khallum had assembled a party of Meghara Arabs as an escort. These were tough fighting men—compact, hard, wiry, with an inborn contempt for city dwellers. Rigid in their religious and social behavior (they regarded circumcision and the shaving of hair from all parts of the body as necessary to manhood), they were expert warriors and horsemen. Cowardice was the greatest sin for them, yet Oudney recorded instances during the crossing when the troop bolted as one man in the face of danger. This strange behavior caused no comment among the Meghara when all could run away without shame. The dereliction of a single man, however, inevitably led to his public humiliation. The culprit would be displayed, bound, in front of the caravan with the bowels and offal of a sacrificed bull draped around his neck as a token of his disgrace.

Love of war, bloodshed, cruelty, and an ability to hold a grudge forever made them uneasy traveling companions, but the fact that these warriors were at their happiest deep in the desert, a terrain they knew intimately, was a boon to the British explorers. For the moment, it was comforting to have as allies men who were feared by everyone else.

To Denham, Bhu Khallum's importance was shown clearly by the deference he was accorded. Half the population of Murzuk turned out to bid farewell to the great merchant, the women singing and dancing, the men executing the characteristic cavalry charge of which Arab people everywhere are so fond—hair-raising to guests, who stood still and watched the rushing horde stop on a penny within feet of them. Of this display Denham commented, with his usual cynicism, that "they charged with every appearance of ferocious courage, but on horses which were half dead from lack of food."

IT WAS A SORRY BAND of explorers that prepared to set off across the Sahara. Oudney's heart was giving him trouble, Hillman was down with dysentery, and Clapperton had a raging fever. The British mission now consisted of four Britons, five servants, and four camel drivers. With the escort of two hundred men, the caravan was three hundred strong (attached also were a number of merchants from Tripoli and Sockna, under the protection of their own armed escorts).

Sick, tired, or both, the explorers assembled outside the walls of the town on November 19, 1822. At dawn on that day, the Bornu mission, with Abu Bakr Bhu Khallum's trade caravan, left Murzuk. The great sand snake would head due south through a great sand sea before reaching Lake Chad. Dispersing the bleak mood of the British was the belief that by traveling in force with such an experienced and powerful Arab leader, they stood a good chance of not getting lost or attacked.

They were accompanied, for a mile or two, by half the townspeople of Murzuk. Ahead of them stretched twelve hundred miles of wilderness so barren that, even today, if a straight line is drawn in an atlas between Murzuk and Lake Chad (their first objective), only one outpost appears on it.

Bhu Khallum was too experienced to take a direct a route, inviting attack. There was a "good track" to Traghan (Taraghin), one of the 109 walled towns of the Fezzan, and they followed it. The "good track" ended there. Onward to Maefen, the caravan stumbled over hard cracked earth, encrusted with salt, where it was difficult merely to put one foot in front of the other. Denham noted salt fields everywhere, covered with scintillating crystals. The next landmark required a trek of fourteen hours over a dreary plain where the camels stopped occasionally to crop *aghul*, the only living vegetation, and the Meghara Arabs vigilantly searched for date palms as sailors at sea look for landfall.

Clapperton and Oudney were in bad shape. Both had contracted fevers in Murzuk, as had Hillman, and all were overwrought. Previous missions had done little to dispel ignorance about African travel. No one used mosquito nets or boiled water or took quinine as a prophylactic against malaria. Having a doctor along served little purpose, for medical knowledge was limited to cupping and taking calomel, or vinegar and water. Their equipment and camels, except firearms, differed little from that in use for a millennium. Survival depended not on medicines and purified water, but on two feet and the human virtues of courage, stamina, and determination.

The tracks they took were lined with human skeletons, often near dried wells. Clapperton registered the mounting toll of bones with fear. Around a desiccated oasis, Denham saw "more than one hundred skeletons, some of them with the skin still remaining attached to the bones—not even a little sand thrown over them." The Meghara Arabs roared with laughter at the concern the white explorers showed over these exposed human remains. "These creatures were only blacks," they said, adding, *"Nam boo!"* (Damn their fathers!).* They played horrific games with the cadavers, using skulls as footballs and making comments on the gender of the scrags. "They began knocking about the limbs," Denham wrote, "with the butt ends of their firelocks, saying, 'This was a woman! This was a child!'"

They were on the infamous slaving route over which tens of thousands of black Africans, taken from their homes in the Sudan, were forced to march to slavery, to Tripoli. It was only too clear that multitudes had not made it. Clapperton recalled how surprised he had been to see a happy slave gang on first entry into Murzuk. The reason for their joy was now clear. *They were alive.* That they would soon be off to be fattened for the markets of Tripoli was a minor worry.

It struck Clapperton that his own party still had a long way to go, and that the Bornu mission might well end up as these dead slaves the Meghara kicked around so irreverently. But if they died, at least they would not be found by subsequent explorers, Clapperton mused, with fetters joining corpse to corpse, each with manacles locked to wrists and ankles.

There was no water now. The travelers had to tighten their belts and dream of the next oasis. Denham's diary became more laconic. He noted one day that a *naga* (a female camel) had given birth on the march, and that the caravan did not halt for so much as a second. The newborn was cared for—after all, it was a camel, a valuable property—but the unfortunate mother was allowed no rest. The calf was briefly carried, and then it, too, was forced to totter along on wavering legs. There was no time for sentiment or compassion. Everyone concentrated on the job of moving on. To stop was to die.

*This could be translated many ways, of which this is the least offensive.

Ill will and squabbling among the explorers added to their miseries and the horrors apparent on the road, with the Englishman Denham in constant conflict with the two Scots. Denham's peremptory orders caused trouble. He belittled his companions and voiced paranoid accusations. Innocent events became, in his eyes, plots hatched against him; his only focus on the expedition came through a distorted lens of personal rivalry.

It was this dreary crossing, with its endless billowing sand and camels dying of exhaustion, that became the setting for the first serious eruption between Denham and Clapperton. In December, somewhere between Murzuk and Bilma (a village 500 miles southwest of the Fezzanese capital), Denham ordered Clapperton, whose naval skill in plotting maps was highly developed, to give him the latitudes of various points. Clapperton refused, saying he would not be subject to "the whim of any man." In fact, he swore that he would deny Denham all surveying observations he made during the expedition. He wrote that Denham "has quarreled with and browbeat every person belonging to the Mission or who has ever been attached to it." Unbelievably, though they saw each other every day, they stopped speaking to each other, communicating only by letter, like an estranged couple still sharing the same house.

In a note datelined "Tents, Jan. 1, 1823," Clapperton informed Denham that "you take upon yourself a great deal to issue such orders [to give him latitudes] which could not be more imperative were they from the Horse Guards or Admiralty, you must not introduce a Martial system into what is civil and scientific, neither must you expect from me what it is your own duty to execute."

These words enraged Denham, whose knowledge of the use of sextant and compass were rudimentary (and whose own computed latitudes were found by later travelers to be wildly inaccurate). The trouble about these constant disputes, so trivial, was that all parties were stuck to one another like survivors on an atoll. Compounding the problem, each man insisted on sending copies of his letters to Warrington, who was expected to forward them to the Colonial Office. Transcripts of their ill-tempered correspondence departed weekly via a messenger service consisting of two Tebu tribesmen who left for the coast with the mail pouch, a sack of grain, a skin of water, and bags tied to their camels' tails to catch the dung they saved for fuel. They traveled in pairs because only one was expected to survive. These messengers risked their lives—and many died—to convey the explorers' malicious and petty squabbles back to Warrington and Downing Street.

As the gaunt Tibesti Mountains, soaring nearly to 11,500 feet, receded away on their left, the track began to show more skeletons, averaging about eighty a day. When they reached El Hammar (Emi Tahmeli), the heaps of bones were so high that the appalled Englishmen noted that "they were countless." Even in the face of this grim evidence, their concern was momentary, for these were men past caring about others. Tortured by thirst, desiccated, their eyes bloodshot and so swollen they could not close them, the explorers reached a place where the Meghara said there was a well, only to find that it had disappeared. As one man, the whole caravan dug frantically into the depression where the main well should have been. Under the sand it was still there. To inexperienced eyes, there was nothing but a hollow. Without guides, the British were certain they would have died at that spot, for all the *guerbas* were empty.

Christmas Day came and went unmentioned. There was no esprit de corps left in the exhausted travelers. Arrival at the next filthy oasis was all they thought about, a place where crippling thirst, heat, and weariness could briefly be forgotten—if they were lucky. Sandstorms engulfed them with treacherous speed. For three days they huddled in rolled blankets, unable to move from hastily erected tents, praying that frail canvas shelters would resist the roaring chaos. Even the Meghara temporarily lost their bearings after this obliterating tempest, which buried half of the caravan's possessions. After two days of running in circles, they found the trail again.

On New Year's Day, 1823, one of the Meghara caught a crippled juvenile hyena. Hobbling it further with cords, he shot it to pieces at close range, chortling and guffawing. Denham recorded the event, appalled.

The explorers soon reached the village of Aney. Huge masses of square stones, so rectilinear that it was hard to believe they had been carved by nature and not by human hands, were used as pedestals for the huts of the inhabitants. The whole formed a bastion impossible to take by direct assault, a perfect retreat for the Tebus, who, though fierce fighters, lived in perpetual dread of Tuareg raids. The only approach to

The naturally fortified Tebu stronghold at Aney. The people of Aney built their homes on top of flat pedestals of rock like that on the left. By withdrawing the rope ladder from above, they flummoxed attackers.

the upper surface of these sheer stone blocks was by rope ladders, which could be hastily drawn up in emergencies. The explorers had heard of the Tebu from Lyon's account and were eager to learn more of this mysterious people—black Africans who had ventured deep into North Africa, and survived.

The caravanners, Arab and English alike, went forward fearing the Tuareg, scourge of the Arab slave trader. Speeding through the desert like a night wind, the nomads regarded caravans as trespassers on their land, seizing their property, or worse. Sheikh Abu Bakr Bhu Khallum believed that precautions against them were useless. He terrorized the British explorers with lurid stories about these "masters of mutilation and torture." The menace of their invisible presence hovered over the men like a shroud.

Nearly a year to the day after the travelers landed in Tripoli they reached Tiggema (Achenouma), a village perched on top of a rock four hundred feet high, with vertical sides. Formations like this are common in parts of the Sahara (such as the stone "forest" in the region of Tamrit), but they were new to the Englishmen, and a pleasant change from the deadly monotony of the ergs and pebbled plains. They had reached the center of a fertile stretch of country, with a drenched wadi running through the middle of it, rich in date palms. There was plenty of fine grass, and over the *trona*, or saltwater lakes, plovers wheeled and called to one another in immense numbers. Clapperton went out to shoot some for dinner. Fresh from a roasting spit, everyone feasted on the birds.

On January 12, the party reached Bilma, capital of the Tebu country, a collection of dingy huts surrounded by a mud wall. Around the village were several more salt lakes. Bilma was the heart of the salt trade and one of the richest salt centers in Africa. The precious mineral was packed into bags and traded throughout the Fezzan. The Tuareg kept a careful balance between raiding and exterminating the Tebu, for they had no wish to kill all the workers who mined this valuable commodity, and the Tebu could be aggressive if provoked. Disinclined to manual labor themselves, the Tuareg were happy to allow the Tebu to perform the backbreaking work and, to a certain extent, prosper. They took what they wanted when they wanted it. The Tuareg saw it as a justifiable tax for, after all, they were the lords of the desert.

It seemed the caravan would never reach Bornu. As the humidity increased, the march became a nightmare of heat and sand and flies, the eternal plodding of camels, and, at night, remorseless cold under glaring stars. They could not go back, and they hardly dared to go forward. By late January, the caravanners began to see vegetation—clumps of weedy grasses and flowers appearing for the first time. The weeks of unrelieved discomfort and torment were coming to an end; they were approaching the southern edge of the Great Desert.

On February 5, 1823, after ninety days in the wilderness, the caravan reached the shores of Lake Chad, a body of water the size of Switzerland never before seen by a white man. Reeds ten feet high lined the banks, hiding the surface of the lake. The papyrus tufts were a reddish green; the water a greenish gray, turning a pale gold in the evenings.

Climbing the crests of low dunes, the travelers could see wide sheets of the great lake, but they had no idea just how extensive it was. The smooth surface reflected the splendor of the sunset—serene, majestic, indifferent, hard. They were astonished they could not see land on the distant horizon.

Denham and Clapperton explored Lake Chad, a body of water the size of New Jersey never before seen by white men. Denham nearly circumnavigated the shallow fresh-water lake, minutely documenting the hydrodynamics of its source, the River Shari, shown here in a sketch by Denham with local fisherman harvesting a catch in their unique canoes and sailing vessels.

"Glowing with the golden rays of the sun in its strength," Denham wrote, "was the great Lake Tsaad, the key objective of our search." He promptly renamed it Lake Waterloo, a name that did not stick. Although Leo Africanus had written of this strange inland sea centuries before, armchair geographers doubted its existence. A lake in the Sahara? Balder-dash! And yet here it was.

By this time, Oudney had chest pains and a bad cough, and Hillman was ill with fever. But sickness and quarrels were momentarily forgotten at the sight of the water.

"By sunrise I was on the border of the lake," wrote Denham, "and very quietly sat down to observe the scene before me. Pelicans, cranes four and five feet in height were scarcely so many yards from my side; immense spoonbills of a snowy whiteness, widgeon, teal, yellow-legged plover, and a hundred species of (to me at least) unknown water fowl."

At the time of the explorers' arrival, the kingdom of Bornu was the most powerful state between the Niger and the Nile. It controlled Lake Chad and one of the main caravan routes to Tripoli, as well as major cities and

Bornu's despotic but much-loved ruler, the great warrior and military genius Sheikh Alameen Ben Mohammed El Kanemi, receiving Denham, Clapperton, and Oudney at his palace at Kukawa, February 17, 1823, from a sketch Dixon Denham made of him on that day.

the royal capital, Kukawa, less than fifteen miles southwest of the lake. To the west, between Bornu and the Niger, lay the Sokoto caliphate, ruled by a Muslim reformer, Sultan Mohammed Bello, "the Beloved of God."

On February 16, 1823 the caravan reached Kukawa. The next day, the English mission was formally received by Sheikh Alameen Ben Mohammed El Kanemi, Bornu's ruler, who had spread Islam throughout his realm. The scene marked the passing of an age. It was the first meeting between the white men who would colonize Africa and a ruler deep in the impenetrable hinterland no European had previously been able to reach.

Now the soldier, the sailor, the surgeon, and the shipwright, in English uniforms set off by turbans and Turkish boots, stood in a darkened room before an African sheikh in a rich blue robe with a gold fringe, who sat cross-legged on a rug flanked by armed guards. The Englishmen were the official emissaries of a European government, the first of an endless line of civil servants who would be sent on African duty for the next 150 years.

On that day and at that moment, the last barrier to the inaccessible African heartland was crossed forever.

Chapter Nine

———◆———

UNDISCOVERED EMPIRES

BEFORE SUNRISE the desert sky turned a leathery brown and then slowly darkened, releasing the outlines of cloud, palates of ocher that massed up from Lake Chad like the veil of ashes on the slopes of a volcano. The city of Kukawa shuttered itself tightly, as if against a gale. Gusts of air and a thin, sour rain were the only forerunners of the darkness that blotted out the day.

Unseen in the gloom of shuttered rooms, sand invaded everything— clothes, papers, teaspoons, in locks, beneath fingernails, a nasty grit on the tongue. . . . Harsh, wailing air dried throats and noses and made eyes raw. Sand settled into the lake like black choking dust into the lungs of a chimney sweep.

Along the margins of wooden doors, thin white drifts appeared, as of young snow. The reeds along the water's edge swayed like ghosts. From time to time a cracked blast of lightning swept down from the heavens and shook the whole city so that one had the illusion that everything—trees, minarets, monuments, people—had been caught up in the eddy of a whirl- pool that would gently suck the whole city into the bowels of the earth.

The British explorers told Sheikh Mohammed El Kanemi that they had come "to see the country merely, and to give an account of its inhabitants, produce, and appearance; as our king was desirous of knowing every part of the globe." They made Kukawa their base for nearly a year, weathering the frequent sandstorms and setting out on exploratory excursions when they could. They exchanged presents with the sheikh, giving him a double-barreled shotgun and a pair of pistols. Clapperton amazed the local population by firing three Congreve rockets* tied to the tips of spears. El Kanemi delighted in their company and insisted on keeping them close by. He warned that leaving Bornu was dangerous, claiming that if anything happened to them the bashaw would invade his country. "The bashaw's letter," El Kanemi said, "orders me to protect you. Once over my borders, in the land of the treacherous Hausas and Fulanis, I can do nothing. You cannot go." He considered the territory south especially hazardous.

The explorers complied. Denham gave the sheikh a music box, which intrigued him. Sensing an opening, Denham asked for permission to explore Lake Chad. To clinch matters, El Kanemi asked for, and received, six of the Congreve rockets, with which he planned to scare the daylights out of his enemies.

Denham went off early one morning to explore the lake. At the town of Bree (Bre) he persuaded the *alkaid,* the chief of the town, to act as his guide. At the lakeshore the cool, clear morning turned swiftly to blazing heat. The shifting inland sea was a swampy world of papyrus and water and countless islands. High grass, tamarind, and locust trees shaded its banks. The shores were teeming with wild animals, a bounty of birdlife, and an orchestra of flying bugs, especially mosquitoes. The first night out, Denham recorded, was purgatory, but on the second, acting on the advice of the *alkaid,* Denham slept inside a ring of cattle and not a single mosquito bit him. It was a trick he never forgot.

Denham spooked three elephants, a male with two females, at close

---

* A powerful rocket of the period used in war, either in the field or for bombardment. In the former case it was armed with a shell or shrapnel; in the latter, with an inextinguishable explosive material enclosed in a metallic case to set fire to buildings, tents, etc., under attack. It was guided by a long wooden stick. Clapperton brought a case of them as part of the expedition's defenses.

range. The females wandered off but the male turned, and for a moment Denham thought he was in real danger. The expected charge never came. Instead, the lumbering bull inhaled a trunkful of sand and, with deliberate and accurate aim, showered it on the explorer. It was an effective defense—by the time Denham cleared his eyes of the stinging bath, the elephants were gone. Later that trip, he came downwind of a herd of 150 elephants and studied them at his leisure, sketching many of them; this time they ignored him.

Lake Chad, about twice the size of Massachusetts at the time Denham and Clapperton discovered it, exercised a weird, hypnotic fascination on Denham.* It was surveyed for the first time early in the twentieth century but remains something of a mystery in the twenty-first, a colossal puddle on the earth's surface which may, at one time, have been part of an inland sea stretching far into what is now Nigeria. Despite its lack of depth (or because of it), the lake is capable of producing ferocious storms that rip across it without warning, much feared by the local fishermen. Such storms can capsize pirogues, the fishing and transport craft made of papyrus reed by the locals. Charts of the lake are useless. The islands of the archipelago on its eastern shore have never been counted, for many appear and disappear overnight. Denham traveled around most of the perimeter of the giant body of water, taking bearings. One of El Kanemi's warriors had told him that circumnavigating the lake on foot would take five months.

---

* The lake is still regarded as one of the oddest geographical phenomena on earth. There are in fact two lakes, but they are so close together that even from the air the division is impossible to make out. Lake Chad has always been regarded as a single body of water, about 150 miles long with a width that varies from 60 miles at the narrowest to 130 miles at its widest point. In Clapperton's day, its area varied from 10,000 square miles in the dry season to more than twice that size in the wet. Today, it is a smaller body of water, with the surface averaging about 6,875 square miles (somewhat smaller than New Jersey). The greatest variabilities charted in recent times occurred in the 1970s and 1980s, with the area dropping to about 10,500 square miles in the mid-1980s, a change apparently related to the desertification of the surrounding region. The shoreline is ever shifting and in places it has been known to move as much as five miles in a single night. It is often impossible to see any water at all owing to the growth of papyrus reeds that clog much of the surface. The lake is so shallow that canoes can punt across it anywhere. It is possible to wade across, although there are occasional depths of as much as fifteen feet. Although the water is shallow, fish of all kinds abound, some said to be as large as sharks.

Only one river, the Shari (Chari-Logone), fed the lake, and none left it. Yet it remains a freshwater lake. The Yobe made periodic contributions during the rainy season, but most of the time the Yobe was only a patchwork of puddles. Narrow channels wove intricate patterns through the forests of reeds. In Denham's time, the men of the islands, the Boudoumi ("men of the grass"), were hairy, physically powerful, and lived apart from their neighbors. They were also piratical, and much feared by El Kanemi's subjects. Denham recorded that they were among the minority of peoples he had heard of who practiced castration to control population. They paid no homage to El Kanemi or the four main tribes surrounding the lake, and they would fight anyone at the drop of a hat. Denham wisely left them alone.

Back at camp, Oudney and Clapperton were so sick they rarely left their cots. Denham was bursting with good health and enjoyed the blandishments of pretty black women who gave him what he called "shampoos"—body massages with oil. These "shampoos" were thorough enough to make him write after one session: "Verily I began to think that I not only deserved to be a Sultan, but that I had already Commenced my Reign."

Denham's romps with local women left him time to magnify his quarrel with Clapperton. Relations between the two men reached the breaking point on April 11, when, in a letter to Clapperton, Denham made an insinuation that permanently poisoned the atmosphere of the mission and forever ruined any hope that the two would get along.

> I should neglect my duty [he wrote], were I any longer to delay setting before you in the strongest light I am able the continued extreme impropriety of your conduct *both public and private.* . . . [W]hen the line of conduct you pursue had the effect of injuring our respectability and National Character in the eyes of those people on whom we are but too dependent for aid in prosecuting the orders of the British government, it becomes necessary to obviate the consequences. . . . [T]he servant of the mess has now complained to me of your having beaten him here, of your having drawn a pistol on him while on the road, threatening to shoot him. . . . [T]he expression I myself heard you use toward this unfortunate person was "You

B——r [bugger, i.e., a homosexual], I'll pick your teeth for rings in
my ears." I have thought it right to state the foregoing facts for your
serious consideration and as far as I know myself without the slightest feeling of ill will.

Denham went on to make other accusations, alleging Clapperton to
have been "rude and violent," using "offensive abuse and degrading epi-
thets," and to have "in my presence insulted and abused" Bhu Khallum
and his officers. Clapperton, an ex-sailor, inured to the hard discipline
and violent language of seamen, swore and cursed, especially when under
strain, and he candidly admitted it. But he was puzzled by the opening
paragraph of Denham's complaint—that curious sentence, referring to
Clapperton's "impropriety of . . . conduct *both public and private.*" Clapperton showed the letter to Dr. Oudney, asking him to support a protest
to the Colonial Office. Oudney, who had often been the butt of Denham's
high-handed malice, happily complied.

You have requested my opinion on a letter from Major Denham,
containing accusations highly prejudicial to your character. I feel
glad I have witnessed most of them and can place them in a light
totally different from him. How your conduct, public or private, has
or will tend to injure the interests of the Mission, I am at a loss to
conceive. . . . In concluding, I cannot but express my indignation at
the vileness of the letter. . . . It indicates a mind void of every drop
of the milk of human kindness, a mind that hordes [*sic*] its venom
to sting when it may find an opportunity—a man that takes memoranda on the conduct of others is one that ought to be expelled from
society, he is a nuisance, he is a curse.

On April 16, 1823, Clapperton and Oudney confronted Denham,
asking that he clarify what he had said about Clapperton's conduct
"both public and private." Denham replied: "Oh you must have heard it
surely. . . . [I]t was the conversation of everyone, our own servants were
talking about it every night over the fire." Oudney said he knew nothing
about it. Denham then dropped his bombshell. He announced that it was

common knowledge among the Arabs of the caravan that Clapperton had had a homosexual relationship with one of his Arab servants.

Clapperton was aghast. To make such a charge in pre-Victorian England, in front of a witness, was more than enough to ruin a man's career, and if proved, to send him to prison.* If untrue, it was the worst possible slander, particularly since Denham must have realized it would reach the Colonial Office, where malicious rumors bred like flies on a carcass. Clapperton asked Oudney to make an immediate investigation, while Denham, having planted his accusation, made plans to go on a slaving expedition with Abu Bakr Bhu Khallum.

Clapperton wrote to Warrington about the incident Denham had apparently been referring to: "When we were encamped at Achenouma [about thirty-three miles due north of Bilma], an Arab . . . came into his [Denham's] tent and told him that I had wanted to commit the foulest crime in nature with an Arab named Abdullahi who was in my service and that the Arab had gone to complain of me."

When Clapperton asked that the Arab be questioned, he could not be found; he had fled the caravan. Clapperton asked Warrington for a full investigation "to clear my name from the most horrid stigma."

Meanwhile, the result of Oudney's probe, in which he was helped by Hillman, surprised no one. The evidence of all who were questioned was that a rumor about "buggery" had been floated by an Arab servant Clapperton had dismissed. Most of the camp servants, including Hillman, had heard the tale and given it no credence. The shower of letters to Warrington continued:

> No one [wrote Oudney] that knows Clapperton, will ever listen to such a charge against him. . . . [T]he whole has so much improbability that the most disinterested would pronounce it a vile, malicious report. . . . Your judgement will direct what is necessary to be done, whether to investigate more into the business, or let the matter rest.

---

* Or worse—sodomy was then a capital crime in the British armed forces, and sailors convicted of "buggery" were routinely hanged.

Though Dixon Denham would accuse him of sexual improprieties with a man, Hugh Clapperton's journals are filled with elaborate drawings of the women (but few of the men) he encountered on the long journey to Lake Chad, including this beauty who posed for him at Sockna, in what is today central Libya.

Regrettably, Oudney added that "Abdullahi is a man above forty and very ugly." Oudney only wanted to show the implausibility of Denham's accusation, but in doing so he implied that had the Arab been younger and less ugly, it would have been harder to disprove. Abdullahi had been hired by Clapperton but let go after the carcass of a young camel disappeared in the night, apparently stolen.

Warrington, more straitlaced in matters of sexual propriety than in his other vices, was as appalled as Oudney and Clapperton and felt it incumbent on him not to let the matter fester. He forwarded copies of the letters to the Colonial Office, with a cover letter, written on November 4, 1823, in his accustomed florid style:

It is indeed painful to be under the necessity of referring to a subject which must be as disgusting to you to read, as it is to me to write. . . . A more infamous, vile, diabolical insinuation to blast the reputation of a man was never before resorted to, and I have not the smallest hesitation, in the presence of my God, to say that it is false, malicious, and conspiring against the future happiness of an individual. . . . Lieutenant Clapperton, I know little of, but in that little, I would with my life answer for him that he would never disgrace human nature by such Foul and Damnable Conduct. Dr. Oudney acquits him, the examination acquits, and Mr. Hillman acquits . . . as to any attempt to reconcile, it would now indeed be fruitless.

The Colonial Office was quick to reply that after a careful study of the documents, no suspicion whatever attached to Clapperton's character. On the other hand, if Denham had other evidence, it was his duty to produce it immediately. If Denham disassociated himself from the charges, "Lord Bathurst has only to express his hope that the discussion may be buried in oblivion." Bathurst wrote personally to Denham that he must either substantiate the charges or return at once to England (a career-ending move).

Denham, realizing his tale-telling had backfired, wrote back immediately that he had always been sure of Clapperton's innocence. In a letter to Warrington of May 10, 1824, he wrote that he himself had "ever believed the report to be a very wicked and malicious falsehood." Characteristically, he could not help adding that the report arose from Clapperton's "constantly associating with the lowest Arabs." Denham concealed from Oudney and Clapperton the fact that he had made this official disavowal, thus leaving Clapperton unaware that he had been cleared. He refused to apologize to Clapperton and the mission proceeded with its members hopelessly at each other's throats. Warrington eventually discovered Denham's omission, rebuking him for it in a letter of August 18: "You Acquit him, and being persuaded of his innocence, it is to be lamented that you did not communicate that Opinion to Dr. Oudney and Lieut. Clapperton. It would have saved them much unhappiness. . . ."

But Clapperton's unhappiness was Denham's joy, and even after receiving this reprimand from Warrington, he did not apologize.

Without excusing Denham's conduct, it should be said that there was probably some truth in his description of Clapperton's short-tempered treatment of the expedition's servants. Clapperton daily lost his temper and often became loudly angry, swearing like the sailor that he was. As Warrington once wrote of him: "I never sat down to table with Mr. Clapperton without feeling a dread that something disagreeable would happen before we separated." It is likely that Denham received more than his share of Clapperton's ill-tempered harangues, peppered with foul language.

To escape the growing controversy over his accusation, Denham decided in May to accompany a large slave *razzia** heading two hundred

---

* A plundering and destructive raid to capture slaves, from the Arabic.

miles southeast into Mandara country, near the town of Bagarmi. The English government was by now squarely abolitionist and Denham had been expressly forbidden to take part in or otherwise sanction slave raids. But he could not resist the call to action.

Under the guise of a pacification mission to help the sultan of Mandara put down invading Fulani tribesmen, two thousand horsemen left Kukawa under the command of Sheikh El Kanemi's top general, a Hausa warrior named Barca Gana. Denham rode in the front ranks with Abu Bakr Bhu Khallum and his troops of Meghara Arabs, who hoped to kidnap hundreds of new slaves for the ghastly march back to Tripoli.

One of the soldiers asked Bhu Khallum whether Denham was a Muslim. "No," said Bhu Khallum, "he is a *miskin* [wretched being]; they do not believe in the book; they do not pray five times a day; they are not circumcised . . . but they will see their errors and die Muslim, for they are beautiful people and will not perish as the devil's children."

Denham's thermometer showed 113 degrees in the shade. The army of 2,000 marched blindly in the dust which rose in choking clouds from horses' hooves. Among the fierce Meghara there was none of the hypocrisy that cloaked slaving expeditions. They were aggressors, and they gloried in it—bandits out for easy pickings, loot, women, and slaves, with

The warlord Barca Gana, on horseback as sketched by Denham, was Sheikh El Kanemi's top military commander. He led a troop of Meghara Arabs, accompanied by Denham, on an 800-mile slaving expedition from Kukawa southwest, deep into the territory of the Fulanis, who were subjects of El Kanemi's principal rival, Sultan Mohammed Bello.

enthusiasm as high as discipline was low. They were sure nothing could withstand their firearms, those wonderful English guns. Backed by the thousands of Bornu soldiers, they clearly were irresistible. All along the route, tribesmen thought so too, and recruits poured in to take their share of the anticipated spoils.

It was typical of the soldier in Denham that he went off, ahead of the column, with six handpicked men, to reconnoiter the "battlefield." It was beautiful verdant country even in the paralyzing heat; villages on their ridges of strategic high ground looked tranquil in the blazing light. Through his spyglass, Denham watched these farmers and herdsmen flee into the mountains as the column approached. Those too slow to run brought gifts of leopard skins and honey, prostrated themselves before Barca Gana, and threw sand over their heads in a gesture of obeisance.

When the alarm sounded, two thousand Mandara horsemen, led by their sultan, joined the Bornu and Arab cavalry. The first resistance was swept aside and a town, with its surrounding villages burned and looted. The stronger young men and women were taken as slaves, but all the rest—men, women, and children—were speared without mercy and flung onto the burning ruins of their homes to die in agony.

The column proceeded to a town where Fulani were entrenched on high ground behind a stream that could only be approached through a narrow pass between two hills, across which they had arrayed a barrier of pointed stakes. As the Arab horsemen rode into the pass, the Fulani launched a volley of arrows, some of them poisoned. Barca Gana lost two horses, shot from under him. Bhu Khallum took a poisoned arrow in the foot. A thick burnous protected Denham, but his horse was wounded.

When the Bornu and Mandara troops saw the Arab horsemen stalled before the shower of arrows and spears, they fell back. The slave raid soon became a rout. With Fulani horsemen in pursuit, Denham followed the others into a wood to take cover. His wounded horse buckled and three angry Fulani caught him and hurled him to the ground. They were about to make a pincushion of him with their spears when a tiny accident saved him. His assailants realized that their victim was unlike anyone else—in fact, he was different from anyone they had ever seen, *and so were his clothes*. Were they to skewer him as he lay on the ground at their mercy,

Denham and Clapperton were astonished by the prowess, ferocity, and sophisticated materiel of the troops of Sheikh El Kanemi and his neighboring rulers, with whom he was constantly at war. This heavily armed Fulani lancer, loyal to a vassal of Sultan Mohammed Bello, is covered with protective gear. He unhorsed Denham and nearly made a pincushion of him, reminding the Englishman of nothing so much as a European knight of medieval times. Note the lethal two-pronged spear.

they would ruin that wonderful suit. So they decided to strip him first, then kill him. In the struggle to remove his clothes, they wounded his hands as he tried to hang on to his trousers. Then his attackers became so absorbed in arguing about who should get which article of clothing that Denham, naked, managed to scuttle away. He slipped under the belly of the nearest horse and ran into the forest.

He came to a stream at the bottom of a deep ravine. As he clutched a branch to let himself down, the branch gave way, dropping him twenty feet over a bank into the rushing water. Half drowned, he managed to crawl out on the far side, and there met Barca Gana and Bhu Khallum with six of their followers, still fighting. One of the two men appointed by El Kanemi to guard Denham, a man named Maraymy, saved his life. He dismounted and threw the exhausted and completely naked explorer across his horse, where Bhu Khallum covered him with a rough burnous. It was the merchant prince's last action. The poisoned arrow that had pierced his foot earlier in the raid now took effect, and he fell from his horse, dead.

Denham, exhausted and only half-conscious, heard Barca Gana shout, "Believers enough have died today; why bother about a *kafir?*" It was a fair question, but Maraymy would not listen. Without his aid, it is likely that no more would ever have been heard of Dixon Denham.

In rags, his flesh wounds irritated by the coarse burnous and the bony horse on which he rode bareback, his skin crawling with lice, his wounds teeming with the fat larva of flies, Denham rode 180 miles back to Kukawa. "I suffered much," he wrote, "both in mind and body, but complained not." In spite of his pain, he was apparently alert enough to record that Mandara women were "singularly gifted with the Hottentot protuberance."*

WHILE FULANI TRIBESMEN were chasing Denham, Clapperton and Oudney, on their good days, were exploring the southern end of Lake Chad to see whether any of the rivers running out of it could be the Niger. The thin streams they found did not qualify, and they came to the conclusion that the Niger terminated in some other lake far south of Lake Chad. Mohammed El Kanemi was still adamant about not letting them travel south. He did give reluctant permission to Oudney to follow the ancient 500-mile road to Sokoto.

In June the wet season began and the mission to Kukawa was stranded. Travel would be impractical until October. With the rains came fever. Malaria sent Clapperton and Hillman to their cots, and Oudney vomited incessantly, able to hold down nothing but sour milk three times a day. Only Denham, again, withstood the debilitating climate, and, as he said, "ate with cheerfulness." The rains stopped, but it took Clapperton and Oudney months to recover.

Dr. Oudney would never see Kano. In his last letter to Lord Bathurst, dated December 10, 1823, he announced that he and Clapperton would set out the next day on their search for the Niger and that "I am a great invalid and hope the present journey will recruit me a little. I am perfectly convinced the prospect of it is what alone has kept me up." On December 14 Oudney and Clapperton left Kukawa. From Kano, 400 miles away, they intended to reach the capital of the Sokoto caliphate and meet its ruler,

---

* Denham was probably referring to attractive breasts, but he could also have meant development of the *labia minora,* or of the buttocks. Whatever his focus, it is apparent that his near-death experience had done nothing to inhibit his always keen interest in the women of Africa.

Sultan Mohammed Bello, for whom they had a letter of introduction from the sheikh of Bornu, El Kanemi, his quondam archenemy.

The two leaders, usually at war, happened to be (briefly) on friendly terms. Since the expedition had no armed escort (the remaining Meghara Arabs, decimated in the slave raid, their leader Bhu Khallum dead, had long since slunk away to Tripoli), they depended on the friendship of the sheikhs whose territories they traversed. A caravan of merchants went with them, the only safe way to travel. There were twenty-seven Arabs and about fifty citizens of Bornu. The Arabs each led a horse as well as rode one, and were prepared to sell either or both.

One absentee was Hillman, who was neither with Denham nor with Oudney. He stayed at El Kanemi's court, where he had become hugely popular. Ever the resourceful sailor and carpenter, he rejuvenated two broken-down brass cannons he found in one of the sheikh's warehouses, built wood gun carriages for them, cleaned them, made ammunition for them, and taught El Kanemi's troops how to fire them. Their projectiles killed no one, but the terror they aroused through noise and smoke made them the "Star Wars" weapons of their day. In one skirmish, El Kanemi's foes had no stomach to face such appalling armaments and surrendered on the spot after the first blast. Hillman then had the idea of making El Kanemi's wives a sedan chair in which they could be carried around town in style by their slaves. This became the *ne plus ultra* status symbol in the kingdom, the equivalent of a Rolls-Royce or a Bentley a century later. Hillman, not much interested in exploration, was nonetheless a deeply resourceful man.

Oudney's caravan to Kano traveled along the pleasant banks of a river in full spate. Tracks of lion and hippo were everywhere, although the travelers rarely saw the animals themselves. Red and white antelopes would barely bother to move out of their path. Clapperton observed that most African game seemed wary of man, but not frightened of him. Flocks of ostriches were abundant, and incalculable numbers of waterbirds circled and called above the lakes.

Roads were flooded and temporary rivers seemed to flow everywhere. The group managed to cross these streams on rafts made of papyrus reeds (of which Chad canoes are still made). It was a precarious and risky business, for all the camels and horses had to go across the same way. Of the company, only Clapperton could swim (in fact, the others had never seen a human swim and were amazed by his demonstration). The women of the caravan enlivened the crossings by raising a chorus of shrill screaming and whooping every time a body of water was spanned.

Towns and villages along this immemorial route—for Clapperton soon realized that this had been a commercial highway for centuries—were at close intervals. Many inhabitants joined the campaign at the sight of the caravan, which swelled in numbers with every mile; it grew to more than five hundred strong women, children, whole households making the journey.

Beyond the Shua territory was a flat country of mimosa bushes. It was while crossing this flat, high plateau that Clapperton made the strange statement—contradicted by later travelers—that the temperature at night was so low in the mornings that ice appeared on the drinking water.

Clapperton, astonished that it could freeze so near the equator, wrote to Warrington on December 27 that "we had such an intense cold that the water was frozen and the dishes and the water skins as hard as boards." Lord Bathurst was incredulous when this news reached England. Word leaked out, and British newspapers opined that it was well known that in the desert in winter the raw mornings were intense, the sun provided no warmth, and the penetrating chill was not driven off by the sun until late morning, and so this revelation was accepted as true.

Clapperton, the red-bearded athletic ex-naval officer who had made his reputation in the snows of the Pacific Northwest, was unperturbed, but the cold weakened the already sick Dr. Oudney. The doctor was terminally ill. He rallied as the caravan reached the borders of the Hausa country, and Clapperton thought he might survive if he could get him to their destination quickly. Unfortunately, at this moment Duncara, an envoy from Sultan Bello, met the caravan. Thinking Dr. Oudney would be honored, he sent out word to surrounding villages that a white doctor with magic powers had come to heal them. Sick people in droves flocked to Dr. Oudney's tent, and the enervated physician, who daily felt worse, was compelled to spend his time treating incurable diseases, from leprosy to sleeping sickness.

The strain was too much for the ailing doctor. He told his friend, "I fear it is all over with me." They left Duncara and reached the village of

Murmur on January 11. There, in a weak, consumptive state, he collapsed and coughed out his lungs. On January 12, 1824, Clapperton helped Oudney to dress.

> He [Oudney] ordered the camels to be loaded at daylight and drank a cup of coffee. . . . When the camels were loaded, with the assistance of his servant and I, he came out of his tent. I saw then that the hand of death was upon him and that he had not an hour to live. I begged him to return to his tent and lay down, which he did and I sat down beside him. I observed the ghastliness of death in his countenance, and with unspeakable grief, witnessed his last breath, which was without a struggle or groan.

Clapperton buried his friend at the foot of a mimosa tree, protecting the grave with a clay wall to keep off hyenas. He performed the burial service himself "with all the solemnity I could give." Clapperton left instructions and money with the local headman for Oudney's grave to be tended.

Though he looked like a man of fifty, Oudney died at thirty-two after two years in Africa, victim of the tuberculosis he had contracted before he left Scotland. The Colonial Office, always miserly, outdid itself in Oudney's case. His mother and sister, entirely dependent on him, received a single payment of 100 pounds sterling in remembrance of a man who had given his life in the service of his country.

Chapter Ten

THE RACE BEGINS

DISHEARTENED, Clapperton pushed on to Kano, the great trading city of the central Sudan whose goods were sold as far away as the markets of the Mediterranean. At the city gates, he spent all night brushing his faded but still imposing naval uniform, polishing its brass buttons, trying to put a sharp crease in his trousers, for no white man had ever set foot in Kano.

He entered the city on Tuesday, January 20, 1824, resplendent in his dress blues, but noted that "I might have spared myself the pains I had taken with my *toilet,* for not one individual turned his head to gaze at me, but all, intent on their own business, allowed me to pass by without notice or remark." It was a frigid reception. The urbane citizens of Kano (no less than modern city dwellers) were hard to impress. Nor did Kano overwhelm Clapperton.

"I had no sooner passed the Gates," he wrote, "than I felt grievously disappointed, for from the flourishing description of it given by Arabs, I expected to see a city of surprising Grandeur: I found, on the contrary, the houses nearly a quarter of a mile from the walls, and in many parts scattered into detached groups, between large stagnant pools of water."

The great walled city of Kano, the largest commercial center in West Africa, at the time of Clapperton's visit there in 1824. Its heavily fortified perimeter measured twelve miles, enclosing a population of about forty thousand.

Clapperton spent a month inspecting the city, whose population he estimated at between thirty and forty thousand. Kano, a major slave trade center, was surrounded by a thirty-foot-high clay wall with fifteen wood gates reinforced with iron plates. The gates were closed at sunset. Vast though it was—the city walls were *twelve miles* in circumference—the city itself was a huge collection of damp huts, honeycombed by twisting, rat-infested lanes. There were large basins of stagnant wetlands into which the city's garbage was piled. These fetid middens held the bodies of animals as well as those of unburied cadavers. Fevers, dysentery, and other diseases were rife. It was a dismal place, foul, with unbreathable air.

In spite of these drawbacks, Clapperton was impressed by Kano's size and its obvious importance as a central market for people who came there to trade from as far away as 500 miles in all directions. Never a prolific writer, he devoted pages of his diary to descriptions of this huge "souk," the incredible variety of trade goods, produce, and manufactured goods he saw.

He took several days to examine the slave market. The stench from pools of sewage and open gutters was overpowering. Clapperton visited the sheds where slaves were kept before shipment north, watching buyers perform their inspection "somewhat in the same manner as a Voluntary Seaman is examined by a surgeon on entering the Navy: he looks at the tongue, eyes, and limbs, and endeavors to detect rupture [hernia] by a forced cough."

Clapperton concluded that "slavery is here so common, or the minds of the slaves are so constituted, that they appeared much happier than their masters; the women, especially, singing with the greatest glee all the time they are at work." Clapperton was not as emotionally ravaged by the horrors he saw as Lyon.

Clapperton observed that Kano had been a busy cosmopolitan center when London was still a village. The city had been attacked so often in its thousand-year history that the surrounding villagers had a long tradition of knowing precisely what to do when war drums sounded. At the first hint of danger they brought their families and possessions into the shelter of the city walls, which had deep pits dug at their outer perimeter, like a moat. In the bottom of this moat were razor-sharp stakes, embedded at such an angle so as to impale anyone who tried to scale the barricades. The fifteen city gates were enclosed within towers, heavily defended. Inside the city, springs provided a renewable supply of fresh water. Cultivated land was set aside to grow food, so that the besieged could not be starved.

Clapperton paid an official call on Hajji Hat Salah, Sultan Bello's vizier in Kano, governor of the city, where he was received courteously enough but without much special treatment. White men, although a new species to the hajji,* were all more or less in a day's work. The visit couldn't compare in importance to the vizier's immediate job, which was to organize a skirmish. Apparently, a local chief had stepped out of line and needed discipline. Hat Salah promised Clapperton the punitive expedition would be over in a week, and that he would be free to take him to Sokoto to present him to the sultan. Clapperton gave the vizier

---

*Hat Salah bore the title "Hajji" because he had made the pilgrimage, or hajj, to Mecca, prescribed as a religious duty for Muslims who could afford it, in those days a long and dangerous journey from Kano. Having performed this duty, such pilgrims were entitled (as they still are) to use, for the rest of their lives, the honorific "Hajji" or "El Hajj" before their names as a title of respect.

a thermometer, delighting the hajji, who called it, not inappropriately, a "watch of heat." In return the explorer got the use of a guest hut next to the vizier's, unfortunately surrounded by a noisome swamp.

Clapperton became ill as the drawn-out days of worried waiting for the return of Hat Salah dragged on. He passed the time eavesdropping in the market. He was particularly interested in a conversation he overheard between two Arab travelers detailing the course of the Niger. They spoke of its great length, strange changes in direction, and its mysterious meta-morphosis into an immense delta swamp through which it entered the Atlantic as a number of separate rivers. Mungo Park had already proved two-thirds of this summary of the Niger's course, but over the remaining third a veil of mystery still hung. Nobody in Europe knew where the river found the sea. Here was a simple and obvious explanation (and the correct one!), but Clapperton, though he recorded it faithfully, did not assign it much importance. He wrote: "I place little dependence on such accounts." Although the extensive, swampy territory known as the Oil Rivers was well known to English sailors, nobody guessed it was the delta of the Niger.

Hajji Hat Salah returned in two weeks a chastened man. The upstart prince he had gone out to thrash had turned the tables on him; Kano's army was vanquished. The hajji was in no mood to face Sultan Bello, and so let his white visitor leave town alone.

Before setting off, Clapperton received news of the lost explorer Friedrich Hornemann, the German sent out by the African Association in 1798 and the first man to cross the Sahara from Egypt by the Fezzan and the Aïr Mountains. Accounts of the crossing had come back to Europe through Arab traders and Hornemann was thought to have reached the Niger River. He disappeared, presumably killed by disease or treacherous guides. An account of his travels as far as Murzuk had been published in London in 1802, but his later journals were never recovered. Clapperton heard from traders in Kano that the facts as known were all true, but the missing journals never turned up.

Weak, gaunt, and light-headed from bouts of malaria, Clapperton pushed on to Sokoto, 250 miles northwest of Kano. He got there thanks to an escort Sultan Bello sent out to meet him, crossing a Hausa state still hostile to the caliphate. Clapperton, trying to look his best when representing his king, entered Sokoto on March 16, 1824, wearing "my lieutenant's coat, trimmed with gold lace, white trousers, and silk stockings, and to complete my finery, I wore Turkish slippers and a turban."

Sokoto was a walled city with two mosques and flat-roofed houses whose waterspouts of baked clay, projecting from the eaves, resembled tiers of guns. It was a smaller, cleaner, more comfortable place than Kano, though also populated by traders and merchants.

Clapperton found Sultan Mohammed Bello sitting on a carpet in a thatch-roofed cottage dressed in a blue cotton robe with a white muslin turban worn like a Tuareg, concealing the lower part of his face. He was reading, alone. The sultan, a youthful forty-four, looking "noble," just under six feet tall, with "a short curling black beard, a small mouth, a Grecian nose, and large black eyes," had a wide reputation as a man of learning. He began a theological discussion with Clapperton, who demurred, saying that he was "a Protestant . . . who having protested more than two centuries ago against the suggestions, absurdities and abuses practiced in those days, had ever since professed to follow simply what was written in the book of Our Lord Jesus."

The sultan returned books belonging to Denham that his agents had retrieved in Mandara during the failed slave raid, including a copy of Sir Francis Bacon's essays and Denham's journal. Bello ingenuously wondered aloud why his old friend the sheikh of Bornu had sent an army into his territory, and why an English explorer (Denham) had joined it. Clapperton replied lamely (and untruthfully) that Denham had merely been touring the country. Dropping this awkward subject, the sultan asked what each book contained. He wanted Clapperton to read aloud to him, saying that he found the spoken sound of English quite beautiful.

Although Clapperton was the first European to come to his court, Sultan Bello was well informed about the civilizations north of the Mediterranean. Clapperton, for his part, had to admit that Europeans knew nothing about the kingdoms of Africa. He stated that "my people had hitherto supposed yours devoid of all religion and not far removed from the condition of wild beasts, whereas I now find them to be civilized, learned, humane, and pious."

That afternoon, at a second audience, Clapperton presented the sultan with presents from George IV, including ornamented pistols, razors, gunpowder, a spyglass, a silver tea tray, a sextant, and a compass. He showed Bello a planisphere of the heavenly bodies, discovering that the sultan knew the signs of the zodiac, some of the constellations, and many of the stars. He was also interested in the sextant, the "looking glass of the sun." Clapperton explained that with the compass the sultan could find the direction of Mecca to pray.

"Everything is wonderful," the sultan said, "but you are the greatest curiosity of all." Then he asked: "What can I give that is most acceptable to the King of England?"

"The most acceptable service you can render to the King of England," replied Clapperton, "is to co-operate with His Majesty in putting a stop to the slave trade."

"What?" asked the sultan. "Have you no slaves in England?"

"No. Whenever a slave sets foot in England, he is from that moment free."

"What do you do then for servants?"

"We hire them for a stated period, and give them regular wages."

"God is great!" exclaimed the ruler. "You are a beautiful people."

Hugh Clapperton was an eager, honest, but naive ambassador for his country, and he faithfully presented England's position on slavery, though he knew this might offend Bello. His arguments seemed outwardly to impress the sultan, who promised his support. Bello agreed, too, that trade between the two nations was desirable.

The African king had a detailed grasp of international affairs. He knew that the English navy had sunk the Algerian fleet in 1816 and that England had begun to colonize India.

"You were at war with Algiers," he told Clapperton, "and you killed a number of the Algerines."

Clapperton replied that they were "a ferocious race," who made slaves of Europeans.

"You are the strongest of Christian nations," the sultan said, "you have subjugated all of India."

Clapperton replied that England had simply given India "good laws and protection."

Though Clapperton was a man of the world and Bello had never traveled far from his borders, it is likely that Bello could see at a glance that his visitor was a man of little finesse or subtlety, but one of integrity. The sultan himself, as a cultured African who ruled a vast kingdom, was master of the two qualities Clapperton most lacked. But in a world where everyone was subtle and finesse was the order of the day, Clapperton's simplicity must have made a startling and positive impression. Bello clearly liked Clapperton.

It was no accident that Bello raised the concern, shared by Arabs, of England's intentions in India, as well as the British attack on Algiers. In the case of India, Bello's advisers believed that England had sent smooth-talking emissaries first, followed by hard-hitting merchants, completing the job of annexation with an armed force. This was the model they feared the English would now use in Africa. (They were right.) To Bello, England had conquered India by trickery. Though he knew the English were empire builders and that he ran risks by establishing ties with them, the sultan was probably tempted by the prospect of trade with what he recognized to be the wealthiest nation on earth. In particular, he seemed willing to run the risk of an English presence in his dominion for the sake of the firearms that would give him military superiority over his neighbors.

He asked Clapperton specifically whether "the King of England would give him a couple of guns, with ammunition and some rockets." Clapperton assured Bello of "His Majesty's compliance with his wishes, if he would consent to put down the slave trade on the coast."

Clapperton, a natural salesman, promoted trade with England as an irresistible opportunity. The sultan, with England's help, would become the greatest prince in Africa. If he built a trade port on the coast, he would have his own navy. The English would show him how to build ships, and with ships he would be able to trade with the rest of the world, send pilgrims to Mecca by the safer sea route, and appoint ambassadors to the capitals of Europe.

The sultan promised to let the English build a town on the coast (an easy commitment for the landlocked ruler to make—his borders did not extend to the ocean). While Clapperton and Bello were talking, it dawned on powerful Arab merchant groups in Sokoto that the British proposals would destroy their caravan trade. Slaves were their main "product," along with gold and ivory, and the trans-Saharan route would remain profitable only if no direct competition from the sea threatened it. Now here was a white man asking for the abolition of slavery and the establishment of a river trade route to the Great Ocean. Clapperton's proposals must have horrified the sultan's Arab advisers and their influential trader friends, and the navy lieutenant was not enough of a diplomat to quell the widespread (and perspicacious) suspicion of Britain's aims.

Sultan Bello's final position was ambiguous. He told Clapperton that he welcomed trade with England, but pressured him to interrupt his trip and return at once to Bornu, warning him of the great danger attendant on continuing south to find the Niger.

"Think of it with prudence," Bello told him.

Bello's men cautioned Clapperton's servants not to risk their lives trying to traverse lands rife with warring tribes. Clapperton discovered that no guide was willing to take him.

The dilemma posed by Sultan Bello's conflicting interests is wonderfully illustrated by his discussion of the Niger. The sultan "drew on the sand the course of the River Quorra [the Niger] which he also informed me entered the sea at Fundah [250 miles north of the Niger-Benue confluence]. By his account, the river ran parallel to the coast for several days' journey, being in some places only a few hours, in others a day's journey from it. Two or three years ago, the Sea, he said, closed up the mouth of the river and its mouth was at present a day or two further south; but during the rains, when the river was high, it still ran into the Sea by the old channel."

This information, more or less accurate, shook Clapperton's belief that the river terminated in a lake, and he asked Bello to have the map drawn on paper so that he could take it back to England. But the map, when he got it, contradicted what Bello had drawn in the sand. It showed the Niger flowing east, toward the Nile, confirming the erroneous ideas of England's leading geographers. Somewhere along the chain of command, from sultan to mapmaker, the river's direction had been diverted, very likely to mislead the British. That could be why Bello refused to let Clapperton proceed; he didn't want further reconnaissance to provide the English with more accurate geographical information.

The sultan brought up the subject of Mungo Park, the only other white man in history to have penetrated his kingdom. In 1805, after following the Niger for nearly two thousand miles (from Bamako to Bussa), the famous Scotsman had disappeared. He was thought to have been killed by tribesmen at Bussa Falls. At the time of Clapperton's meetings with Bello, Park's death was still a mystery. He was supposed to have been killed by arrows from tribesmen as his canoe got wedged between rocks at the head of the falls, but Bello said of this hypothesis that "it was the wet season and a canoe could not have got caught in the rocks." Park's missing journal, he added, was safe with the sultan of Yauri.

Yauri was only a five-day journey from Sokoto, but the sultan would not allow Clapperton to go there to retrieve the papers. The whole country, he said, was in a state of upheaval. This was certainly true, but it was unfortunate, for the last part of the Scot's famous journal has never been found. Clapperton believed that the suppression of Park's notes was the deliberate policy of Bello. He wrote that "the Arabs conspired to prevent me finding [Park's diary], which might lead to England stepping in and stealing the Soudan trade." No doubt it was possible, but if so, why would Sultan Bello have mentioned Mungo Park at all? It is likely that Bello, with an exaggerated opinion of the powers of the British, thought they knew far more about Park's fate and Bello's domains than they did. His initial candor about the Niger's course is another indication of this. Certainly, Park's arrival in the area had been a momentous event, akin to the landing of extraterrestrials. Bello would have found it virtually impossible not to mention it.

To proceed in defiance of the sultan's wishes into hostile territory while he was ill and weary and encumbered by mutinous servants was more than Clapperton could manage. After two months in Sokoto, he started back on the road to Bornu on May 4, 1824. The sultan asked him to return, and promised to send an escort to meet him at any point along the coast. He gave Clapperton a letter for George IV and accorded him an affectionate farewell. Bello's letter agreed to put a stop to the slave trade "on account of the Good which will result from it, both to You and to Us," in exchange for English weapons. Justifiably elated over the success of his diplomatic mission, Clapperton headed for Kano, traveling mostly by night because he feared thieves.

The trip was a nightmare: he lost his way; horses and camels died under him; food and clean water gave out; fever increasingly sapped his remaining strength. At one town, nine men and six camels died of exhaustion, yet Clapperton did not fail to record every incident of the wearisome trek. A friendly chief offered him the pick of his seraglio. Clapperton, unable to refuse but not wishing to get embroiled in a relationship from which he might not easily extricate himself, chose the oldest woman offered to him. When she arrived at his tent, she brought two younger women. One of these nursed the ailing white man "with such devotion and skill" that he got well.

Back in Kano, he was received a second time by the ill-tempered Hajji Hat Salah, who organized a formal luncheon for him. It was a strange meal; as it was Ramadan and still daylight, only the white guest could eat. Clapperton was urged to enjoy the meal by his fasting host, who said, "*Rais* Abdullah,* eat, for you are a hungry *kafir!*" The vizier was likely smarting from reports that Clapperton had become Bello's confidant while he, ruler of Kano, was in eclipse. A *kafir*, while it only means a nonbeliever to a Muslim, is by no means a polite way of describing one.

The road from Kano to Bornu was choked with traffic, ponderous caravans of Tuareg and merchants from Senegal, Tripoli, and Ghadames, all trying to reach safe harbor before the rainy season, heralded by terrific displays of thunder and lightning. Arriving at Murmur, Clapperton visited Oudney's grave and was outraged to discover it desecrated. Clapperton, who could become explosively angry when crossed, turned momentarily into a madman. He tracked down the village elder, whom he had paid to care for the grave, and thrashed him with a whip, realizing only later how foolhardy this had been.

Ten weeks after leaving Sultan Bello, Clapperton reached Kukawa, depleted and sick. Denham had preceded his arrival at camp, back from a second disastrous slaving expedition.

DENHAM HAD HAD his own share of disappointments in the period he was alone. When Clapperton and Oudney left for Kano in December 1823, Denham was still lost on his expedition with Barca Gana, but on

---

*"Abdullah" was Clapperton's traveling name. *Rais* simply means "chief" or "boss" and is still a common honorific in North Africa and the Middle East.

his return to Kukawa he tried to determine whether the Niger ran into or out of Lake Chad. A caravan from Tripoli arrived, bringing him an assistant—a twenty-two-year-old ensign from Malta, Ernest Toole. The young man had made his crossing of the Sahara in an astonishing fifteen weeks and was still suffering from the strain. Denham and Toole left to explore Lake Chad anyway. Toole was so sick that he had to be strapped to his camel. Ill though he was, he seemed determined to continue with Denham, who was so consumed by the novelties of the lake that it did not occur to him that Toole was unfit for travel.

A palpable excitement fills his notes as he records that the Shari River, after the rains, was in spate, the trees green and full-foliaged, drooping down to the sparkling sheet of the lake, its surface broken by the snouts of crocodiles slithering quietly away, and the snuffling heads of herds of hippos so numerous they covered acres of open water. Denham could rejoice, for the first time, as the undisputed leader of his own expedition. He writes of the millions of wildfowl darkening the evening sky in their flight, the vast size of the lake, the Chadian desert stretching left and right to the far horizon unbroken by sight of land across the water. The lake, he realized at last, was oceanic in its extent. Denham took his fleet of pirogues across the hot, sweet-smelling muddy waters and through forests of tall papyrus, bamboos, and giant grasses.

The canoes were cramped, and they leaked. By day, the sun glared down in the torrid, humid heat. At night, mosquitoes from stagnant pools pinged in roving billions. Toole was getting worse, and "Columbus" (who suddenly appears again in the journal) became sick himself, but never stopped trying to nurse the young newcomer back to health.

Toole was destined to become one of those young and eager volunteers whose sole achievement was to join the growing list of British casualties in the cause of African exploration. He died at Ngala, off the southern tip of the lake. "A cold shivering had seized him," Denham wrote, "and his extremities were like ice. I gave him both tea and rice-water; and there was but little alteration in him until just before noon, when, without a struggle, he expired, completely worn out and exhausted."

Realizing too late and not for the first time that he should have used better judgment, Denham returned to Kukawa alone. In May another young assistant arrived, none other than Warrington's protégé, John Tyr-

whitt, the profligate romancer of Italian beauties they had left behind at
Murzuk. Though he, too, was exhausted by his travels, Tyrwhitt was still
a hail-fellow-well-met who looked like he would be more at home at a
London embassy than in the wilds of Africa. He entertained the camp
by playing the flute every evening. His instructions were to remain at
Kukawa as British vice-consul at a salary of 300 pounds a year (what he
would spend it on was another matter).

Denham was peeved to hear from Tyrwhitt that Warrington had called
him "unpopular," and on June 25 he wrote to his brother Charles railing
against "these insinuations by a man 1500 miles off who knows no more
of the Interior of Africa than you do of the inside of the Lying In Hospital,
who gets Drunk every night, and who Harasses the Minds of those he is
bound to support with his Influence, that is the English Influence, for he
has None in Tripoli, and when they have nothing but bad water to drink
is rather unkind and ungenerous."

Denham took Tyrwhitt on an excursion along the southern tip of Lake
Chad. On their return, they found Clapperton back, looking so awful
Denham didn't recognize him. "It was nearly eight months since we had
separated," Denham wrote, "and although it was midday I went immediately to the hut where he [Clapperton] was lodged; but so satisfied was
I that the sunburnt sickly person that lay extended on the floor, rolled in
a dark blue shirt, was not my companion, that I was about to leave the
place, when he convinced me of my error, by calling me by name: the
alteration was certainly in him most striking."

Together again at Kukawa, they found that the old hatreds still smol-
dered; they soon stopped talking to one another. Though their tents were
a few yards apart, Clapperton informed Denham in writing of Oudney's
death.

Communicating solely by letter, they could agree only that it was time
to head north to Tripoli, and from there back to England. Both wanted
badly to go home, where they each had solid achievements to report. As
soon as he had recovered his health, Clapperton was determined to return
to Africa and continue his dialogue with Sultan Bello. Denham had other
plans: to parlay his experiences into a major book, bask in the limelight,
and achieve leapfrog advancement in government service, perhaps as the
governor of an African colony.

Tyrwhitt was given the choice of going back with them. Although the deaths of Oudney and Toole must have been vivid in his mind, and the sight of the malarious Clapperton cannot have been reassuring, Tyrwhitt decided to stay.[*]

On Tuesday, September 14, 1824, Clapperton, Denham, and Hillman set out across the desert along the same route they had taken twenty months earlier. They now faced, once again, a slow and painful journey across some of the worst country of the Sahara. The way back seemed a longer, harder march, with nothing but dates to eat. The camels bruised their padded feet on sharp rocks in the stony track; many died. Clapperton, weakened by malaria, suffered terribly. In spite of their common misery, nothing, it seemed, could improve relations between Clapperton and Denham. They did not share a spoken word during the whole 133-day crossing. Ten miles outside Tripoli, on January 25, 1825, the parched explorers saw a tent set up by Consul Warrington to greet them. Soon they were washing down anchovy sandwiches with "huge draughts of Marsala wine in glass tumblers," experiencing the particularly intense sensation that comes from climbing out of a deep valley of pain to a threshold of pleasure. "It was quite indescribable," Clapperton wrote.

Back in Tripoli, Clapperton immediately drafted a letter to Warrington requesting that he open a formal inquiry into the charges Denham had made against him of homosexuality. He was astounded to hear that Denham had, months earlier, withdrawn the accusation.

Warrington wisely persuaded Clapperton to let the matter drop, but the explorer then learned of a far more ominous threat: Lord Bathurst had sent another explorer, Captain Alexander Gordon Laing, on a Timbuktu-Niger mission.

This was devastating news. In Sokoto, Clapperton had felt the Niger and Timbuktu within his grasp, merely days—weeks at most—away. Had Bello permitted it, he would already have clinched the prize, he thought. He realized now that he risked having it snatched from his hands by a younger man, an interloper who had never set foot in the Sahara.

---

[*] A fatal decision. Alcohol, loneliness, and fever sent Tyrwhitt to his grave only a few months after Denham and Clapperton left for the Mediterranean. His father's reaction in Malta is not recorded.

Like Mungo Park and others before him, Clapperton now became obsessed with Africa. Planning his next moves as he returned to Tripoli, he had not calculated that he was about to be caught up in a frenzied race with a fellow explorer, one he considered a poacher on what had become, because of the hardships already invested, his private hunting preserve. Though he had never met Laing, he recognized out of the blue that he detested him. Here was a man unworthy of the homage that would surely be accorded the discoverer of Timbuktu. Clapperton's misfortunes—his malaria, his corrosive quarrels with Denham, the abominable death of his friend Oudney—all of these, instead of making him lose heart, had strengthened his determination to find the elusive river and the fabled town. Now all this was threatened, and by a mere tyro.

Who would reach Timbuktu and the mouth of the Niger first? Clapperton was determined that it would be he. Adding to his frustration, the Colonial Office, unaware of the resentment Laing had aroused, ordered Clapperton to "commit to paper whatever part of that important information you are in possession of which must tend considerably to assist the operations and labors of Captain Laing."

Clapperton, enraged, refused this request. Why should he share secrets he had learned at such terrible personal cost? Warrington convinced him that the consequences of this stubbornness would be harsh, as Lord Bathurst had an icy and diminishing tolerance for the vanity of explorers. In the end, Clapperton reluctantly complied.

Clapperton and Denham returned to England in June 1825, after an absence of three and a half years, to heroes' welcome. They were promoted (Clapperton to captain and Denham to lieutenant colonel) and presented to George IV, who feted them at a weekend at Sandringham, the royal estate in Norfolk. The press compared them favorably to Marco Polo.

In the England of their time, they were deemed successes. Considering the tensions involved, it is surprising they accomplished as much as they did. Though they failed to find Timbuktu or the termination of the Niger, they were the first Europeans to reach the kingdom of Bornu and stand on the shores of Lake Chad. They helped chart the African interior (chiefly owing to the accuracy of Clapperton's surveys), about which nothing useful had been written since Leo Africanus in the sixteenth century. They had survived in the heart of Africa for three years, no small feat in itself, and demonstrated that the difficult "Tripoli route" across the Sahara to Bornu was passable by Europeans in Christian dress without insuperable dangers. They had proved that the mandate of the bashaw of Tripoli ran to Bornu (though not beyond), and that the Bornu kingdom and Sokoto caliphate were each important states, advanced and undiscovered civilizations, and great entrepôts of trade.

Yet in its main goal the mission was a costly failure. Timbuktu remained undiscovered by Europeans and the question of the Niger's termination remained unanswered. Complicating the Niger question, each of the explorers had a different and conflicting hypothesis. Oudney died convinced that the Niger emptied into a mysterious lake south of Lake Chad. Denham, who had explored more of Lake Chad than the other two, still believed the Niger was somehow connected to the great inland sea. Clapperton, on the basis of his talks with Sultan Bello, was converted to the idea that the Niger flowed into the Bight of Benin. Five years would pass before one of the three hypotheses was proved right.

Having tasted celebrity, Clapperton was impatient to get back to Africa. This left Denham to write the account of the mission for publication. In this he not only cut all of Oudney's interesting and useful report of the journey made to Ghat, but he watered down the contributions of both Oudney and Clapperton so that anyone reading his first draft would have surmised that the whole expedition had been carried out by one man, though here and there he acknowledged his comrades by interlarding the narrative with catty remarks about them. Fortunately, Sir John Barrow, secretary of the Admiralty and soon to become founder of the Royal Geographical Society, along with the publisher of the book, John Murray,* one of London's most eminent editors, reviewed the manuscript. By comparing Denham's draft with notes left them by Clapperton (including

---

*John Murray (1778–1843), the son of the famous publisher of the same name, produced almost all of the most distinguished African travel books published in English in his lifetime. He was Laing's publisher, as well as Sir Joseph Banks's, Clapperton's, Denham's, Tuckey's, and Lyon's. Few men have done more (except Frank Cass, in the twentieth century) to inform the English reading public about Africa.

Oudney's journals), they discovered the interpolations and excisions. Barrow reinserted some of the contributions of Oudney and Clapperton and cut most of Denham's petulant carping.

Still, in *Narrative of Travels and Discoveries in Northern and Central Africa*, published in 1826, it sounds as if Denham traveled alone. The wealth of new material on the African interior made it a classic of exploration, but a flawed classic, for Denham succeeded in belittling the contributions of his partners while magnifying his own.

Ironically, Denham, the self-proclaimed commander-in-chief of the mission, died before the solution to the mystery of the Niger became known. After capturing the popular admiration with his book, he was elected a fellow of the Royal Society and became the toast of London and a familiar guest at Lord Bathurst's dinner table. He accumulated honors and was appointed governor of Sierra Leone in 1828. His return to West Africa proved his undoing, for he died there of fever the same year, aged forty-three.

In reassessing Denham's role today, it is hard to dissent from the verdict of one of the greatest amateur historians of African exploration, E. W. Bovill, who wrote of him in the early 1960s: "It remains difficult, in the checkered history of geographical discovery, to find a more odious man than Dixon Denham." Denham, in the end, showed himself to be a duplicitous careerist with powerful friends who got him his place on the expedition roster and promoted him afterward. He succeeded in suppressing Clapperton's account of the mission, at least for a time. Consequently, until the discovery of Clapperton's journals years later, Denham's account was the primary source dealing with the expedition.

WHEN HUGH CLAPPERTON sailed to England in the spring of 1825, his ship's wake must have crossed that of his rival, Alexander Gordon Laing. Laing had boarded his vessel in Falmouth in February to take him to Malta, and from there to Tripoli. Clapperton knew it was too late, if he was to catch up with Laing, to make his return journey from the north, so he persuaded Lord Bathurst to let him take the more dangerous path inland from the West African coast. From the swamp-infested shores of Sierra Leone, he would travel overland 450 miles due east to Timbuktu.

Dixon Denham, Clapperton's nemesis, as he appeared shortly before his appointment as governor of Sierra Leone in 1827.

This would cut 700 miles off the trip and give him, he hoped, the chance to overtake Laing.

To make up for time already lost, Clapperton persuaded the Admiralty to let him ship out on the speedy HMS *Brazen,* a sloop leaving for the West African coast to join the anti-slavery patrols then intercepting slave shipments to America. The *Brazen* left Spithead on August 28, 1825. Clapperton had been home less than three months.

For his part, Lord Bathurst had high hopes that Clapperton would meet Laing in the African heartland, where the two men could join forces, greatly enhancing their chances of success by acting in concert over what Bathurst reckoned to be the smaller probability that either man would succeed alone. In the meantime, if they wanted to scramble to see who would be first, so be it. So long as it resulted in bonanzas for the British Crown, personal ambition, in Bathurst's mind, was a perfectly acceptable spur for explorers, and cheaper than money.

The race was on.

Chapter Eleven

OVER THE RIM OF
THE WORLD

DAYS BEFORE LEAVING TRIPOLI, Laing received the letter of advice Clapperton had been ordered to write by Lord
Bathurst. It infuriated him. Counsel from a competitor, conde-
scending at that, was the last thing he wanted as he set out on his great
journey. The tone of the letter bent toward the patronizing. Clapperton
advised Laing to be "kind and patient with the natives," to take plenty
of presents, and not to "meddle with local women." Laing thought the
language supercilious, haughty, disdainful—implying that Clapperton was
the superior explorer and that Laing was a novice.

Laing complained to Warrington that "we need not ghosts to rise from
their graves to tell us such simple stuff." He set out for Ghadames with
the shadow of competition dogging him.

To avoid bandits, Sheikh Babani mapped a circuitous route that
doubled the distance from Tripoli to Ghadames from 500 to 1,000 miles.[*]

---

[*] Satellite imagery shows that, as the crow flies, the distance between Tripoli and Ghadames
is about 275 miles. The shortest land trail, to this day, is about 500 miles, given all the twists
and turns occasioned by obstacles in the desert.

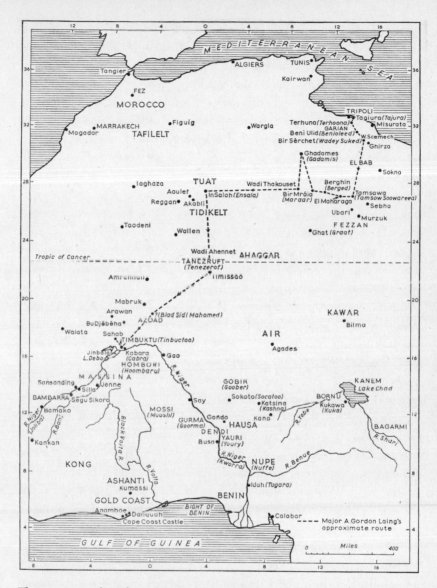

The route across the Sahara, from Tripoli to Timbuktu, taken by Major Alexander Gordon Laing, as reconstructed in meticulous detail by the British amateur historian E. W. Bovill in the 1960s.

Incredibly, Babani was still promising to get Laing to Timbuktu within ten weeks. The bashaw had allegedly paid Babani 4,000 Spanish dollars to see Laing safely to Timbuktu, but the sheikh told Laing he was doing it without pay and constantly dunned him for money. Everyone in the caravan appeared intent on extracting something from Laing. "I never met with such a set of greedy vagabonds," he wrote to Warrington.

Though he was dependent on Sheikh Babani, Laing had his own retinue of loyal men. With him were his Caribbean-born servant, Jack le Bore, and two West African ship's carpenters: Roger, "a good-humored rough fellow, picking up Arabic fast," and Harry, "a quiet, nobody disturbing sort of lad." Laing also took camel drivers, a freed slave named Bongola, and a Jewish merchant and interpreter, Abraham Nahun. Eleven camels carried this menagerie. They were dressed as Muslims, mainly to avoid arousing comment from strangers, but "lest it should ever be supposed that we attempt to pass ourselves for what we really are not," Laing wrote, he proposed to read prayers to his servants on Sundays, "on which days they would appear dressed as Englishmen."

Jack le Bore had been with Laing a long time. Laing records that he was "originally a native of Santo Domingo, and having entered into the French army as a trumpeter, was present at Austerlitz and many other of the important victories of Buonaparte. . . . He was taken prisoner in a French line battle ship by Sir Alexander Cochrane; after his exchange, he served in almost every country in Europe, and, at the peace, made his way back from Denmark to England, whence he volunteered for the late Royal Africa Corps, in which he served as bugle-major." He met Laing on the Gold Coast and went with him to Falaba. His experience as an explorer in Africa was more extensive than Laing's. He had the Scotsman's absolute trust.

The two naval carpenters worried Laing. "My two sailors," he wrote, "although superior to the general run of the class to which they belong, are nevertheless exceedingly thoughtless, and give me much unnecessary trouble in watching them, for heedless of the dangers which attend such doings in these countries they will run after the ladies and entail annoyance and inconvenience upon both themselves and me." He brought them along because he intended to navigate the Niger and they would be needed to make a vessel. In his baggage he also carried naval plumb lines for sounding the river depths.

Laing's expedition, officially christened the Timbuktu Mission by Lord Bathurst, had dual objectives: to find Timbuktu and the mouth of the Niger. Laing, like Clapperton, considered himself the successor to Mungo Park, and he set out to complete Park's work by discovering the main course of the great river and its termination. The still-undiscovered city of Timbuktu, which Park had asserted lay close to the river, was clearly the key to the Niger. From Timbuktu Laing and his mentors thought it would be possible, in spite of what had befallen Park, to follow the Niger to its mouth. At least its middle and lower course could more likely be traced from that point than by groping blindly in the wholly unexplored heart of the continent. Above all, Laing was impatient to reach the river before Clapperton, who he feared would "snatch the cup from my lips," as he put it in a letter to his confidant, Bandinel.* By traveling through the dry desert from the north, he believed he had an excellent chance of succeeding.

From the walls of Tripoli, Laing's caravan crossed the semidesert flanking the coastal oases, a district sparsely populated by Bedouin tribesmen. They were traveling toward Beni Ulid, to the southeast, instead of directly toward Ghadames, to the southwest. The travelers picked their way past patches of green where rainwater had collected behind heaps of broken stone that had once formed Roman dams.

In this, the earliest stage of the long journey, the most prominent point on the horizon was a diminutive mountain, a dark and forbidding rock frowning over the southern end of the Tripolitanian oasis. This mountain was said to warn of the approach of caravans from the south, its other side, for when it "sang," Babani said the locals knew a caravan was about to come into view. The noise was likely produced by wind blowing through crevices of the torn rock.

They reached Beni Ulid on August 1. Here they found a letter from

*Laing's close friend James Bandinel (1783–1849) was at the time employed as a clerk in the Foreign Office. He had earlier explored Melville Island in the Arctic and later became a prolific writer contra the slave trade. He preserved many of Laing's letters, a collection that later become the property of the Royal Society, where it remains.

Warrington that had overtaken the caravan. It told Laing that Clapperton was making a journey eastward from the Guinea coast and hoped to reach Sokoto, where he would meet his old friend Sultan Bello. Warrington expected Laing to make his way to Sokoto from Timbuktu so the two travelers could join forces. Laing was affronted by this idea, which he termed "hare-brained" to his fellow travelers, and sent a tepid reply back to Tripoli.

On August 13, Laing departed Beni Ulid. The explorer and his party negotiated steep, dry watercourses that in geological times had drained the plateau northeastward into the Gulf of Sidra. Leaving the coastal plain, they spent days climbing and descending the steep rocky banks of a range of wadis, or dried riverbeds. Then they began the torturous crossing of the Hamada el Homra, the "great red wilderness," a seemingly endless, waterless plain spreading over 40,000 square miles whose surface was covered with sharp flints reflecting a blinding, merciless sun. On this plain, previous caravans had left their dead behind in such numbers that Laing could follow his route through the trackless waste simply by following the bones lining the way.

For five days in the Hamada el Homra, the horizon stretched around the travelers in an unbroken line, as at sea—one indefinite plain as far as the eye could reach. The wind sighed mournfully among the polished stones. The arch of sky, steel blue to the edge of the horizon, domed the endless disk of red rock over which the caravan slowly made its way. It was unlike any land Laing had ever seen.

A mountain range barred the road to the south, rising in a vast plateau of chalk 1,800 feet above the plain, a mighty sheet of rock 360 miles from east to west and about 140 miles broad where the road crossed it. For days they crawled past the skirts of these black hills, the Jebel es Sawda.

The caravan was marching close to the rocky massif to the south, but soon those mountains curved in a great arc away from the most direct course to Ghadames and the caravan was confronted with what looked like another eternal plain. Its dimensions were magnified, low on distant horizons, by isolated peaks and tabletops of rock. These made for confident navigation, for they were marked on the crude charts Laing had obtained in Tripoli and London, but their greatest effect was to provide a scale to the panorama, reducing men and camels to fleas. The travelers felt themselves creeping toward a far rim of the world that might never be reached, across pure and unbounded space in which they had no hope of encountering anything from the world left behind. No one would offer them comfort here.

The surface of the plain was rock littered with red stones and bits of chalk. Over the eons, heat and cold had shattered the exposed veneer of this rocky floor and an incessant wind had carried away all loose particles of sand. The surface was swept clean, as if with a broom, and the smooth stones appeared varnished from the polishing action of drifting sand.

On most days, Laing's caravan set off early in the morning, usually well before dawn. They camped in the heat of the day when the sun lit the sky ablaze and the horizon trembled. During late afternoon and dusk, once the suffocating heat had abated, the caravan resumed its journey, traveling into the night. The sun was their only timekeeper (though Laing carried several functioning nautical chronometers). Distances were measured in days, never in miles.

The daily routine varied little. Morning prayer was the opening business, followed by the first tea of the day, weak and syrupy, a desert staple. Breakfast usually involved *zummita* paste[*] or a ball of foul-smelling dried fish steeped in camel's milk. Next came rounding up the camels, let loose to forage for what they could find. This could take hours, depending on how far they had wandered. If there was no forage, the camels ate what they carried on their backs, remaining hobbled through the night, their bony legs tied together painfully so they could move only a few yards from camp. With loads restored, the caravan moved out, the baggage masters checking to see that loads did not shift. They mounted their own camels only when satisfied that nothing could fall loose.

Around noon Babani usually called a halt and the camels were unloaded again and left to find food. After prayers, more tea was brewed and "lunch" (usually more *zummita* and some dates) was served. After an hour or two, the handlers rounded up the camels and the caravan plodded on until after dusk. The evening devotions were longer and the evening

---

[*] *Zummita* is roasted ground barley or a mixture of roasted barley flour, dates, and butter usually carried in a leather pouch. To this day, desert travelers typically dilute a little of this mixture with water in the palm of the hand or in a tin cup and make a paste which they consume before continuing on their way. It is the "fast food" of the Sahara.

meal more substantial, usually including camel or goat meat, milk, and more dates—and, of course, tea. They seldom pitched tents (except for Laing); the caravanners simply wrapped themselves in their blankets and slept on the sand. The far slope of the closest dune served as latrine—too often distressingly nearby; it was the wise man who exercised caution when walking at night. Hands were washed with sand, not water, and no other cleansing of bodies took place until the caravan reached its destination. Chewing on fiber kept teeth and gums healthy; stalks of sugarcane were specially brought for this purpose.

Hunger, a need for food that was persistent, gnawing, and demoralizing, rivaled thirst as the caravanner's enemy. As a rule, Europeans did not find desert cuisine sustaining or appetizing: "It is a point of great politeness with the Arabs to tear the meat for a stranger, as well to squeeze up the *bazeen* [a Tripoli dish made with barley, onion, olive oil, and lamb] with the sauce for him," Lyon wrote of his trip. "And as this is sometimes done with unsavoury fingers, hunger becomes an absolute requisite to induce a novice to touch an Arab meal."

The appetite of a Saharan traveler, like that of his camel, was elastic. In the desert, he might live for days, even weeks, on little more than dried dates, a handful of *zummita* mixed with water and a little rancid fat for flavoring, and salt. Food was so scarce in the Sahara that a plague of locusts, regarded as a disaster in the agricultural regions to the north, was welcomed as a gift from heaven in the desert by the men, who gathered them up by the sackful. They could be broiled, fried with red peppers, salted, or preserved in oil.

The temperature at midday usually hovered around 120 degrees. There was a shortage of water, and water ruled all life in the desert. Humans needed two gallons daily. A supply was carried on the backs of camels in goatskin bags called *guerbas,* but drinking the water from these required a strong stomach. The water was muddy, tinged red from the leather, and full of foreign matter (including goat hairs). It was tepid, even hot, and tasted of sulfur and magnesium. Laing found it nauseating at first, but thirst soon made him less squeamish.

In the vastness of the Sahara, finding a well required great skill and a measure of luck. Whole caravans of a hundred men had simply vanished like ships in the ocean because their calculations were off by a hundred yards. Once wells were located, the real work began, as they were often covered over with sand. Digging out clogged wells was an operation that could take days, and the suffering from thirst became more intense beside a well (because one knew the water was so near). Even after hours spent in excavation, the well might be found dry, or containing barely inches of muddy water, hardly enough for men, much less for animals. The hole might be a deep one with no bucket and rope to draw the water, or, if provided, the water might be so spiked with chemicals it was undrinkable.

At the sight of a well, the caravan usually dissolved into a stampeding rabble. The animals could smell the water before the men saw it, and both beasts and men ran toward the well or oasis. "I was presented with a hallucinatory vision," wrote a French explorer, who watched one parched caravan rush toward a water hole. "Children crushed in the stampede let out heartrending cries, camels, donkeys, zebus rushed with their heads lowered into the mob to get closer to the precious liquid; the women called for water with agonized cries; a terrifying spectacle, a Dantesque vision."

Travelers were too thirsty to examine the water they were drinking closely, and this may have been a blessing. Water holes were small pools idyllically set among golden dunes and shaded with date palms, "peeping from amidst the hills of sand, like a few evergreens amidst the snows of December," as Laing once wrote. On closer inspection, the water was revealed to be covered with a thick green scum liberally peppered with animal droppings, and often containing the marinating bodies of dead camels. The wisest travelers dug wells beside these oases. Those who drank the polluted and sulfuric water straight were plagued by stomach disorders and might suffer kidney failure. But even polluted water was precious; quarrels broke out over who got the sewage-like liquid.

The desert west of Beni Ulid was reported to be rife with plundering tribes, and so Babani, whose camels were loaded with merchandise, insisted on making a dogleg of the route, going south to Tamsawa (Tesawa), only twenty-five miles from Murzuk, and then turning back to the northwest to head for Ghadames. It didn't seem to matter whether they traveled by day or by night; Babani never lost his way.

Crossing the reddish, wind-scarred sandstone, biscuit-colored and dusty, the caravan's passage was oddly silent, even secretive. Camels' feet made no noise on the dunes, and even on the *hamada* or ergs their soft feet made a padding sound. Leather creaked; water sloshed in the skins; camels grumbled and moaned like old men.* The caravanners talked softly with their neighbors and sang mournful dirges. Even when the pace picked up—when a water hole loomed nearby or the sun beat overhead and shade was within reach, or simply because the drivers suspected some unknown peril—sound rose only slightly.

Rarely did shouts ring out, the crack of whips punctuating irritated curses. Camels that would not go faster were induced to extra exertion by an exquisite cruelty: drivers sliced into their necks and poked the fresh wounds, gouty with congealed blood, with a sharp stick. Riders who pitilessly goaded their camels also goaded themselves. Babani said that a man who is indifferent to pain (because he has long grown used to it) is unlikely to recoil from giving pain to others. In the desert, human beings willingly inflicted apparently limitless pain on themselves. And yet they remained, in all other respects, kindly men.

When the route was clearly marked, following the dry bed of a wadi or leading to a distant escarpment, the travelers dismounted and walked together. Their gait resembled that of the camels: shambling, loose, and long-legged, covering the ground efficiently. Hot air trembled over the land, reflecting the sky in every depression, distorting distant objects into moving, fantastic shapes. Hollows in the rocks appeared as dim blue lakes and wandering camels became dark palm groves or strange hills. These were the games of the "*hamada* devils," Babani told Laing, games they played to terrify and mislead luckless caravans. It was an environment given to letting the mind wander, to mesmerization.

In nineteenth-century Saharan Africa, the caravan, more than merely a mode of travel, was the heart and pulse of desert commerce. Merchants like Babani who fitted them out were solely responsible for its losses and gains. Great care was taken in the selection of camels and the men who accompanied them. Caravans varied in size, from lone nomadic traders who trudged beside a solitary "ship of the desert" to great trans-Saharan trade caravans with thousands of camels, donkeys, goats, sheep, and dogs.

---

* "The souls of the damned," a Coptic metropolitan of Khartoum once said, "speak through the throat of the camel." It is a sound Paul Theroux has aptly called "that frightful groan, that awesome, existentially discontented noise."

The largest caravans were infrequent since they took a year or more to outfit and a great deal of money, invested by Arabs and Jewish merchants, to set up. Lesser caravans whose sheikhs believed in the safety of numbers delayed their departures for months just to attach themselves to one of these moving cities.

Sunbaked Ghadames, Laing's destination, was close enough to the coast—usually no more than twenty days distant by camel on the direct route from Tripoli—that it had long figured as an important crossroads in the caravan trade. From Ghadames ran the route to the Sudan by way of Ghat and Djanet. By reason of its location alone, Ghadames was a city of many *fonduks** and a common stopping place.

Laing's thousand-mile roundabout journey took him into the northern Fezzan. He was still in the heart of the great desert of the Idehan Fezzan, crossing into the Tinrhert Hamada, another flat, rocky wasteland the size of Kentucky, when, on August 28, 1825, Hugh Clapperton departed Spithead, the ancient English sea terminus on the eastern flank of the English Channel between Southampton and the Isle of Wight, on HMS *Brazen*. Two weeks later, on September 13, eight weeks after leaving Tripoli, Laing approached the sequestered oasis city of Ghadames from the south, having succeeded in avoiding marauding bands. His party had maintained an unshakable pace of seventeen miles a day across some of the most unforgiving terrain in the world.

AFTER NEARLY TWO MONTHS in the wilderness, Laing saw Ghadames "situated like an island in the ocean, in the midst of an extension between plains, and enveloped in a green mantle of date trees." Upon sighting the city walls, Laing ordered his retinue to dress in white Turkish shirts with English linen trousers. He put on "light European dress" and a blue military cloak, and the group entered the town of 6,000 people, Laing wrote, "as Christians and subjects of His Majesty the King of England." Crowds came out to meet them. Their reception was "truly cordial, decent and respectable."

Ghadames, pearl of the desert, was one of the oldest Saharan cities. For centuries this medieval citadel had resisted assaults of sand and

---

* A *fonduk* is a business establishment in northern Africa, or an inn or hotel.

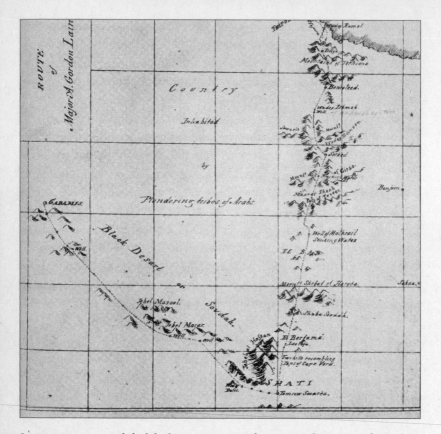

Laing was an accomplished draftsman, preparing this map on the two-month trip from Tripoli to Ghadames. One can see clearly how far out of his way he went to avoid bandits, and the range after range of mountains he had to negotiate. This map was saved because Laing had the good sense to send it to Warrington by courier from Ghadames, and Warrington forwarded it immediately to Lord Bathurst aboard a British warship. Maps like this were considered beyond price in London—British lives were literally sacrificed to obtain them—for whoever possessed such maps gained detailed knowledge of the strange, unknown world called Africa, and held an advantage over European competitors for colonial domination of this last great frontier.

climate, its limewashed mud-brick walls and close-set covered alleys providing protection from the heat and cold of the stony wasteland. Ghadames was known for inventive architecture, designed to fight the extremities of the Sahara. Houses were made of mud, lime, and palm tree trunks, constructed with covered alleyways between them and adjacent roofs, granting passage from one house to another in complete shade and privacy, much like the skywalks that connect modern office towers. The city was a labyrinth, lit by gardens and squares open to the sun. Though the town had always been a stopover on the caravan routes crossing the Sahara, its importance had peaked with the slave trade, and this traffic had already begun its decline when Laing arrived, shrinking the city's economic base.

Scattered over low hills, Ghadames seemed abandoned. The heat was fierce, even for September, and a deep silence gripped the narrow streets. At its worst, Ghadames appeared as an improvised anthill, attracting the poor and the desperate from the harshness of the desert. And yet, Ghadames, the ancient city, had a timeless appeal. Defended by high walls, its peculiar remoteness, and scores of triangular rooftop crenellations soaring above labyrinthine alleys, it offered the peace of an immemorial refuge.

Laing's equipment was already badly damaged; the ether in his hygrometers had evaporated, his naval chronometers had stopped, "and a camel, having placed his great gouty foot upon my rifle one night as I lay with it by my side in the ground, snapped the stock in two." The animals had suffered as much as the men, for along the route there had been "as little herbage for them as in the bottom of a tin mine in Cornwall," Laing wrote. Yet if he regretted having taken on his ambitious journey, he showed no sign of it. Laing spent his days visiting buildings, making drawings, and talking to the denizens of mosques and libraries. He wrote long letters to Emma. A message from Warrington caught up with him, reassuring him that "your dear wife, you may believe me, is well and happy *as it is her duty to be* [emphasis added]."

As far as Laing could tell, Ghadames had not been visited by Lyon, Clapperton, *or any European* since the Romans had occupied it a millennium and a half earlier, making it the southernmost African frontier of the Roman Empire. While there was evidence of earlier settlements, Herodotus and Ibn Batuta record that the first Roman garrison was established there around 20 B.C. The Romans found it a difficult post to hold, however, for the Berbers of that era were as tough as those of 1825. By the fourth and fifth centuries, Ghadames became an episcopate under the Byzantine Empire, and four bishops served there until the Arab invasion of 667. The Arabs established Ghadames as a trading center, and in the sixteenth century, Ghadames became a satrap of the bey of Tunis. By Laing's day, the influence of the bashaw of Tripoli was already ascendant (by 1860, Ghadames would be completely controlled by Tripoli).

Sheikh Babani was fond of the city, and said that as pearls imprisoned the languid light of moonbeams, so Ghadames, pearl of the sand sea, throbbed with the life of the sun. It was the water of the oasis, not light, that gave life to all things in Ghadames, flouting the desert, which could rob only the city's crystalline and transparent air, but not its land, of moisture.

Braced for misery, Laing had arrived at Ghadames sick with fatigue. Through a dilapidated gate, the traveler would enter "the dark intricate labyrinths of [the] closely built town." The streets, covered passages running beneath the houses, were so complex that it was impossible to negotiate them without a guide. They opened periodically onto squares surrounded by stone benches where old men sat and gossiped. A plain mosque graced the central plaza, along with the governor's residence and a few shops.

Laing was fascinated by the houses of the town; he sketched dozens of them. Contrasting with the streets, which contained mounds of rubbish, they were clean and comfortable, though spare. A central room on the first floor acted as a courtyard, with all other rooms leading off it. The central room was lit by an ingenious hole high in the ceiling, letting in sunlight that reflected off the white walls, thus illuminating the whole room. The top floor in most houses was reserved for women. These dwellings combined a certain elegance with practicality. "Of square construction with terraced roofs, and only dead walls exposed to view," Laing wrote of them,

> the interior of the houses exhibits nevertheless a degree of comfort, and occasionally even of elegance, the walls of the house being plastered with considerable skill, divided into paneling of oblong

squares, painted ornamentally, with recesses in which are fixed
pier glasses [and] small earthen ornaments. . . . The rooms on the
ground floor have no other light than that admitted by the doors
which open into the square courtyard, but those in the upper stories
have the advantage of skye light.

White daylight poured onto the city walls, blinding yet reassuring. In
the desert, sand entwined, concealed, bewildered, tormented—goaded by
impetuous winds. Not so in Ghadames, where the sand was snowy and
soft, an accomplice to truce with a desert that threatened just beyond city
walls. In Ghadames, the sea appeared unwittingly in the colors used to
paint the city. The cobalt of the deep ocean and the turquoise of waves
against the sunlight defined the doors of the houses, painted blue. Even
the sun, sinking into the blue horizon, enveloped the walls of the houses
in a magical web of reflected tints of blue.

Chapter Twelve

—————◆—————

CLAPPERTON CATCHES UP

H ANMER WARRINGTON held Hugh Clapperton in high regard, and that was a frequent and intense source of irritation for Alexander Gordon Laing. At times, it appeared to Laing that Warrington was encouraging the more experienced sailor to rob him of what he hoped would be the capstone of his career.

When Laing landed in Tripoli in May 1825, Warrington had already recommended that Clapperton, who had recently sailed for London, be sent back to Africa to search for the lower Niger from the Bight of Benin. The suggestion made sense from the standpoint of British policy, but it interfered with Laing's personal plans, which involved reaching the same place via Timbuktu.

Even more irritating—indeed, truly unendurable—was the train of correspondence from Warrington that dogged Laing as he crossed the Great Desert, letters suggesting that with Clapperton also in the field and likely to meet him en route, he would be able to cut short his journey and share the honors of discovery with his rival. That was the last thing Laing, thirsting for glory, wanted to do. Warrington was completely blind to this, or chose to ignore it.

"I have endeavored," Warrington wrote to Lord Bathurst after Laing left Tripoli, "to implant on the mind of Major Laing the cheering prospect of meeting Clapperton at Sockatoo." Months later, he wrote to Laing, "You will certainly meet Clapperton at Yauri which I should think will render it unnecessary for you to go to Benin." And two weeks later: "If you recollect, I always said you would meet Clapperton at Yauri & I think it more than probable now. He is an honest and good fellow & you will find him so.—When you meet him the course of the Niger is ascertained & I do not perceive the necessity of your going to Benin."

It was galling to Laing, now well into his perilous journey, to be told by his father-in-law that he expected Clapperton to forestall him in the main object of his expedition. Nonetheless, Laing's confidence remained unshaken. "I understand," he wrote to James Bandinel, his confidant in the Foreign Office, "that Captn. Clapperton has gone to the Bight to make the long looked for discovery, but he might have saved himself the trouble for the disclosure of that long hidden secret is left to me, as I hope to prove by March or April next."

Laing, for his part, would bide his time and go his own way, which he thought would be more worthwhile than "running a race with Captain Clapperton, whose only object seems to be to forestall me in discovery—Shou'd he succeed in reaching Tombuctoo, which I doubt much, I shall have much pleasure in meeting him." Laing believed he would reach Timbuktu first, and he must have enjoyed imagining Clapperton's reaction when he found Laing there, at the city gates, waiting to greet him.

The Colonial Office, like Warrington, hoped that Clapperton would run into Laing somewhere in Africa, unaware that Clapperton also had no desire to meet the man he considered a challenger. Clapperton, too, had been told to proceed from Sokoto to Timbuktu—but only if Laing hadn't made it there first. Lord Bathurst's instructions (which Laing never saw), dated July 30, 1825, were explicit on this score: "You will also, during your stay in Central Africa, endeavour to visit the city of Tombuctoo, provided you shall not have heard that Major Laing had already accomplished that object," words he must have found galling.

There are sound reasons for thinking Clapperton was as jealous of Laing as Laing was of him, each man regarding the other as an unwelcome interloper. Warrington, who, to his great credit, was more committed to the results of exploration than in who would achieve them (notwithstanding his daughter's vested interest in Laing's success), had asked Clapperton, before returning to London, to leave him with any information about the interior helpful to Laing, who was shortly expected from Malta. That Warrington took the trouble, as he did, to record this request in a letter to Clapperton, then a guest in his house, suggests that he had been instructed to make it by the Colonial Office, and that he had already done so orally and received an unsatisfactory answer.

This is what he wrote:

To Lieutenant Clapperton. R.N.

Sir,
    Having read to you the contents of a dispatch from the Right Honble Earl Bathurst of the 7th Dec. last, containing the information of the intention of His Lordship to send out an Officer direct to Tombuctoo to explore the course of the Niger.—I beg leave to submit to your consideration the propriety of your committing to paper whatever part of that important information you are in possession of which must tend considerably to assist the operations & labours of Capt. Laing & facilitate the object of the mission entrusted to Him—Probably a sketch of Bello's map would be of the greatest importance accompanied with your Opinion & Advice & it only rests with me solemnly to assure you on my honor that whatever you may entrust to me will remain an inviolable secret with exception of communicating it to Capt. Laing on his arrival.

With great esteem and friendly consideration
I have the honour to be
Sir,
Your Obt. & Faithful Servt.

[signed] H. Warrington

Clapperton responded to Warrington the following day, when he must have received the written request, but he did not refer to it, possibly confirming the notion that he had no intention of helping Laing if he could avoid it. When Clapperton got back to London, he discovered that the colonial secretary, to whom he looked for further patronage, was in no mood to tolerate his pigheaded thinking. In August, Laing, who had reached Beni Ulid, wrote to Robert Wilmot Horton (Bathurst's deputy) acknowledging, in a slightly acid tone, a letter "transmitting a copy of the opinions and suggestions which Lt. Clapperton had been called upon to furnish for my guidance. . . . [T]heir general tenor has been anticipated and acted upon."

Still smoldering over the letter he had received days earlier from his rival, Laing finally sent Warrington an amusing account of what Clapperton had said and what he thought of it. "By the bye," he scrawled,

I have received hints from the Colonial Office, furnished by Clapperton, evidently wrung from him for my guidance. They amount to this:
"I must cordially co-operate with you." *Bono!*
"I must wear Turkish dress" just as "I must be kind and patient with the natives." 'Tis not my nature to be otherwise.
"I must not take observations secretly." The sun does not shine in sly corners!
"I must not speak disrespectfully of the women." I wonder how he found this out? I might have been a century in Africa and never made such a discovery!
"I must not meddle with the females of the country." Prodigious!
"I must have presents to give away." Sound advice!

Having posted these sarcasms back to Tripoli, Laing struck off across the desert. "I care little for any information that Clapperton cou'd communicate," he wrote to his friend Edward Sabine. "I smile at the idea of his reaching Tombuctoo before me—how can he expect it? Has he not already had the power? Has he not thrown away the chance? I cannot

think what were his ideas—a man to be within two days of the Niger, and
to come back without ever seeing it—I think I may safely aver, that had
I been at Sakotoo—the problem wou'd have been long ago solved—and I
feel certain that to me the honor of the solution is left."

In fact, some of Clapperton's advice may have been wrong, if not
outright dangerous. Mungo Park and many who came after him into
Muslim territory often paid with their lives for refusing to conceal their
Christian faith. And yet whether to penetrate these Muslim lands as an
undisguised and professing Christian or a disguised and bogus Muslim
became a highly controversial topic in British drawing rooms, where there
were bound to be references to the treatment of Mungo Park who was, as
he wrote, "obliged to suffer, with an unruffled countenance, the insults of
the rudest savages on earth."

Some thought Laing would have been safer had he avoided wearing
a "plain Turkish dress," theorizing that no Englishman could credibly fool
the local Arabs and would only invite their wrath by trying. Sir Richard
Burton would prove them wrong thirty years later when he entered Mecca
surreptitiously in 1855, but Burton was a master of disguise, spending
hours on his makeup. Before his voyage, he took long baths in a spectrum
of dyes to imbue his pale English skin with precisely the right color. He
also submitted to the agony of circumcision. In Laing's day, there was no
consensus on how English explorers should present themselves in their
African travels. There seemed to be deadly potential costs no matter what
the approach.

LORD BATHURST WAS IMPRESSED by Clapperton's enthusiastic
description of the newly discovered "Soudan lands," and the respectful
attention the explorer had received from Sultan Bello in February 1824.
Bello's promise to end slavery, and his invitation for an English consul and
doctor to be sent out to Funda, had an authentic ring. British diplomacy
had, as yet, nothing to do with African potentates, but the future seemed
promising. Without hesitation, Bathurst commissioned Clapperton—who
was eager to return to Africa as quickly as possible—to organize his second expedition to consolidate the work of the first. Its purpose would be
to work out details with Sultan Bello for opening trade between Britain
and the Hausa lands, and to further abolition of the slave trade.

At Clapperton's insistence, the Admiralty provided transportation for Clapperton and his party aboard the exceptionally fast sloop HMS *Brazen*. The logbook for the *Brazen* on August 28, 1825, reads: "Came on board Captains Clapperton and Pearce & Messrs Morison and Dickson and 4 Domestics on a Mission to the interior of Africa."

Accompanying Clapperton (without question, this time, chief of the mission) were Captain Robert Pearce, a naval officer who was second-in-command, Dr. Thomas Dickson, a Scottish surgeon, and Dr. Robert Morison, a naval surgeon who was also a naturalist.

It was now the practice on African missions to take along a doctor, although precedent showed that, far from guaranteeing the health of the explorers, doctors were the climate's first victims (indeed, Oudney and Ritchie had both been doctors). Notwithstanding the many expeditions sent to find the Niger and the large number of men who died of malaria and dysentery on these, no progress had been made in the treatment of tropical diseases by 1825. Fevers were believed to come from putrid air, and malaria had yet to be connected to mosquitoes. Fevers were all treated the same way, with bleeding, calomel, and emetics. Quinine was known as "a strengthening agent after fever or dysentery," but using it prophylactically had as yet occurred to no one.[*]

The logbook's casual mention of four servants concealed the identity of a man who was to become one of the greatest of West Africa's explorers: Richard Lemon Lander. Except for John Ledyard of Connecticut, the explorers searching for Timbuktu had until now all been army or navy officers like Clapperton and Laing, or physicians like Mungo Park. Lander, the accidental explorer, rose from working-class origins and came to Africa as a menial. He was born in 1804 in the Cornish town of Truro, the fourth of six children. His father kept a pub called the Fighting Cock and his grandfather had been a well-known wrestler at Land's End in Cornwall. Lander left home at nine (for reasons he never revealed), and two years later went "into service" for a merchant who took him to the West Indies. He later went to South Africa as the servant of a colonial commissioner. In 1823 he returned to England, but he had become enamored of Africa. He wrote:

---

[*] Indian tonic water was not invented until 1870 to disguise the unpleasant taste of quinine. The first "gin and tonic" made its appearance at British colonial clubs the following year.

Richard Lemon Lander, Clapperton's servant and later his friend, in Arab dress, aged about twenty-five. With his brother, John, he returned to Africa to trace the course of the lower Niger River to its delta, thus solving a mystery that had puzzled geographers for centuries. Like Clapperton, he was claimed by Africa; he died in 1834, before he was thirty.

There was a charm in the very sound of Africa that always made my heart flutter—whilst its boundless deserts of sand; the awful obscurity in which many of the interior regions were enveloped; the strange and wild aspects of countries that had never been trodden by the foot of a European, and even the very failure of all former undertakings to explore its hidden wonders, united to strengthen the determination I had come to.

When he heard that Clapperton was setting out on a second mission, he volunteered to join him. Friends tried to dissuade him, citing the dangers and diseases, but Lander believed that "all men think all men are mortal but themselves." He went to see Clapperton, who seemed "the very soul of enterprise and adventure." Clapperton hired him on the spot. Lander, twenty-one years old when he left for Africa, was experiencing hero worship for his new boss. As the younger man observed, "It would not have been well for any haughtiness or reserve to be manifested toward me under such circumstances, merely because accident had thrown me into a lower rank of life than my master. . . . [S]uch, happily, was not the disposition of Captain Clapperton; the differences in our respective conditions were willingly levelled . . . and for my part I may justly say . . . that I would willingly have laid down my life for the preservation of his."

CLAPPERTON HAD LEFT SULTAN BELLO in Sokoto in May 1824 with the understanding that he would return by sea to the Gulf of Guinea. "Let me know the time," the sultan told him, "and my messengers shall be down at any part of the coast you may appoint, to forward letters to me from the mission, on reception of which I will send an escort to conduct it to Soudan." From Bornu's capital of Kukawa, before setting off for Tripoli, Clapperton had confirmed to Bello in writing that he planned his return no later than July 1825. He hoped to land at Whydah (Ouidah), a natural harbor close to present-day Cotonou, Benin.

When he got back to London (in June 1825) after an absence of more than forty months, Clapperton set to work impatiently to get back to Africa as quickly as possible, in spite of recurring attacks of what he called "the ague" (probably malaria). It was, of course, already far too late to rendezvous with Bello's messengers in July, but Clapperton still hoped to reach the coast in time to make the 450-mile overland trip to Sokoto during the dry season. He stayed in England just long enough to outfit his second expedition and receive his new instructions from Bathurst.

These instructions contained a long section on the suppression of slavery, charging Clapperton to "endeavour by every means . . . to impress on his [Sultan Bello's] mind the very great advantages he will derive by putting a total stop to the sale of slaves to Christian merchants . . . and by preventing other powers of Africa from marching koffilas [slave caravans] through his dominions. You will inform him of the anxious desire which the King your Master [George IV] feels for the total abolition of this inhuman and unnatural traffic."

The Colonial Office directive reflected a slow turnabout in British slavery policy that can be credited to successful lobbying by abolitionists for many years. The Quakers had launched the campaign in 1783, after the rebellion of the American colonies in 1776 weakened vested proslavery interests. Within a quarter century, a band of ardent reformists succeeded in changing the attitude of a nation. In the House of Commons, William Wilberforce, "the nightingale of the House," led a lifelong crusade against slavery. Abolitionists spread the humanitarian gospel of the age: the rights of man and the immorality of the ownership of humans. They gathered evidence on the inhuman treatment of slaves, organized a nationwide boycott of West Indian sugar, and drew up petitions to Parliament.

At the same time, the economic underpinnings of slavery were weakening. In Britain, transformation from a mercantile to an industrial economy was under way, and the great trading companies found that their interests lay in opening new markets for industrial goods rather than in supporting slavery. Even before abolition, Liverpool was already diverting ships from the slave trade to cotton.

One might take with a grain of salt the view of one well-known historian of eighteenth-century England: "The unweary, unostentatious, and inglorious crusade of England against slavery may probably be regarded as among the three or four perfectly virtuous pages comprised in the history of nations." The truth is, abolition also made sound business sense. Great Britain was, after all, a nation of capitalists.

The Danes, who had slave-trading posts on the West African coast, declared slaving illegal in 1802. The English, whose ships were the chief carriers of West African slaves, abolished the trade in 1807, and the last English slaver, *Kitty's Amelia,* sailed out of Liverpool on July 27 of that year. Parliament passed an act mandating "all manner of dealing and trading" in slaves in Africa be "utterly abolished, prohibited and declared to be unlawful." An 1811 bill made it a felony for any British subject to engage in "the carrying trade."

Voting for abolition was one thing, but persuading other slave-trading powers to do the same was another. From having been the nation most actively engaged in slaving, England became the most zealous enforcer of its suppression. The trade continued to flourish well into the second half of the nineteenth century, as long as North and South America continued to absorb all the slaves Africa could supply. Long after the United States prohibited the importation of new slaves in 1808,[*] and after Europe agreed to abolition at the Congress of Vienna in 1815, the trade survived illegally.

England, the poacher turned gamekeeper, formed a Blockade Squad-

---

[*] Ratification of the Thirteenth Amendment to the U.S. Constitution, abolishing slavery in its entirety, would have to wait another half century, until December 1865.

ron (soon to be tagged the "Coffin Squadron") to intercept slavers in the coves and hidden harbors of the West African coast. Skirmishes at sea and diseases from land took a hellish toll (giving the squadron its nickname). Between 1822 and 1830, of 1,568 sailors and soldiers in one detachment in West Africa, 1,298 (82 percent) died there of "climatic fevers," 125 died on the voyage home, and half of the survivors died of tropical diseases after returning to England. Only 57 men (less than 4 percent) were discharged as "fit." With grim humor, Bathurst (Banjul), Gambia, was known colloquially as "half die."

This was the context within which Clapperton was ordered to persuade Sultan Bello to give up slavery. The English government, now vigorously engaged in the suppression of the slave trade, found a new use for explorers who could spread the message of abolition deep into the African interior, at the source of supply.

Clapperton was also told to pursue commercial and geographical goals. He was to promise Sultan Bello that once the road was open from the coast to Sokoto, "he will receive whatever articles of merchandise he may require at a much cheaper rate than he now pays for those which are brought across the long desert." And so it may have seemed an afterthought that Clapperton was ordered "to trace the course of the river which is known with certainty to flow past Kabara, or the port of Timbuktoo, and which has been known in modern times by the name of Niger." The afterthought remained Clapperton's own priority; he was, to the end, an explorer.

WITH PACKING CRATES FULL of rich gifts for Sultan Bello, the Clapperton party embarked for Africa from Spithead at the end of August. Clapperton had rested for less than ninety days, but he seemed confident to go to one of the world's most notorious death traps (the west coast of Africa was not called the "white man's grave" for nothing), with his strength still sapped by his first expedition. After pursuing and capturing several Spanish slavers along the coast and sending their cargoes to Sierra Leone (where the slaves were freed), the *Brazen* reached Whydah on November 23.

Dr. Dickson was put ashore to explore the interior of Dahomey. Dickson had such a vitriolic temper that Clapperton, who had the same problem, warned him: "The conquest of the people to you will be guided solely by your behaviour toward them. Set a guard over your temper, my dear Dickson, and never let it lead you into error." It was unheeded advice, for news later reached Clapperton that at a village called Shar, Dickson "had a serious misunderstanding with a party of natives, and his life being threatened by its chief, he was so violently exasperated that he attempted to throttle the individual; which, being observed by his followers, they fell upon the unfortunate doctor, overcame and slew him." The story must have reminded Clapperton of his own outburst at the grave of Dr. Oudney.

In December, the *Brazen* landed the rest of the expedition at the slave-trading station of Badagri, 60 miles up the coast. Leaving the *Brazen*, Lander put a bugle to his lips and played "Over the Hills and Far Away" as sailors on the decks cheered. The explorers went over the side into canoes ready to take them through the terrific Atlantic surf to shore, an event that nearly ended in tragedy. One of the canoes overturned and some of the party might have drowned but for the prompt action of two Africans.

Clapperton's party left Badagri for the long haul overland to Sokoto—a distance of 475 miles as the crow flies, twice that on foot. The explorers engaged a British trader named Houtson to guide them. There was no sign of Sultan Bello's messengers, but Clapperton was not discouraged. He was three months late, after all. Houtson promised to take them to Katunga,* about 150 miles north of Badagri, through friendly Yoruba country. They took canoes for the first leg of the journey along the Lagos River. When the Lagos had taken them as far inland as it could, they went into the great triple-canopy rain forest on foot.

The explorers immediately made an elementary mistake, inexplicable given Clapperton's earlier experiences in Africa. Though he had previously crossed deserts and savanna and had little personal knowledge of the vast, gloomy wilderness near the ocean, he must have suspected something, as all Englishmen did, of the damp "night humors and miasmic vapors"

---

* Katunga will not be found on any modern map. The capital of the Yoruba was destroyed in the civil wars of the early nineteenth century and renamed Oyo. Present-day Oyo is about 100 miles south of Old Oyo, the site of the old city of Katunga.

so feared in this area. But lured by the astonishing beauty of the tropical night, he and his men slept out in the open. Mosquito hordes did their unhealthy work. Clapperton was racked by fever within days; he became so ill he had to be carried in a hammock.

Exacerbating his illness, Clapperton discovered that inhabitants of the region had a different attitude toward strangers than the gregarious Yoruba. Where the Yoruba had been helpful, the men of the coast and the forest, while insatiably curious, did nothing to assist the already struggling white men. At every village the explorers were welcomed festively with singing and dancing that went on all night (to the dismay of the exhausted travelers), but that was the extent of their aid.

The villagers stared, sniffed, poked, and tried to examine the genitalia of the white men, but never offered food or shelter. Soaked each night by the rains and heavy dew, footsore (Clapperton's feet were raw from wearing new boots), and uncertain of his path, Clapperton found that his ability to hold the expedition together was falling apart. The men were separated from their baggage; it would go by another route and not catch up for days. It was impossible to hire forest people to carry those too weak to walk; Clapperton himself could barely totter. Captain Pearce and Dr. Morison were in even worse shape and Lander could barely stand. They reached Laboo (Lalo), only miles from their starting place, in despair.

Clapperton found men to carry Morison and Lander, who were past walking, but when they reached the village of Jannah (Jonah), the bearers abandoned them in an empty hut. Clapperton and the trader Houtson arrived just in time to see Lander go crazy from sunstroke. He ran around camp berserk. To subdue him took the combined strength of the whole party. Dr. Morison predicted that Lander might not last the night. By morning he was better, but Pearce and Morison were now ill in his stead. Clapperton suggested that Houtson take them both back to the coast, but the invalids refused. They had to be carried in hammocks.

Two weeks out of Badagri, Lander was so sick that he recorded, "I was bled in the temple; but the doctor, who was himself suffering from fever, being unable to hold the instruments steadily, inadvertently thrust it into my skull. This accident occasioned the most excruciating agony and made me shriek with pain." Lander became delirious and had a violent fit, attacking Clapperton. Dr. Morison and Captain Pearce "looked more like walking spectres than living human beings," Clapperton wrote.

Pearce was a slight, fair man "whose frame was much too delicate for the arduous task that he had undertaken." Dr. Morison was coaxed into returning with Houtson to the ship in Badagri in the belief that his health would improve by the sea, but it was too late. He died of fever before he reached the coast. With the mission barely under way, both its physicians were dead. Taking a pair of doctors along, as this expedition again proved, provided about as much protection against illness as the fetishes the Africans believed would protect them—perhaps less.

In spite of chaos and death, Clapperton and Lander were diligent in keeping their journals, recording details of the march. Jannah emerges in Clapperton's pages as "a great place for woodcarvers" (as it remains to this day). It was also active in the slave business. Most of the indigenous men, at the time of the arrival of the explorers, were away on a slave raid to supply a Brazilian brig then anchored at Badagri. Clapperton mentions watching looms at work and visiting dyehouses, finding the indigo of high quality. The whole countryside was well ordered and well governed. They stayed for six days, resting.

The next weeks were harrowing. The rains came in a deluge, the mud at times reaching the horses' shoulders. That Clapperton allowed his expedition to start into the West African forest belt just as the annual rains were imminent is a good indication of the hurry he was in.

The dead Morison's servant, an English seaman named George Dawson, remained with Clapperton, but he was delirious and kept repeating that he had deserted his family only to die in a strange land, death crowding life out of him the way the forest trees squeezed the light out of the sky.

He did die, in a particularly bizarre way. Night had fallen and his companions were sleeping, except Dawson, who was raving, blaming himself for the criminal mistake of abandoning his wife and children. As Lander tells the story, "[T]he medicine chest was lying open by Dawson's side and he perceived it. Pointing to a phial, he desired a black attendant to fill him a glass of its contents; which being promptly done, he eagerly swallowed it. . . . [A]bout a quarter of an hour afterwards, not hearing

Dawson's groans, I asked how he did; but receiving no answer, I went to his bed-side, and found him a cold and stiffened corpse. Pearce awoke and said: 'What? Is Dawson dead? Well, poor fellow, his sufferings are over; I cannot long survive him.'"

The bottle contained ether, and Dawson died instantly from the poison. In the night, the death yells of the African porters, amplified by the sharp tattoo of rain beating on leaking beehive huts, petrified the survivors, themselves sick and exhausted and near death.

Chapter Thirteen

———◆———

THE IVORY MINIATURE

A **CONDITION** of Laing's appointment was that his journey to
Timbuktu be made under the guidance of that old comrade of
Lyon, the Tuareg Hatita ag Khuden. Laing arrived in Ghadames
to find the elusive guide (he had refused to go to Tripoli) waiting for him.
He reported to Warrington that "I have completely won over Hateeta's
heart with the presents I have given him." The foremost gift was "from the
King of England, a fine scarlet Goldlaced Burnoose which delighted him
so much that he gave me his spear and said I will take you safe through
Tuarick [Tuareg] country and will afterwards go to Tripoli to see my friend
the Consul."

The Colonial Office's insistence on Hatita as guide was a surprising
stipulation. At the time, little was known about the Tuareg, thought to be
a wild, remote, and predatory people. Hatita was unusual, in no way more
so than in his inexplicable liking for infidel English explorers. He had
associated himself with the British, on and off, for five years, beginning
with Lyon in 1820. A later British explorer writing in the 1850s, who knew
him only as "a rather tiresome oldster," described Hatita as "an extremely

pacific man in his conduct, and greatly liked for his peacemaking disposition." Whatever spell he cast on the British, he had cast on his own.

Hatita had offered to accompany Lyon to "the Negro Land" (by which
he meant the Hausa territory near Lake Chad). To Oudney and his companions, he had asserted that "he could by his influence alone, conduct
us in perfect safety to Timbuctoo, and would answer with his head. . . ."
These statements, coming from a much-respected African, were repeated
in London and came to the ears of Lord Bathurst, whose heart was set
on solving the frustrating mysteries of African exploration. To Bathurst,
Hatita's promises sounded like the words of a prophet, and he came to
be viewed in Downing Street with something bordering on reverence: the
one guide who could unlock every gate that barred the way to the center
of the continent. Thus it transpired that Bathurst insisted that Laing be
accompanied by Hatita. It was not a request.

Warrington accordingly summoned Hatita to Tripoli, but nothing
could induce him to come. Instead, he joined Laing at Ghadames and
agreed to stay with him only as far as Tuat.* To get from Tuat to Timbuktu,
he would have had to follow a dangerous road, controlled partly by the
Chaamba Arabs, traditional blood enemies of all Tuareg, and partly by
two Tuareg tribes (the Hoggar and the Ifora), both sworn enemies of his
own tribe, the Ajjer.

Of Hatita's many services to explorers, the first was to give them a
genial welcome, a courtesy rarely available in these hostile lands. He
had an engaging facility for adjusting himself to strange European ways.
He was skilled in protecting his patrons from the endemic violence to
which, as Christians, they were frequently exposed; and from a curiosity
so intense it was almost as bad as violence, precluding the most basic privacy. Hatita's ability to win the confidence of Englishmen gave him a certain cachet among his own people, for while the white men were despised
as infidels, their wealth, their arms, and (oddly) their recent reputation for
having driven Napoleon out of Egypt accorded them a grudging respect.

---

* "Tuat" is still the Tuareg name for the region comprising all the oases in the western part of
what we know today as the Algerian Sahara, including the oases of Gurara in the north and
Tidikelt in the south, as well as the trading hub of Insalah. Laing and Warrington often used
"Tuat" interchangably with "In Salah" in their letters.

Hatita took pride in being called, as he was throughout much of the Sahara, the "Friend of the English" or the "Consul of the English," and in his old age he even suggested that he actually be appointed British vice-consul at Ghat.

When Laing met Hatita in Ghadames, he was relieved to have another guide he could trust. He was already quite pleased with Babani, in spite of the constant dunning. He wrote to Warrington on September 13, 1825, that

> Babany is a man of the most sterling worth, who is to be found to morrow exactly as he is to day; he is quiet, harmless, and inof-fensive, but a man of infinite determination withal, as I have had occasion to observe on one or two occasions. . . . He either is much attached to the English, or he is a better actor than Talma,* for he has shewn so much apparent friendship and performed such disin-terested acts of kindness . . . that I must acknowledge a kind and generous heart. He is a man of mighty importance in Ghadames, being nothing less than its Governor,† a circumstance which I was ignorant of till this morning, but which, on being made acquainted with it, you may be assured did not disappoint me. I am lodged in one of his own houses, a very snug dwelling with a fine garden and extensive yard for my camels, all of which he is to feed at his own expence during the period we sojourn at Ghadames. He is no advocate for extravagance, but rather recommends the semblance of poverty in passing through the country. He thinks it is the surest and safest way of travelling, but in places of importance which we shall have to call at, and where advantage may be likely to arise out of it, he recommends a well timed liberality, and in this respect his ideas correspond exactly with my own.

Despite his optimistic tone, Laing's hardships were far from over. Rumors were already circulating throughout Ghadames that Laing would proceed eventually to In Salah. This gossip had certainly reached the

---

* François Talma was a French actor and friend of Sarah Bernhardt.
† Sheikh Babani, though a prominent merchant and resident of Ghadames, was never its governor.

ears of any potential raiders who might hold up the caravan once it left the city.

And yet, it was not the threat of angry Arabs that now most jeopardized Laing's mission. Laing's most difficult trials in Ghadames, once he recovered from his desert crossing, were the tribulations of his heart.

Emma was much on his mind. Warrington made an overt effort to prevent Laing's marriage to his daughter, but there may have been more going on than met the eye. In a strange letter to the Colonial Office written in March 1829, Warrington said that "the life of Major Laing and probably of my daughter, rendered it necessary that I should consent to the marriage previous to his departure. By so doing, and the determined measures I resorted to rendered abortive, thank God, his fatal intentions. I send by this occasion all the original correspondence with Major Laing at the time to Mr. Amyot. . . . Afterwards Mr. Amyot can commit them to the flames or keep them for me." A decade later, in July 1840, Warrington said in a letter to a man who was thinking of writing Laing's biography: "Mr. Amyot is in possession of the correspondence that caused the marriage with my daughter. . . . But of course one circumstance of a very delicate nature must be suppressed."

What were Laing's "fatal intentions" that Warrington had "rendered abortive"? And what was the "circumstance of a very delicate nature" which had to be suppressed? The great amateur English historian E. W. Bovill, who catalogued all of Laing's papers in the early 1960s, was unable to trace the missing letters to "Mr. Amyot." Possibly they were destroyed.

Certainly, the set of conditions attendant to Laing's marriage would have been enough to try the emotions of a less sensitive man. Did the young people, in their precious moments together, have some premonition of the short days allowed them? Did Emma feel that with this gallant, amusing, and lovable man gone from her, with only their "troth plighted," she might lose him forever? Did she, in fact, hope for a child?

Madame de Breughel, the Dutch consul's wife, wrote of the time preceding Emma's wedding in a memoir she later published:

Emma fell ill, and all the family were plunged into despair. The Doctor was immediately called, and, after an examination, he concluded that It was a case of poisoning. Tortured by violent cramps,

Emma admitted that she had wished to finish her life, since her father had refused his consent to her marriage with Laing. She had therefore poisoned herself. She was immediately offered an antidote, but in spite of her agonies, she refused it until her father had given his consent to the marriage.

It is also evident that Emma, genuinely distraught, wanted to frighten her father. In this she succeeded, but only partly. Warrington agreed to marry the couple in his capacity as consul, but would do so only conditioned on their solemn agreement not to cohabit until Laing returned. It is very remotely possible that Laing, too, threatened to kill himself unless permitted to marry Emma, though this would be a strange act by a man of such overweening ambition. On the other hand, Laing had a tendency to what was then called "melancholia," or, in more modern terms, depression. He suffered from a "liver complaint," a term used in that era to describe a psychological condition, not an actual illness of the liver. There was a complex, artistic, questioning, imaginative, slightly feminine, and wayward side to Laing's character, an unusual dimension in a man of such stupendous physical and moral toughness. His letters also show that he was given to extremes of enthusiasm and pessimism.

Laing and Emma spent exactly seventy days together from the night of their first meeting to the morning of his departure. They were often alone, without a chaperone. Had they wanted to, they could easily have found the privacy to make love. It is remotely possible that at the time of Laing's departure for Timbuktu, Emma feared she might be pregnant and that Laing pretended to threaten to kill her and then kill himself unless Warrington allowed them to marry.

Warrington agreed to perform the ceremony only "under a most sacred and solemn obligation not to cohabit [as he put it] until they could be remarried by an ordained priest." Their last hours together, we know, were passed under the stern eye of Consul Warrington and the timid eye of his wife. On the other hand, would it truly have been possible for Warrington, a man who drank heavily every night and who slept profoundly, to prevent a determined young couple, just married, from consummating their marriage? In fact, even given the pre-Victorian times and mores, it seems incredible that they had not become lovers long before.

THE STORY of the ivory miniature sheds an interesting light.

After Laing's departure, Emma asked the Spanish consul, Joseph Gómez Herrador, an amateur artist, to paint a tiny portrait of her on a smooth lozenge of carved ivory similar to one Laing had given her of himself on the day of their wedding, one of many small gifts they exchanged on that day. She planned to send it, along with her letters, as a good-luck charm for her "dearest Laing." When it was finished, the Warringtons held a family conference. The focus of discussion was this: Should a piece of pink silk "twice the size of a dollar" or a piece of white paper be placed beneath the ivory?

Papa Warrington argued that the delicate tinge of the pink silk was more effective and produced a stronger likeness than "the pallid and melancholy appearance" produced by the paper. On this rare occasion, his wife and daughters overruled him, maintaining that the pink tint made Emma look like a milkmaid, whereas the pale and dejected look imparted by the white paper made her appear "more interesting."

When Hatita joined Laing, he carried the ivory miniature with him, conveyed to him by couriers from Tripoli, together with a packet of letters from Emma. In her letters, contrary to her father's assurances, Emma pleaded that the strain of constant and increasing anxiety about Laing was driving her to the brink of madness. Gazing at the tiny portrait in his stifling room in Ghadames, Laing reacted exactly as Warrington had predicted. He was shocked by her deathly mien. He had a grim night, one of sleeplessness and foreboding. The next morning, September 29, Laing lost his nerve and decided on the spot to abandon his mission and return to his wife. He wrote an emotional letter to his father-in-law announcing his revised intentions.

> While I am writing thus boldly, my heart throbs with sad pulsations on account of my dearest, most beloved Emma. You say she is well and happy, but I fear, I feel, she is not. Good God, where is the colour of her lovely cheek, where the vermillion of her dear lip? Tell me, has Mr. Herrador, or has he not, made a faithful likeness? If he has, My Emma is ill, is melancholy—her sunken eye, her pale cheek and colourless lip haunt my imagination, and adieu to resolution.

Was I within a day's march of Tombuctoo and to hear My Emma was ill, I wou'd turn about, and retrace my steps to Tripoli—What is Tombuctoo? What the Niger? What, the world to me? Without my Emma? Shou'd anything befall my Emma, which God forbid, I no more wish to see the face of man; my course will be run—a few short days of misery, and I shou'd follow her to Heaven.

I am agitated, but you will bear with me I hope. Never since this terrestrial ball was formed was there a man situated as I am—never, never, and may no man ever be so placed again—it requires rather more than the fortitude which falls to the general lot of mortals, to enable me to bear it—I must again entreat that you will.

"Bear with my weakness, my brain is troubled."—I must lay down my pen awhile . . . Oh, *that picture!*

Warrington exploded when he read this. He upbraided Emma for sending Laing letters she must have known would make him feel guilty about his decision to leave her. But before the consul had a chance to respond to Laing's decision, his son-in-law wrote again, in a letter carried by the same courier, to say that he had changed his mind a second time. He would continue his journey to Timbuktu after all.

Warrington père expressed glee at this news. He forgave Emma and wrote cheerfully to Laing: "The importance of the mission, the certainty of success and the honor and glory in reserve for you will inspire you with everything necessary to accomplish the object. Your dear Emma is well and happy, be assured, and for God's sake do not think otherwise, and make yourself unhappy."

Had Emma deliberately picked the backdrop that made her appear pale and sick because it signaled to Laing her feared pregnancy? And had Laing understood this secret message (Oh, *that picure!*) regarding her "interesting" condition only too well?

IN A LONG LETTER written just before his departure from Ghadames dealing with his travel plans, Laing penned an ominous phrase: "The Bashaw's authority finishes at Ghadames." Laing recognized just how alone he was going to be in the next leg of his journey. But in spite of (or because of) his emotional turbulence, Laing's next letters are exuberant, almost maniacal. He joked in one that "I have attained great celebrity as a medico [among the Ghadames locals]. . . . I shall, like the apothecary who had only two drawers in his shop, one for magnesia and the other for money, do little harm." Another letter to Emma's father railed against his competitor, showing a growing obsession with his mission: "Clapperton may as well have stayed at home," he wrote, "if the termination of the Niger is his object."

He had developed a tremendously optimistic, some would say unrealistic, schedule.

> I expect to go through in the following order with regard to time—
> Tuat, October 28th—Tombuctoo, December 10th—where I shall
> remain till the 1st January, when I shall cross the river, and traverse
> a desert of ten journeys [ten days' travel], which will bring me to
> Wangara, and the Lake where I presume the Niger terminates—a
> month more, the middle of February, and I am on the coast, where,
> if I find a Man of War, I shall instantly embark, calling at Sierra
> Leone and Gibraltar on my return, for letters. . . .

The discovery of Timbuktu and the source of the Niger—and the precarious emotional and physical condition of his wife—these were the opposing themes that battled in Laing's psyche during his long wait at Ghadames. In yet another letter —this one about money, camel-loads for the caravan, and gifts for the sheikhs on the route—he paused to ask if, when he returned to Tripoli, he would be released from the promise his father-in-law had extracted from him:

> Very Private,
>   Will you still consider it necessary to keep me to the promise [he
> wrote Warrington] which you have from me in writing [his emphasis]
> (and which wou'd be sacred was it merely verbal) or will you absolve
> me from it? Do not be offended at my putting such a question—As
> I merely do it to prevent a disappointment which might take place
> was I to return to Tripoli without being so liberated; for I made a
> solemn promise to my Dear Emma, the night of our separation, (that
> melancholy night which you will well remember), never again to part

from her when it shou'd please God to restore us to one another. . . . I
therefore trust that you will understand me, that I ask for the sake of
information and to prevent an awkward dilemma hereafter.

Was he concerned that Emma was already pregnant? "The promise,"
presumably, was that he would not sleep with her until their marriage had
been solemnized by an Anglican priest, though this is not precisely clear
from the context.

With these thoughts turning somersaults in his head, Laing left Ghadames on November 3 after a stay of fifty-one days. "At length, my dear
Consul," he wrote on that day, hastily, while a messenger waited,

I have it in my power to say that I am on the road to Tombuctoo—The camels are all loaded, and only wait for me while I give
you notice of the event.

Then, after a line about his plans for the journey, with a poignancy
which later events would only accentuate:

My mind forebodes nothing ill—I have a strong presentiment that
my Dear Emma is well, but it is truly painful to remain so long in
the dark. Had I but a single line from her dear hand, I shou'd mount
my camel satisfied.

Of course, she had written many letters to him, but they were weeks,
even months old. Laing was concerned about her condition *at that*
moment, again suggesting the possibility of her pregnancy.

Then an unrelated event took place that seemed to restore his sense
of well-being: in that month, November, as evening fell over the wastes
of the Sahara, a large comet could be seen moving southward across
the heavens. Each night, Laing watched its silvery wisps in the sky as it
moved slowly down toward the horizon: "I regard it as a happy omen," he
wrote. "It beckons me on & binds me to the termination of the Niger and
to Timbuktu."

The caravan had left Ghadames for In Salah (Insalah, in present-day
Algeria), traveling southwest along the edge of the eastern sand sea (the

Great Eastern Erg in what today we know as southern Tunisia). The journey was arduous. Only caravanners who had crossed these lands all their lives could tell one sand dune from another. Laing watched the forward guides run to the top of a sand hill, so that within minutes they seemed to be a long way off, minute white-robed figures signaling from the top of a mountain.

The fear of Tuareg was unrelenting, despite Hatita's comforting presence. Paradoxically, as Hatita's role made clear, Tuareg also made trade possible through their protection as escorts. In return for fees, these warriors, mounted high on their lurching camels, accompanied caravans to the outskirts of their territory, providing safe-conduct. If paid enough, they accompanied the caravan through adjoining districts where they might be called upon to fight their own kin. They did battle on these occasions as for their own cause, with the ferocity of lions. And yet, during the march, they were prone to treat those paying them as captives or servants. If a Tuareg saw something of an Arab merchant's that appealed to him, that object quickly changed owners.

Five hundred miles separated In Salah from Ghadames by the crooked route Babani and Hatita insisted on taking. There were many nights when shadowy figures loomed out of the swirling obscurity of the desert, men on camels plodding steadily through a veil of sand. They passed within yards of Laing's camp, but no one called out or raised a hand in greeting. Their tall camels had impossibly long and knobby legs and an imperious look, snorting and burping as they moved like derelict old men with bad digestion.

The nomads riding them were draped in blue, and veiled, only their eyes showing. These were the deep-desert Tuareg, the lords of the Sahara.

Each carried a long staff pointed downward at an angle past his mount's neck, and broadswords in leather scabbards. Many had rifles slung over the shoulder. Water in goatskin bags sloshed faintly against the animals' sides.

These figures moved through the camp silently and then vanished into the shroud of the desert, nothing to mark their passing, as elusive and mysterious as wraiths. Where were they going, these Tuareg nomads of the remote desert? Where had they come from? On what errand? And

A Tuareg mounted on his swift mehari dromedary near Murzuk, from a sketch by George Lyon in 1820. Twenty veiled men like this one joined Laing's caravan, uninvited, in the dangerous crossing of the Tanezrouft.

how, in this trackless land of no horizons, in this minuscule universe at night of maybe twenty feet, did they know their path? They headed north, but to the north was nothing but weeks of difficult traveling to nowhere. To the south waited the hellish Tanezrouft, but to the north—nothing— nothing but a thousand miles of desolation that ended with the sea.

Laing was now traversing lands well beyond any influence of the bashaw, lands controlled by raiding tribes who lived on the plunder of caravans. He succeeded in his crossing without incident in four weeks, in spite of frequent stops to replot the route. On December 3, Laing reached In Salah. News of the coming of a Christian traveler had preceded him, and large crowds were assembled to meet him—the first European to visit the territory.

A mile from the oasis, "upwards of a thousand people of both sexes came out to greet me. I have been in the habit of late of covering my face *à la mode* Tuareg, as a convenient protection against the sun, and as nothing but my eyes were yesterday visible, the curiosity of the multitudes was not gratified and my poor attendants were beleaguered by a thousand questions—Is he white? Is his hair like a Turk's? Has he a beard? Can

he fire a gun without a flint?" The local sheikh welcomed Laing and gave
him use of a house.

Three months had elapsed since Laing set out, and yet he was only a
quarter of the way to Timbuktu. He occupied himself studying the customs of his hosts. Laing tried not to think of the chasm of time as well as
the great distances that increasingly separated him from Emma.

"Indeed," he wrote to her in a letter that was surely more honest
than the one he had recently penned to her father, "I so much despair
of hearing again from Tripoli that I no longer look back. My whole ideas,
my thoughts, my prospects, are *forward,* driven by *ambition,* for I cannot
enjoy a moment of happiness till I return to you."

The anticipation of Clapperton breathing down his neck may have
played a part in Laing's renewed resolve. Though he didn't mention his
competitor, he took pains to reaffirm his goal. "Do not think I despond,
My Dearest, or that my enthusiasm which, for a while, lay Dormant, is in
the least abated. No, I am still the African traveller, and as eager as ever
for discovery, *though I lament every moment which my enthusiasm inclines
me to devote to it* [emphasis added]."

He must have realized the risks he would soon be taking. The ergs,
or seas of sand, were bad enough, but the most dreaded part of the
Sahara, even among seasoned travelers, was the Tanezrouft, southeast
of its equally dreadful partner, the Erg Chech. These were lands of fear
and loneliness where any man foolish enough to wander by himself was
certain to die. Each one covered 70,000 square miles, an area twice the
size of Scotland. Of the pair, the Tanezrouft was the most frightening, an
endless level plain with not so much as a single blade of grass.

This was the wilderness that lay ahead.

Chapter Fourteen

———— ·•· ————

THE WIDOW ZUMA

WHEN DAWSON DIED of ether poisoning, Clapperton's party was 150 miles due north of the point on the coast, in the Bight of Benin, from which they had started. They were mired in the great swampy forests of the Yoruba.

The rain stopped and the expedition resumed its march. Just as the explorers' prospects seemed most bleak, they came to the far edge of the jungle and into a well-cultivated country of hills, valleys, and trees. In this rural district the villagers were more friendly and cooperative.

The outlook improved, but it was too late for Robert Pearce, who had contracted fever in the jungle. He became delirious and had long imaginary conversations with his mother, asking her questions that he then answered for her. He fell into a stupor and died, aged twenty-eight, two days after Christmas, a holiday not noted in any of the journals. Clapperton read the burial service surrounded by his shrinking band of men. Less than 200 miles from their point of departure, Dickson, Morison, Pearce, Dawson, and several of the African porters were already in their graves—a disastrous beginning for Clapperton's second expedition.

Peaceful Chiadoo (Igboho) put new life into the survivors. Looking toward the rugged mountains, they were uplifted by the thought that, though a strenuous hike lay ahead, it would surely be an easier path than through the soggy vegetation. With renewed courage they marched through a hard, almost alpine terrain. Steep overhangs and cliffs, craggy paths, and high summits made progress slow, but it was liberating to the men, who had felt stifled for so long, losing their footing in the tangled brambles of the rain forest. "We almost forgot our misfortunes," Clapperton notes.

Within a week they reached what is today the northern boundary of western Nigeria, the end of the country of the Yoruba. It was then (and today) intensely cultivated and densely populated. "There are large towns every four miles," wrote Clapperton, who was delighted to find the local people "as industrious and law-abiding as those of England." It was well intended chauvinism. He was now stronger and riding on horseback. His two white companions (Houtson had returned to them after Morison died on the route to Badagri) were healthy once more, the country exceeded his expectations in its beauty and security, and the whole adventure seemed to have turned into something akin to a jaunt through Switzerland in the summertime.

Bucolic villages and fat cattle abounded. This was Clapperton's vision of what a great pastoral people in Africa should be like. Even his sense of humor, so rarely evident, came to the fore. At Toko, the explorers visited a minor king with no less than *two thousand* wives—"a true mountain king," was Clapperton's comment.*

The sense of pastoral security vanished with the arrival of a rowdy escort from the sultan of Katunga: robust warriors armed with spears, bows, and arrows, who shattered the peace with dissonant singing and shouting. Behind them, Clapperton recorded, exhausted but doggedly persistent, came an orchestra of (to his Western ears) unbelievably bad

---

*If this seems opaque, it is because pre-Victorians had to resort to complex wordplay to indulge in off-color humor in print. Far from referring to Grieg, Ibsen, or to the legend of Peer Gynt (whose Mountain King had only one wife), allusions that might have been the English reader's first inference in 1825, the joke is "a true *mountin'* king," i.e., they were traveling on a flat savanna, well beyond mountains, so "mountain" could only be understood as "mounting" (his many wives). How tedious to explain!

musicians, unable to keep pace with the soldiers but raising a cacopho-
nous racket.

At the end of this leg of their trek, the explorers broke away from
their escort momentarily and, from the top of a ridge, looked down upon
Katunga, the capital of Yorubaland. They were the first white men ever
to do so.

They reached Katunga on January 23, 1826 (less than two weeks after
Laing had departed In Salah). They stayed six weeks, recovering, with
the exception of Houtson. He got as far as Katunga, as promised, only to
inform Clapperton that he would have to go home—he was a businessman, after all, with a trading post on the coast to manage, and he feared
too long an absence from his untended wares. He got back to Badagri
safely but, with grim irony, immediately contracted a coastal fever and
died from it. "Like the characters in Mozart's *Farewell*,'" wrote Lander of
the party's original number, "they have dropped off one by one."

The king of Yorubaland, one Mansoleh, gave his visitors an audience
seated in state on the veranda of his "palace," which looked much like all
the other huts to the white men, surrounded by his four hundred wives.
Red and blue umbrellas on long poles protected the sovereign from the rays
of the sun, while musicians wailed "earsplitting discords." The most impressive thing about Mansoleh was his crown, a wonderful headdress which,
on close inspection, turned out to be made of cardboard—a white swindler
on the coast was doing a flourishing business selling cardboard crowns,
"exactly the same as worn by King George IV of England," to local chiefs.

Mansoleh's subjects brashly crowded the newcomers. Clapperton,
taking his role as George IV's emissary seriously, refused to kneel before
the ruler, and while this breech of etiquette astonished the king, it did not
appear to annoy him. As soon as his white guests were comfortably settled
in their huts, the king returned their visit accompanied by the court musicians and about half the population of the town. Clapperton paid tribute
to the people of Yorubaland, saying how kind they had been to him and

---

* Lander was likely thinking of Haydn's Symphony no. 45, the *Farewell* (much influenced by
Mozart), where the final violinist sits alone on the stage as his counterparts, one by one, take
their leave of him on the platform to return to their families. There is no "Mozart's *Farewell*."

his men during their journey, and how helpful he had found the headmen of the villages to be.

King Mansoleh was delighted—too delighted. He developed so great an interest in his English guests that he concocted every excuse for delaying their departure. The roads were dangerous, he said; there were too many war parties at large; the tributaries of the Quorra River (the local name for the Niger) were in flood; there were impassable swamps—and so on. Meanwhile, slave caravans came and went, noisily, and without trouble or delay.

Clapperton used the enforced idleness to keep up his journal. He wrote of "the malpractices of a sly, lubberly, fat and monstrous eunuch—Ebo," the king's principal counselor. Mansoleh himself was impulsively generous and hospitable, and heaped presents on his guests. The gifts were mostly in the form of food, but little of it got past the watchful guard of the "despicable eunuch." The caravan had not seen the last of Ebo, who would cause great trouble on the return journey.

Clapperton and Lander provided the first detailed information about the trade, industry, and government of the country, as well as the music, entertainment, court etiquette, marriages, and funerals as practiced by the Yoruba. One particular art form was enormously popular at every level of society: pantomime theater, which went on for hours and which the white visitors found both ingenious and funny. They soon became characters in the daily dramas, like celebrity drop-ins in a modern soap opera on television.

In time Mansoleh relented and gave the explorers his laissez-passer to continue their journey. They moved on astride lean, bony horses, crossing the Moussa River on March 11, the frontier between the Yoruba and Borgu (today found in northern Benin and northwestern Nigeria). Clapperton had to swim across, towing Lander (who could not swim). In Borgu villages, they noticed that crocodile eggs were impaled on the pointed tops of beehive huts. These were considered strong *ju-ju* against the predations of crocodiles. The two white men realized belatedly that they had nearly become lunch for famished river reptiles.

As they approached Kaiama, the capital of Borgu, Lander again came down with dysentery. He was barely able to walk when an escort arrived

from the chief of Kaiama, a wild troop of warriors mounted on magnificent horses. They made Clapperton nervous, for Mansoleh had warned
him that the people of Borgu were "the craziest and most untrustworthy
gang of cutthroats in all Africa." Despite their recklessness, the escort
appeared good-humored. They sang, shouted, and charged their horses,
Arab style, the whole way, but did not fail to conduct the white visitors
to their city in safety.

Yarro, the king of Kaiama, had a hut ready for them and visited immediately. To Clapperton's embarrassment, the king entered with his six
youngest wives, all of them naked. Female beauty, Yarro proclaimed, had
no right to hide itself behind clothing; as soon as it became necessary for
a woman to clothe herself, he said, you knew that she was past her prime.
The women themselves were nubile, exquisitely attractive, and appeared
ingenuously unconscious of being unclothed.

When the chief offered Clapperton his daughter, he accepted her.
He stayed with her six days, noting that, aged twenty-five, "she was much
past the meridian in this country. . . . I went to the house of the daughter,
which consists of several coozies [thatched huts] separate from those of
the father, and I was shown into a very clean one; a mat was spread; I sat
down; and the lady coming in and kneeling down, I asked her if she would
live in my house, or I should come and live with her: she said, whatever
way I wished; very well, I said, I would come and live with her, as she had
the best house." The citizens of Borgu expressed surprise that the explorers traveled without women.

Kaiama was a joyful place. Games, racing, celebrations, and an
uninhibited mixing of the sexes seemed to go on from dawn until dark
(and, surmised Clapperton, probably long after dark). Clapperton was
perplexed by the wide range of European goods evident all over town,
although nobody in Kaiama had ever before seen a white man. The arrival
of a Hausa slave caravan, en route from Dahomey to Kano, provided the
explanation. The caravan leader, a wily Arab of obviously wide experience
in Africa—imperturbable, impressive, and dignified—claimed to have
met Clapperton in Kano on his first visit. Clapperton neither remembered
nor trusted this man, declining his offer to take the explorers' baggage on
to Kano. The Arab's deputies traded pots and pans and other manufactured goods with the locals.

Clapperton and Lander left Kaiama with regret. By British morals of that era, it was a sinful city, but the Kaiamians themselves hardly seemed to appreciate the fact, and it was apparent to the visitors that a more cheery people would have been hard to find on any continent.

The explorers were approaching the kingdom of Wawa. They crossed the river Oli, rocky and turbulent, to be met by yet another band of riders, this one sent by Mohammed, the sultan of Wawa. The town of Wawa, surrounded by a high mud wall and deep trench, was the capital of the kingdom. The roads were wide, straight, and clean and the buildings, all on the beehive principle, made it "the neatest and best-regulated city in the interior," according to Clapperton. It was an important intersection in the system of highways linking Ashanti, Dahomey, Badagri, and Jannah to the west of the Niger, with Nyffee, Hausaland, and Bornu to the east.

Clapperton and Lander met the most interesting character of their journey in Wawa, a rich widow named Zuma (the Arab word for honey). It soon transpired that she was determined to marry one or the other of them. The story of Zuma can only be understood in the frame of the local male ideal of feminine beauty, which was bulk. The ultimate compliment that could be paid a Borgu woman of the era was that she would make "a good load for a camel."* By that yardstick Zuma had no rivals. Clapperton described her as "a walking water-butt." She pursued both men relentlessly, seriatim.

Zuma's father had been an itinerant Arab. Though her skin color was not appreciably lighter than that of any other inhabitant of Wawa, she considered herself white, and as a member of the white race, she was determined to marry a white man. A politically ambitious woman, she had been left wealthy by the death of her first husband, and therefore powerful. She spent her time scheming to depose her sultan, who retaliated periodically by throwing her in jail.

She initially tried her charms on Clapperton, but all he would do was sing Lander's praises, which had the desired effect of diverting her to the Cornishman. Clapperton wrote of her: "The lady was dressed in a white,

---

* A healthy, well-fed, well-watered camel can safely carry up to 350 pounds over long distances. Zuma likely weighed at least that much.

coarse muslin turban, her neck decorated with necklaces of coral and gold chain; the one with rubies, the other with gold beads. Her eyebrows and eyelashes were blackened, her hair dyed with indigo. Her hands and feet were also dyed with henna, and her breasts were tremendous. She was as fat as a barrel of lard and she was as black as charcoal."

Zuma then devoted her attentions to the cherubic, fresh-faced Lander, appearing daily in his hut in her finery, all henna and coral and indigo and gold beads. The effect was lost on the young man, who saw her as "a moving world of flesh, puffing and blowing like a blacksmith's bellows."

When Lander refused to visit her hut, her passion shifted again to Clapperton, who finally accepted her invitation because, he claimed, he wanted to see the inside of her house. He found her comfortably installed amid pillows and carpets, wielding a grass fan in one hand and a whip in the other, attended by a hunchbacked female dwarf, daintily picking kola nuts from an English pewter mug. Zuma declared her love and proposed marriage. When she saw the consternation on Clapperton's face, she reassured him that the difference in their ages was no obstacle.

"This was too much for me," recorded Clapperton, "and I made my retreat as soon as I could, determined never to come to such close quarters with her again." But the widow kept hounding him, and "I could only get rid of her by telling her that I prayed and looked at the stars all night. . . . She departed in a flood of tears."

With the failure of her frontal attacks, Zuma turned to stealth. She presented one of Clapperton's porters, who collected new women wherever he went, with a pretty young slave selected from her household. This gift gave her a claim on the young man, whom she planted as a spy in the explorers' camp. Sultan Mohammed, who was keeping a careful eye on his difficult subject, was incensed when he learned of this. Zuma, he warned Clapperton, with her great wealth (she had 2,000 slaves) and her irresistible allure, would inevitably try to marry Lander now that Clapperton had refused her, and Lander, if she succeeded, might be declared king by the local inhabitants. He, the sultan, would then be banished or executed. In the event, Mohammed's anxiety was unnecessary. Lander, realizing that Zuma was serious in her pursuit of him, rebuffed her. "Poor widow Zuma," he wrote, "I almost fancy I see her now, waddling . . . the very pink and essence of African fashion."

Clapperton tried to take off alone for the Niger, leaving Lander to bring on the baggage later. He was eager to verify the information given to him by Bello about Mungo Park's death, and made straight for Bussa Falls. Unfortunately, as soon as he left Wawa he was followed by Zuma. This again inflamed Sultan Mohammed, this time to such a degree that he impounded the white men's baggage. Lander was forced to stay behind to keep an eye on things. When Clapperton heard this, he had no choice but to return to the capital. He arrived with the tireless Zuma dogging his heels.

The widow's entrance was overpowering. Upon a fine horse, gorgeously dressed in a red silk mantle, red trousers, Morocco boots, and festooned with charms hung about her body, she was preceded by drummers decked out in ostrich feathers and followed by a large train of armed guards. This time, she was no longer an object of mirth to the two white men. She was both impressive and formidable, and the sultan's fear of her became, for the first time, fully comprehensible to Clapperton.

He realized belatedly that she had to be taken seriously, and ordered his servant to return the young woman Zuma had given him as a present, an affront so boorish that even the resilient Zuma understood that he meant to insult her. Indignantly, she let the white men go, and as Lander put it: "We saw no more of the generous, the kind-hearted, the affectionate, the ambitious, but above all the enormous widow Zuma."

Disgusted with the white men, Zuma apologized to her sultan for her behavior, and he gave the explorers their baggage and his *teskera*—written permission for them to go on their way. In the end, Clapperton must have been flattered by Zuma's attention, because when the expedition finally left Wawa in April, he no longer ridiculed her. He wrote of her with the admiration and the respect her intelligence and persistence deserved. He said that "had she been somewhat younger and less corpulent, there might have been great temptation to head her [political] party, for she has certainly been a very handsome woman, and such as would have been thought a beauty in any country in Europe."

Lander wrote of the inhabitants of Wawa that "the whole place appeared to be [populated by] the most roaring, drunken set of any town I have ever seen. Chastity is non-existent and sobriety is not considered a virtue; yet the people are merry and behave well. All night, until morning, nothing is heard but fiddles, Arab guitars, castanets and singing." Yet, despite their sometimes critical remarks (likely for the consumption solely of prudish English readers), it is clear Clapperton and Lander were very comfortable in Wawa, perhaps proving again that British explorers of the period were almost never as straitlaced as their hagiographies portrayed them to be. And if Hugh Clapperton had a homosexual bent, as Denham had alleged, it was certainly not evident on this trip.

The country between Wawa and Bussa,* which was only twenty miles away, was hilly and wooded—a land of scarlet birds, of monkeys screaming at each other from every bough, of vibrantly colored butterflies, of snakes and turtles, and of trees with trunks the size of buildings. The view was dominated by a lone mountain Clapperton christened Mount George after his king (forgetting, of course, that the mountain had carried a local name for thousands of years). The explorers headed for Yauri, the village on the Niger where Mungo Park had gone ashore to give presents to the king before he was ambushed and killed. Along the way, Clapperton stopped at Bussa, where Park had died, and it was there, on March 31, 1826, that he saw the Niger for the first time. Oddly, the object of his long quest neither inspired nor exhilarated him; he wrote in his journal simply: "At 3:30 arrived at a branch of the Quorra."

Clapperton interrogated the natives in Bussa about Park's death and met with an evasiveness he considered evidence they were trying to conceal something. He and Lander visited the rapids where Park's "schooner" had foundered. The deluge of water foaming over rock outcroppings sounded like a forest of tall trees shaken by a mighty wind. According to the account of a local headman, Park's vessel, the *Jolibar*,† had become impaled on a rock at the head of the falls. The two white men aboard (only two of the original party of fifty that set out from the Gambia had survived this far) threw themselves into the water and drowned. The people of Bussa, lining the bank, could render no aid (this had a ring of truth, for as Clapperton well knew, it was the rare African of that era who could swim). According to the headman, nobody fired a musket or pulled

---

* The old town of Bussa, and Bussa Falls, is now underwater as a result of the construction of the Kainji Dam in the late 1960s.

† "Jolibar" is one of dozens of West African names for the Niger River.

a bowstring. On the contrary, the people had been sad, "keeping up their lamentations all through the night."

There was a piece of information at the end of this man's story that raised the hairs on the back of Clapperton's neck: the sultan of Bussa, said the headman, had salvaged the canoe the next day, and in it were found some papers and a quantity of meat. The villagers, not wanting to waste this meat, had a feast, and all of them died. White men, as everybody knew, were cannibals, and the meat must have been human flesh.

Clapperton inspected the place where the *Jolibar* had reached the end of its incredible 2,000-mile journey. "We visited the far-famed Niger or Quorra," Clapperton wrote, "which flows by the city, and were greatly disappointed at the appearance of this celebrated river. The Niger here, in its widest part, is not more than a stone's throw across at present. The rock on which we sat overlooks the spot where Mr. Park and his associates met their unhappy fate."

The people of Bussa obviously regarded this place, at least in Clapperton's presence, with reverent wonder and a touch of fear. One of them confided that the headman's account to Clapperton was just a cover story—there really *had* been a fight, just as Clapperton suspected. Mungo Park had opened fire with his muskets and the men of Bussa replied with arrows.

Still not satisfied and seeking more detail, Clapperton called on the sultan of Bussa and requested the full story of the Scottish explorer's death. The sultan seemed uneasy at this question, so plainly put. He himself, he explained, had been a boy at the time, and the man who knew the history of the episode was the sultan of Yauri, who, incidentally, had sent canoes for Clapperton. They were waiting now, and the sultan would be delighted if he would go back with them to Yauri. Before leaving, Clapperton asked the king whether he had any of Park's books, papers, or belongings. The king replied that he did not.

In fact, Clapperton did not go to Yauri. It is hard to understand what kept him back, and he does not reveal his reasons in his notes. He had been eager enough (the previous year), to make a special trip from Sokoto to see the sultan of Yauri, but Bello warned that the journey was too dangerous and had prevented it. Now here he was, within hours' paddling distance of Yauri, and he says only that he could not spare the time.

This is baffling, especially since he noted in his journal that although everybody treated him with great kindness, on the subject of Mungo Park all were evasive. Yet Clapperton himself failed to visit the one man who could, presumably, have told him exactly what happened on that fatal day twenty-two years before.

Even more astonishing, according to Bello, the sultan of Yauri had Park's journals and papers, for which, one would have thought, Clapperton would have been prepared to lose a month, let alone a day or two. There must have been something about the proposed trip that raised Clapperton's concern, a concern he did not put in writing and that remains unknown to this day. It is possible, of course, that he was simply unwilling to allow anything to divert him from besting Laing to Timbuktu.

In any event, Mungo Park had set a terrible precedent that was to haunt subsequent explorers. Driven to the edge of sanity, Park had massacred many Africans, forgetting that he, not they, was the trespasser. It was an indelible first impression that his successors would fail to erase in the decades ahead.

After inspecting the place where the *Jolibar* came to grief, Clapperton noted shrewdly that even if the canoe had not struck a rock or been attacked, it could not have survived the terrific rapids of the river. Lander, too, inspected Bussa Falls, capturing wonderfully the atmosphere of the place:

> It was nearly sunset when I got into the canoe in which I was ferried across the stream to Bussa. The evening was calm, clear, and beautiful; the fireflies had already begun to shine and buzzed the air. The hollow roar of crocodiles was heard from the borders of the current, and the declining sun tinged the surface of the water with a rich hue of crimson. The sound of sweet-toned instruments and the hum of human voices mingling in concert and wafted from the city I was approaching produced a soothing and delightful effect; and as the little canoe was propelled slowly through the lazy stream, the music seemed like a symphony of angel voices floating from the sky.

This is a departure from the stark, utilitarian prose typical of Lander and Clapperton. It is all the more impressive when one takes into account that even men of the officer class, like Clapperton, were little more than barely literate.*

The next day, April 10, at a place called Komie (Komi), where the Kainji Dam now stands, the two white men crossed the Niger at what was called King's Ferry and saw the last of Borgu territory. Both were reluctant to leave. Clapperton had been told that the Borgu had the worst reputation of any of the African tribes. "They have not lived up to that reputation," he wrote. "I have travelled and hunted with them and been at their mercy for weeks." Lander called them "strictly honourable, good-natured and cheerful; always benevolent and ready to sacrifice personal comfort for their white visitors."

As they traveled, Clapperton heard from all interlocutors that the Niger River flowed south into the sea, but his instructions were to head north and find Sultan Bello in Sokoto, and he personally very much wanted to renew his friendship with the great African king. The main road to Sokoto was via Kano, which they reached on July 20, 1826. They had taken more than three months to travel three hundred miles, averaging under three miles a day, slogging through stifling jungles and boulder-strewn plains.

At Kano, Clapperton learned that war had erupted between the Sokoto caliphate and the kingdom of Bornu. A famine had devastated Bornu, and the sheikh (the familiar El Kanemi, who had been so impressed by Hillman's martial inventions) had sent fine horses to Kano as an oblique way of calling attention, through ambassadors who accompanied the horses, to their predicament. Instead of helping, the governor of Kano (the foul-tempered Hajji Hat Salah, who, the year before, had slandered Clapperton in a luncheon toast) ordered the Bornu ambassadors bound hand and foot and publicly butchered alive in a market square.

Other cities to which El Kanemi had sent horses returned them with bundles of spears—a way of saying that if the sheikh wanted grain, he would have to come and fight for it. Outraged, Mohammed El Kanemi assembled an army and marched on the caliphate. War had raged ever since.

---

* As late as 1850, less than 5 percent of British sailors were literate, a figure that would rise dramatically as cheap printed books soon became widely available.

Having come this far, Clapperton now had to decide whether to move forward despite hostilities that greatly increased the risks he faced. It was a decision that would take him five weeks to make. In those long days and nights, while mulling over his prospects, he must have asked himself what had become of Laing. Clapperton likely thought often of his rival, wondering if he might find him in the next valley, across the next bend in the hills, ensconced in a hut in the village just ahead in the wilderness.

In fact, the entrepid Scot was very far away, and in terrible trouble.

Chapter Fifteen

------·◆·------

TREACHERY IN THE TANEZROUFT

AFTER A MONTH AT IN SALAH, Alexander Gordon Laing wanted to get moving again. Yet Sheikh Babani showed a reluctance to leave the desert oasis. The Arab leader was strangely irritable. He argued with Laing about money, protesting that he had not been paid. Further, Babani claimed that the caravan's camels needed rest and their loads redistributed. When Laing pressed him, the sheikh "burst into tears indicating," Warrington wrote later, "that his heart failed him in what he was about to do."

The other members of Laing's party were also in no hurry to leave this place of plenty, which, had they seen it on their first day out of Tripoli, would have seemed overpoweringly drab. After weeks in the desert, In Salah appeared to everyone as a corner of heaven. But they knew they had to leave, and so they drank the crystal-pure water from local wells, savoring it, as Laing continued to bicker with the head of his caravan.

Hatita was not much help; he was going no farther. Laing sent the Tuareg guide back to Tripoli with the mail on December 8, for he would have been useless in the Hoggar country, where the Hoggar Tuareg would certainly have recognized him as an Ajjer and killed him on sight. Hatita's departure left Laing despondent, telling Warrington,

> I despatch Hateeta tomorrow, and shall leave the remainder of this sheet till then. I like Hateeta much. I never met a better man in any country, and certainly never a more disinterested man. Use him according to his deserts my dear Consul, and you will use him well.

Laing tried to generate enthusiasm for setting off among the merchants, some of whom had been waiting ten months to go south, but this effort, too, failed. These experienced desert travelers, no strangers to local conditions, told him that Tuareg bands were roaming abroad. These were dangerous, deadly men. No one was willing to risk crossing the desert until rumors of their presence had abated.

The waiting was insupportable. On January 1, 1826, in a letter to his friend Sabine, Laing added a postscript asking for books: "When Denham's work is published, I wish you would tell [John] Murray to send me a copy, as well as of Lyon, to Sierra Leone [where he expected to end his journey]—the *Travels of Edrisi,* a copy of Ptolemy and Herodotus also, if he can possibly procure them."* The boredom and delays gave him time to worry about his wife, a pastime that was "driving him to distraction." In a letter to Warrington before Christmas he wrote:

> Shou'd you have now in your possession, or hereafter receive any letters addressed to me in the interior, pray return them to the Colonial Office, whence I have desired that they may be forwarded to Sierra Leone, to which place I must request of you for the future to address to me. Continue writing to me regularly, and giving me every kind of information which you think will be interesting to me. You know there are many subjects to which I am indifferent, there-

---

*Dixon Denham's *Narrative of Travel and Discoveries in North and Central Africa* came out under the Murray imprint later that year. George F. Lyon's *Travels in Northern Africa* had been published by Murray in 1821. Laing's *Travels in the Timanee* had just been published (also by Murray, in 1825), and it is typical of him that he did not ask for a copy of his own book.

fore do not accuse me of dictating, when I say that I shall be happy if you enlarge most upon matters relating to my Dear Emma, and the mission upon which I am employed. In both of these subjects we are I believe equally and reciprocally interested. Do not I pray you, omit to apprise me exactly of the state of health of my Dearest Emma, whose image ever occupies my thoughts, is ever before my eyes. I feel in its full force the truly peculiar and delicate situation in which I have left her, and the bare idea is oftentimes nearly sufficient to drive me to distraction: My only consolation arises from the consciousness that it was necessary to the happiness of us both. If it pleases God to spare us for each other, (and that it will so please Him I have implicit faith) I shall devote the remainder of my life to atone for the unhappiness I have occasioned her, in my future endeavours to render her as happy as it is possible for me to do. . . .

On the day after his arrival at In Salah (December 3, 1825), Laing had apprised the Colonial Office of his intention to resume his journey no later than December 10—just long enough to rest the camels. The days rolled by; Christmas passed; New Year's Day came. For Laing, racing against Clapperton to reach Timbuktu and the Niger, waiting any longer became out of the question. At last, he decided to set out alone across the dreaded Tanezrouft, the heart of the desert, a land known as "the place of thirst." It covered 70,000 square miles of barren rock and sand, the deadliest leg of the journey south. Laing's ignorance concerning the route and his inflated self-confidence blinded him to the risk he was about to take. He wrote that he was "determined upon setting out *solus* in four days more, come what will, come what may."

And then, a strange thing happened: the traders, seeing that a lone Christian who did not know the way showed less fear than they, were shamed into joining him. "The merchants having become acquainted with our determination plucked up courage," Laing wrote.

On January 9, thirty-eight days after he had arrived, the caravan of forty-five men and one hundred camels left In Salah to cross the mournful kingdom of sand. They headed for the Hoggar, the great mountain nucleus of the central Sahara. For two interminable weeks,

An Arab merchant on horseback in Africa. These intrepid entrepreneurs were the lords, and often the scourges, of those black-populated regions whose commerce they dominated.

they waded through loose, granular sand, the camels nearly knee deep in the shifting particles, dark sandstone ridges flanking the track their only guideposts. This was the desert of the European imagination—high sand-hills down whose slopes the camels plunged in a wavering zigzag, kept upright only by the camel boys tugging their tails; high sandhills that loomed over the exhausted travelers like ranges of mountains.

The Sahara daily became more dangerous, and yet Laing's fascination with it bordered on mesmerization. Fully seduced by its bleak beauty, he was elated. He wrote Bandinel, apparently not recognizing just how serious the matter was, of the peril he was now in for having been mistaken for Mungo Park:

An extremely ridiculous report has gone abroad here that I am no less a personage than the late Mungo Park, the Christian who made war upon the people inhabiting the banks of the Niger, who killed several, and wounded many of the Tuaric, and although at the first blush its statement, you may feel inclined to treat it with the same levity which I did, and smile at the absurdity which cou'd for a moment favor the belief of such a report, yet when I inform you that there is a Tuaric in this place [a village south of In Salah] who received a Musket shot in his cheek in a *rencontre* with Park's Vessel, and who is ready to take his oath that I am the person who commanded it, and when you consider that the great discrepancy in point of time (I being only 31 years of age, and the expedition of Park having taken place 21 years ago) is a matter of no moment among people who do not trouble themselves with investigation, you will regret it as much as I do now, absurd & ridiculous as it may at first appear, for I cannot view without some apprehension the difficulties in which it may involve me in my attempts at research hereafter on the great artery of this unexplored continent. How imprudent, how unthinking; I may even say, how selfish was it in Park to attempt making discovery in this land, at the expense of the blood of its inhabitants, and to the exclusion of all after communication: how unjustified was such conduct! What answer am I to make to the question which will be often put to me? What right had your countrymen to fire upon and kill our people?

Laing understood much that had eluded his fellow Scot, and he was determined not to replicate Mungo Park's errors.

From time to time, little vortices of sand imitated the spume of the ocean, and it occurred to Laing that the challenge of the desert was not unlike that of the sea. The familiar perils were all there—bad weather, loss of bearings, exhaustion of supplies, even going down with all hands. A caravan engulfed in sand might not descend as far as a ship sinking to the bottom of the ocean, but the effect was oddly similar, and the odds of rescue distinctly less. The Sahara was twice the size of the Mediterranean, and emptier. Its vastness was inconceivable: 3,500 miles separated Cap Blanc on the Atlantic from Port Sudan on the Red Sea—3,500 miles as the crow flies, to *walk* that distance was to double it.

In two weeks the caravan reached the Hoggar country, an endless rubbled plain the size of Texas with boulders the size of tall buildings. On this waterless, bone-hard plateau, the sun's rays beat the ground as upon an anvil. Except for the unwonted acacia and a malignant species of crow that tormented the camels and stole precious supplies, no living thing inhabited this land—except the Tuareg. Laing thought it the most desolate region in the world. He described it as "a Desart of sand as flat as a bowling green and as destitute of verdure as Melville Island [in the Arctic Circle] in the depth of winter." The merchants were still so frightened, he wrote, that "during four days that we were in a constant state of alarm, expecting every moment to fall in with the much dreaded [Tuareg], every acacia tree in the distance being magnified or rather metamorphosed by the apprehensive Merchants into troops of Armed Foes." Though the

caravan was isolated and at greatest danger, to Laing the fears of his comrades seemed exaggerated. "Receiving daily advices from Tuat [In Salah]
of the perilous state of the road," he wrote, "my situation was not the most
enviable, exposed as I was to the [hostile censure] of the whole *kaffila,*
for subjecting them and their property to such hazard, when by a little
patience in waiting at [In Salah], till the road became good [i.e., safe] they
might all have gone in safety."

Though explorers and geographers could not know this at the time
(and would not for many decades, until satellite photos revealed the fact),
the sand desert forms only one-seventh of the whole brooding wasteland
of the Sahara. The rest is made up of plains of pebbles and rock like
the Tanezrouft. Movement along these iron-hard surfaces was torturous
in the merciless heat. Huge outcrops of rock alternated with mountain
ranges extending hundreds of miles and rising thousands of feet, denuded
of vegetation. Changes of temperature were violent. At sundown, the
thermometer fell thirty degrees in ten minutes, a drop accompanied by
explosive salvos as pebbles cracked in the sudden loss of heat. The prevailing winds, the khamsin* and simoom, rose in terrific gusts. Over the
centuries, these winds had flattened mountains. At night, their searing,
chafing eddies dried out canyons and withered life.

Laing could not hinder the sand. A tin plate left on the ground was
covered in seconds with a thin gritty film. Sand filled the ears and nose,
reddened eyes, and infiltrated clothing. Sand clogged every crack and
crevice. There was sand in the tea glasses, sand in the food, sand in the
scientific equipment, a dispiriting grit on one's tongue, a malevolent sting
in the eye. . . .

Whenever the wind picked up, visibility lessened. One might see
thirty feet. Caravanners hunched against whatever shelter they could
find, waiting. Some put their heads on their knees, barely breathing.
Camels snorted and gnarred.

After wind, water was the ruler of the Sahara, and its incidence in the
Tanezrouft was as yet unexplored. There were few oases, each boasting
settled life of a sort, usually in a village behind white mud walls. In the

---

* In modern times, this wind is well known for stripping vehicles of paint and pushing sand
particles into supposedly airtight cameras and watches.

water holes, there were catfish. In some inhabited lands (like In Salah), rain had been unknown for as long as eighteen years running, but rain was no stranger to the desert. Sometimes it came down in blinding, icy torrents. Then the wadis became cascades; mammoth pools formed in valley bottoms while overnight millions of white and yellow blooms appeared in the desolation. Tamarisks, an evergreen shrub with roots as deep as eighteen feet, and the pasture grass called *ashab,* so loved by camels, would gain new life.

But there was no rain now. They plodded on. On January 26, Laing wrote the Colonial Office that the caravan had come under the aegis of some friendly Tuareg, and "Timbuktoo began to appear within our reach, the merchants began to calculate their gains, and apprehension having entirely subsided, [there was] a profusion of thanks and benedictions. I have little time at present to say more than that my prospects are bright and expectations sanguine."

In a postscript added January 27, Laing noted ominously:

I had just finished the above when two Hookgar [Hoggar] Tuaric arrived at our encampment with accounts that a party of their tribe had fallen in with the Ghazi [Muslim fanatics] . . . yesterday, at a well about 30 miles West from us, & engaged them with advantage, killing several, and taking from them a hundred and sixty two Maheries [*mehari*⃰ camels]. This intelligence is extremely satisfactory, but the Ghadamis Merchants are much afraid that the victors, whose arrival we are compelled to await, will make exorbitant demands upon them for the service performed. . . .

The fears of Ghadames merchants proved justified. Twenty heavily armed Hoggar Tuareg joined the caravan, appearing out of nowhere. Their blue veiled faces evinced no acknowledgment of Laing's party. They were greeted with distrust, but no one dared turn them away. They had simply materialized through the veil of sand. One evening, a few days after their arrival, Laing fired at a crow. Sheikh Babani told him not to reload his

---

⃰ The swiftest breed of dromedary, the racehorse of the desert, used mainly as saddle animals rather than as beasts of burden.

rifle, suggesting that since they were out of danger, Laing should turn his gunpowder over to him. Inexplicably, Laing agreed, and Babani later gave the powder to the Tuareg. The next day the caravan stopped by a well at a place called Wadi Ahnet* to water the camels.

The travelers were approaching the center of the stony plain, caught in an undulating savanna of shallow sand. Wadi Ahnet, when at last they reached it, seemed sick unto death. Its palms were raddled and thread-bare; below them lay a narrow marsh covered with a fetid brown crust. Mosquitoes swarmed in voracious profusion. The remains of a pitiful fort, gutted and crumbling, occupied rising ground behind the marsh. This was the Saharan oasis at its worst—a salt-caked malarial swamp. The sun at midday weighed on the caravan like lead. The mosquitoes thrummed.

Wadi Ahnet was strangely filthy for such a remote place. Outside oases, damp, dirt, and decay were not found in the Sahara. A man or animal might collapse, and whatever the reason, the immediate cause of death was nearly always thirst. The body was desiccated even before life had passed out of it. Long before flesh decomposed, vultures would pick bones dry. Within hours, all moisture was gone. Clean again, pure again, the dry sand would sparkle.

Laing knew of only two other environments where one was conscious of this aseptic quality, that of lofty mountains and the Arctic, the realm of his friend the explorer Bandinel. That is why he compared the desert to Melville Island in winter, "as flat as a bowling green and destitute of verdure." The ambience of the Arctic and Sahara were strangely similar, and so was the state of mind they engendered. Polar snows and desert sands: both immaculate, untouched by humanity and indifferent to it. Explorers came to them if not as trespassers, then strictly on their own terms—terms which, if not accepted unconditionally, led to death.

After Wadi Ahnet, Laing and his party faced many waterless days across an inferno of rock, but they were buoyed by the thought of their impending arrival at the great caravan city. The merchants thought of nothing else, unless it was the possibility of attack from hostile Tuareg. In this desolate passage, they faced their greatest danger; a looming, unseen threat that

---

* Wadi Ahnet cannot be located precisely on today's maps, but it probably lay in the district of Ahnet, about 150 miles south of Insalah, near Adrar Nahalet in modern Algeria.

made everyone restless; a danger they were helpless to redress, one that whittled away at their composure. They could not deviate from their route, and they could not trust their veiled escorts. To stop meant certain death. But not to stop possibly entailed death also—at the hands of marauders.

The travelers became numbed by the void, by the vast distances that remained, the heat, thirst, hunger and discomfort yet to be endured. It required a mighty will to load the camels and strike out each day. Men retained their sanity by sinking into a dream world. The imagination took over, substituting fields and forests where only baked *hamada* loomed, preparing gargantuan meals to ease the pain of hunger, inventing clear, cool streams to slake tormenting thirst. Laing grew sick of

> these desert, forlorn, black looking plains, these *Libya deserta*. The eye of the traveller roams in vain over the wide, unvaried superficies, in search of some object to rest upon, till at length wearied by a repetition of the bleak and tedious sameness, he is willing to pull one of the folds of his turban over his eyes, and to shroud his head in his Burnoosa, allowing his mind, which refuses to expand upon the exsiccated objects around him, to shrink within itself, and to anticipate in imaginative hope, more genial and enlivening scenes.

To the physical stamina and mental toughness required of a caravanner in the Sahara, there was a third important quality: courage. Everyone in the caravan viewed the Tuareg escorts with increasing apprehension. The discontent of these swarthy riders seemed to grow as the journey's miseries increased. They were bored; they wanted plunder. Asking no one's permission, they sometimes disappeared for hours or days.

At night, they seemed to stalk the camp, moving silently on the periphery of sleeping men and camels. A brief creaking of leather, the breathy burping of their animals, and then they were gone, vanishing into the shroud of the desert, nothing to mark their passing.

Tensions in the caravan grew; nerves were taut; there was a sense of impending disaster.

Laing's presence further complicated matters. Equal relationships did not exist among Saharan caravanners. Desert society was a narrow ladder upon which everyone had a place, and no two people shared the same rung. This hierarchy was a necessary part of caravan life, integral to its ability to function as a cohesive, moving village. In normal circumstances, Sheikh Babani would have had no difficulty finding the correct place in his caravan for a passenger. But the presence of a *nasrani* made the circumstances highly abnormal, complicating everything. On the one hand, as a traveler who was undoubtedly rich (in Babani's eyes, all Englishmen were rich), Laing occupied a place near the top of the ladder. On the other hand, as an infidel from a country populated by unclean *kafirs,* Laing was lucky to be tolerated at all, and surely merited the bottom rung.

And then there were the Tuareg. They were armed, and this was their country. One traveled through the Sahara at their pleasure. Could the band of twenty Tuareg escorts be trusted?

"The sacred word of a Targui," Laing recalled Yusuf Karamanli warning him, *"is like water fallen on the sand, never to be found again."*

And yet, Laing and the caravan depended on the Tuareg, for only a Tuareg who had lived in the Sahara all his life could differentiate one boulder from another.

FIVE OR SIX DAYS after departing the squalid oasis of Wadi Ahnet, on the night of February 2 or 3,* Laing retired to his tent early, his servants nearby. It was twilight, the desert swept by a cold, steady wind. The land was a neutral tawny color, spreading under a darkening sky. Loose canvas on Laing's tent flapped with disquieting monotony. In the dark, Laing could feel the tarpaulins trembling overhead. His cot was shaken as if at sea in rough weather. Around the camp, camels moaned with stentorian, unearthly cries.

Under cover of this noise and the darkness, the Hoggar Tuareg surrounded Laing's tent. In one volley, they fired into it with muskets. They cut the canvas and cords and fired again into the gloaming, rushing at Laing's cot before he could reach his sword. Struck in the hip by one of the balls and surprised in his half sleep, Laing was barely able to sit up before Tuareg were hacking savagely at his body. He fell to the ground, bloodied and unarmed. With curved scimitars, the Tuareg slashed. Laing stopped moving.

---

* The exact date has been much debated, but never fixed with certainty.

IN A SHIVER OF PERCEPTION, Laing understood that Sheikh Babani had betrayed him. This had been a long time coming. In a letter to Warrington dated December 13, 1825, from In Salah, he wrote that he had "some hints respecting the Sheikh Babane, whom I did not consider as acting up to the agreement which he entered into with you at Tripoli. . . . This circumstance has caused me a good deal of uneasiness as well as dissatisfaction." Babani was plainly unhappy and felt he had been cheated. The bashaw had *allegedly* paid Babani handsomely to protect Laing (though Babani denied ever getting a penny). Laing had taken note of the sheikh's growing resentment for weeks, but he failed to anticipate its terrible result: motivated by his own frustration and avarice, Sheikh Babani had apparently come to an "arrangement" with the Tuareg. Probably in return for some of Laing's camels and a portion of his merchandise and presents, the Tuareg gang agreed to murder the Christian explorer. Sheikh Babani would pocket the rest, and be rid of the troublesome white man and an uncollected debt that was driving him to distraction.

ROUSED BY THE NOISE of the attack, Laing's servants tried to help him, risking their lives. Having subdued Laing, the attackers went after his assistants with their swords, instantly killing one of the carpenters and the interpreter, Abraham Nahun, and wounding the remaining carpenter in the leg. Hamet, the camel driver, was crippled by a saber cut but survived. Laing's West Indian servant, Jack le Bore, and Bongola, the freed slave, ran off and hid in the dunes.

After stealing what they found in Laing's tent, the Tuareg gang of twenty fled on their camels, shrieking and shouting in manic triumph. Sheikh Babani, paralyzed with fear, huddled near Laing's tent, where he had been silent witness to the butchery. The Ghadames merchants now joined him as spectators. None was molested; none tried to help Laing.

When the attack was over, Laing was unable to lift a finger, but he was not dead. In the first hour after the attack, the desolate night grew colder, wrapped in silence and solitude.

Laing's wounds were beyond ghastly. He took five saber cuts to the head—three on the left temple, from which bone was chipped; one on the left cheek, which fractured the jawbone and split his ear in two (portions of which dangled by bloody ropes of tissue); and another over the right temple. He also sustained a horrible gash on the back of the neck, a musket ball in the hip, five saber cuts on the right arm and hand, and three broken fingers. The carpal bones of his right wrist had been crushed into a gravelly mush, and the hand itself was cut three-quarters across. There were three cuts on his left arm, the humerus of which was broken, and a deep gash on his left leg.

Within the hour, Jack le Bore came back to his master's side and began dressing his wounds. The loyal West Indian soon had a great blaze of desiccated acacia branches roaring by the camp, helping to keep Laing warm. One of Babani's nephews, Alkhadir, perhaps motivated by shame for what his uncle had done, helped Jack tend to the wounded and bury the dead. Slumped that night against what remained of his baggage, Laing was beyond responding to his fears. He could not think. When the campfire went out, lamps pierced the darkness with a wan, fatiguing glare.

During all those dreary weeks in the desert, Laing had been revived by the magical half hour of the sun's decline. Most beautiful of all were those evenings when the horizon glowed with green, yellow, and blood-red rays, in which the thin crescent of a new moon barely cleared the ground before slipping back again in pursuit of the sun. The evening he was attacked had presented just such beauty, the colors staining wisps of high, stratospheric cloud. Henceforth, Laing would recall the Tuareg attack just after dusk—and the twilight held magic no longer.

Though desperately ill from his wounds and near death, within hours of the attack he decided to go on with the expedition. The next day dawned cold and clear. Stunned and dehydrated from loss of blood, Laing realized the extent of his wounds and that he would need help, but none of the caravanners rendered aid. Terrified at the bad luck the *nasrani* had attracted, the Arab merchants left without him. Only the survivors in Laing's entourage—Jack le Bore, Harry the carpenter, the wounded camel driver Hamet, and Bongola—stayed with him. So too, against all expectations, did Sheikh Babani, who belatedly remembered that he was responsible for Laing's safety, and that the bashaw's wrath could be lethal.

Swathed in bandages, Laing had to be lifted onto his camel and tied down with leather straps to keep him upright in the saddle. The desolate world of the Tanezrouft still loomed endlessly ahead. Before the attack, they had been marching close to a rocky massif that ran northeast in the central Hoggar, but now this compact group of mountains curved away in a great arc to the right, off course. They were confronted with passage across an eternal plain whose dimensions reduced Laing's tiny party of men and camels to infinitesimal proportions. They were like microscopic insects creeping forward toward a rim of the world that might never be reached, across unbounded space. They had no hope of encountering anything that might offer comfort.

Laing's powers of recovery, strong in the Ashanti wars in West Africa, were diminished by the strain of his journey, but still formidable. He had twenty-four wounds, of which eighteen were severe. He feared he would be disfigured for life and dreaded Emma's reaction when she saw him again, if he survived. His moods changed alarmingly, moving between extremes. Sometimes he was unruffled, almost apathetic, then he would be overtaken by interludes of agitation and hysterical crying.

We do not know what Laing wrote in his diary, for it was later lost, but a diary is often the last place to look if you seek the truth about a person in great distress. Laing's letters may have held more candor, and many of these, from the days just after the attack, have survived. After resting a day or two, he had recovered enough to write to Emma, a letter he penned laboriously with his left hand.*

"I have stopt in the sun to write. Pray excuse it, for I am in great haste. I write with only a Thumb & Finger," he mentioned casually, "having a very severe cut on my fore Finger. You will, I am certain, excuse me for addressing you upon so sorry a piece of paper when I tell you that it is the last piece which I have out, everything being shut and tied up for this long, tedious Journey to Timbuktu, which appears, thank God, now drawing to a close." Laing explained that a friendly Tuareg who was going to Tuat would take the letter, which would show that he was safe and in good health. "I am now in Latitude 23," he added, "and with God's help I shall be in Timbuktu in twenty days' time, and in two months' time I hope to reach the coast." He said nothing at all of the attack, fearing that it would needlessly frighten his wife.

Even here at its most desolate heart, the desert did not disappoint.

---

* Laing was right-handed.

Its immensity overwhelmed everything, enlarged everything, and in its presence, beneath the icy purity of a sour sky, the wickedness of human beings was overshadowed. Though Laing had been robbed of his belongings and was desperately weak, he was determined to cross the four hundred miles that remained of the plateau.

As soon as the letter to Emma was sealed, the tiny caravan set out again. Though it must have seemed at times that they would never arrive at the other end of the Tanezrouft—the march by now was a nightmare of heat and sand and flies, and at night, a merciless cold under glaring stars—Laing felt oddly renewed. He could not go back, and so he dared to go forward, buoyed by some mysterious inner strength.

CONDITIONS GREW WORSE. In the evenings, camels and men collapsed into a mass of animal wretchedness, men and beasts tangled together on rock and sand, reeking of stale urine and dung. For nineteen days the caravan moved leadenly across the desert, Laing swaying in agony and sickness. At last, sometime in April, the ragtag troop reached an oasis known as Azaud, where they were welcomed by a friendly Arab chief and marabout, Sheikh Mokhtar of the Kunta Arab tribe. The merchants who had abandoned Laing had preceded him, and a week later the main caravan left for Arouan. On Sheikh Babani's advice, Laing stayed behind with Sidi Mokhtar to rest. In the event, he stayed for three months.

To get to Mokhtar's camp, Laing had covered 400 miles in less than twenty days—more than 20 miles a day of travel—a truly staggering achievement for so grievously wounded a man.

Even in the comparative safety of the camp, a new disaster hit the expedition. An epidemic of dysentery (or yellow fever, as Laing incorrectly termed it—the symptoms included jaundice and black vomit) broke out in Mokhtar's camp and killed half the population, including Sidi Mokhtar himself, the traitorous Sheikh Babani, Harry, the surviving carpenter, and most painfully of all, Laing's most valuable assistant and longtime friend, Jack le Bore, who had traveled with him around the world.

Laing, now utterly alone except for Bongola, was sick himself for nine days with the gruesome intestinal illness. After Mokhtar's death, Laing was at the mercy of a young sheikh, Mokhtar's son, Sidi Mohammed, who was the opposite of his father—"fanatically anti-Christian, uncharitable in every way and a thief to boot," according to Laing. The weeks rolled endlessly by as Laing slowly, agonizingly regained some of his strength.

As Hugh Clapperton approached the Niger River in early May, Laing was scrawling a note to his father-in-law describing his injuries more truthfully than he had to his wife:

[Camp] Sidi Mohammed, May 10th 1826

My Dear Consul,

I drop you a line only, by an uncertain conveyance, to acquaint you that I am recovering from very severe wounds far beyond any calculation that the most sanguine expectation could have formed, & that tomorrow please God I leave this place for Tinbuctoo, which I hope to reach on the 18th; I have suffered much, but the detail must be reserved till another period, when I shall "a tale unfold" of base treachery and war that will surprise you: some imputation is attachable to the old Sheikh [Babani], but as he is now no more I shall not accuse him: he died very suddenly about a month since, and there are some here who look upon his demise as a visitation: be that as it may, he has by this time answered for all. Since the robbery committed by the Tuaric, I have been very badly off for funds: I have succeeded in getting a small advance of 270 Timbuctoo Mitkallies (which by the bye are a dollar each in value) from the nephew of the Sheik [i.e., Alkhadir], who is a remarkably fine young man, & who has shewn me much attention all along, but more particularly since the death of his uncle. As he will carry my dispatches from Tinbuctoo you will have an opportunity of seeing him, when I shall recommend him to your best notice and attention—When I write from Tinbuctoo I shall detail precisely how I was betrayed & nearly murdered in my sleep, in the mean time I shall acquaint you with the number and nature of my wounds, in all amounting to twenty four, eighteen of which are exceedingly severe. To begin from the top, I have five sabre cuts on the crown of the head & three on the left temple, all fractures from which much bone has come away, one on my left check which fractured the jaw bone & has divided the ear, forming a very unsightly wound, one over the right temple, and a dreadful gash on the back of the neck, which slightly scratched the

windpipe: a musket ball in the hip, which made its way through my
back, slightly grazing the back bone: five sabre cuts on my right arm
& hand, three of the fingers broken, the hand cut three fourths across,
and the wrist bones cut through; three cuts on the left arm, the bone
of which has been broken, but is again uniting. One slight wound on
the right leg, with one dreadful gash on the left, to say nothing of a cut
across the fingers of my left hand, now healed up. I am nevertheless, as
I have already said, doing well, and hope yet to return to England with
much important geographical information. The map indeed requires
much correction, and please God, I shall yet do much, in addition to
what I have already done, towards putting it right.

     So much is official, & I shall feel obliged by your sending a copy of
it to Lord Bathurst, as I write with my left hand with much pain and
difficulty and shall not upon that account communicate till my arrival
at Tinbuctoo. Private. I have many charges of complaint against the
memory of the old Sheik, all of which you shall know in due time; he
has never repaid the 400$ he borrowed from me at Benioleed; he bore
no expence of any sort upon the road, and when I was laying without
expectations of living, he took my best gun, sent it to Tinbuctoo & sold
it for a hundred dollars, the original cost in England—I write to no one
but you; May God bless you all: I dare not yet trust myself with my feel-
ings, for which reason I have not attempted a line to my dearest Emma:
I shall make the trial at Tinbuctoo; & in the mean time remember me
with kindest love & beg her to think nothing of my misfortunes, for all
will yet be well.

Yours ever truly

A. Gordon Laing

It took eight months for Laing's letter to reach Tripoli, in November.
In September, Emma had received the undated note from her husband,
the one in which he had written about having cut his finger. This was the
first news of Laing in Tripoli in five months, and it obscured completely
what he had suffered. Reassured by this deceptive note, Consul Warrington, who had already heard rumors of an attack in the desert, wrote
to Lord Bathurst that "[i]t . . . affords reason to credit the report of the

Attack & it is very satisfactory to know that the wound He has received is of no consequence." Two months later, Warrington received the letter written in Sidi Mokhtar's camp (above), and shortly after that, the wounded camel driver Hamet, who had returned to Tripoli on Laing's orders with more mail, also reached the coast and gave Warrington an eyewitness account of the Tuareg butchery.

Despite his weakened state, Laing held out, reporting to Warrington on July 1 that "my fever yielded at length to the effects of blistering and calomel. I am now the only surviving member of the mission and my situation is far from being agreeable." But as he slowly recovered from his wounds and illness, there was an ominous change in the tone of some of Laing's letters, indicating that his many misfortunes had begun to affect his emotional balance. After months of enforced idleness at the camp, he complained that "with a mind sadly depressed with sickness, sorrow, and disappointment, I lift an unwilling pen to acquaint you that I am no further on my Journey than I last addressed you. . . . I regard my situation here as Captive. . . . I am subject to dreadful pain in my head arising from the severity of my wounds." He now believed, he said, that he was a man of genius ordained to discover Timbuktu. He wrote that unless he reached the city, "the world will ever remain in ignorance of the place, as I make no vain glorious assertion when I say, that it will never be visited by a Christian man after me!" a statement that must have raised eyebrows at the British consulate. And he wrote Emma, "I shall do more than has ever been done before and shall show myself to be what I have ever considered myself, a man of enterprise and genius." Clearly unsettled by his trials, Laing had made the object of his mission even more important, if possible, than it had been before.

In late summer, Laing felt strong enough to continue, but El Mokhtar's son, Sidi Mohammed, who now ruled the camp, tried to persuade him to go back to Tripoli. His efforts were futile. Laing, growing paranoid, wrote Warrington that he suspected someone in the camp of stealing twenty Spanish dollars from him. "I have also been shewn knives, forks, beads, snuff boxes, looking glasses without number &c which I know to be mine, that the villain has been selling."

Laing swept aside Sidi Mohammed's arguments, and in late July or early August the young chief had no choice but to let Laing leave, providing a strong escort. In return, Laing promised him the equivalent of a thousand Spanish dollars. "I have now obtained permission to proceed to Timbuctoo," he wrote just before departing the camp, "at the expense of everything I have got, but I had no alternative."

On this, the last stage of his great journey, Laing was also accompanied by Alkhadir, Babani's nephew, and Bongola. To Laing's relief, they soon left the sandy wastes behind. The face of the land improved day by day, with flowering grasses, trees, and vegetation taking the place of endless dunes, bleak stones, and rocky hills. Red and yellow roses bloomed; deep purple strands of bougainvillea draped the trail. They stopped to enjoy interludes of shade provided by green, living trees, a luxury not known for months. They were moving directly south now, toward the sun, and every dawn had a more entrancing clearness, a more caressing warmth, and the bronze color in the human faces Laing saw took on a deeper tint, the dark blue-black of tropical sub-Saharan Africa. They left, at long last, the exhausted, dust-powdered sky of the Sahara.

Laing found himself in game country, surrounded now by vast herds of wild animals, the very landscape he had dreamed of but despaired of finding. Antelope and guinea fowl roamed forest-covered hills. The caravan frightened away a herd of gazelles, but Laing managed to shoot one. With the retreating gazelles went a pack of hyenas; from a safe distance, they watched their prey with a sardonic mirth, whooping and laughing with the demented intensity of hyenas.

Laing contemplated the mystery of the addax, the powerful beast of these parts, the only living creature, it was said, that could live for years without a drop of water, making it the lone animal that did not have to observe the law of those who live in the desert: *Aman iman*—"Water is life." To Laing, this was the harbinger of the promised land—the Niger and Timbuktu. The desert was dying. He stopped among the trees and scrutinized, as though they were divine glyphs in the soft earth, the tracks of ostriches. He lowered himself to the ground and realized he was trembling, trembling with a hint of that hysterical happiness that grips those who have had a close brush with death.

Laing's party thought they were over the worst of the desolation, but the Sahara held one last terror for them. The herds of game distracted Laing so much that he was surprised by a vicious sandstorm, the worst of the desert crossing. It continued unabated for two days, during which nobody could move. The tiny party huddled in their inadequate robes, the universe a whirring mass of sand that blotted out the sun. Laing retreated again into his own head, his last refuge now, for he had seized upon a profound truth: no sandstorm could counter the fact that the desert crossing was over, and that he had survived.

After spending more than a year in the desert, having come close to madness and death, Alexander Gordon Laing was finally within miles of his destination. He had reached the southernmost edge of the world's greatest desert and was walking on the red, moist, lateritic soil of black Africa—rich, vital, fertile, inexhaustible.

Timbuktu itself, he could now be certain, would soon spread open its gates to him.

Chapter Sixteen

————◆————

TROUBLES FOR
CAPTAIN CLAPPERTON

IN APRIL 1826, while Laing recovered from his wounds in Sheikh Mokhtar's camp, Hugh Clapperton was pondering whether to leave Kano and make a beeline for Sokoto. As he weighed his next move, the filth and congestion of Kano caused him to fall ill, as he had on his first visit to the city. Clapperton was soon confined to his hut. He quickly grew bored lying on his cot. Though he could barely walk, he spent hours sitting up in bed catching up with his travel notes. He and Lander had walked through a succession of warm rains on the way to Fulani territory, and his notes are full of vignettes of the great pastoral landscape. Absent the nastiness of war, this Africa was one of sunshine and soft air washed clean, newborn leaves and buds, pioneer birds and flowers.

Though sick, he felt excited to be again among the Fulani. To Clapperton they were Africa's greatest people, and Sultan Bello was, without a doubt, Africa's greatest ruler. Even in those suburbs of Kano plagued by the war, Clapperton discovered pleasant things to write about. He comments on little walled villages, each with its own "fetish house," although many of the people professed Islam. There was iron in the local hills, and most villages boasted a competent blacksmith. Iron utensils were commonplace.

While Clapperton recuperated in bed, Lander toured the Kano district, biding his time. He was impressed by the colossal termite mounds, twenty feet high and as tough as reinforced concrete, which he called "Gothic cathedrals in miniature." He was also amused to see some of the literate men of the city earning a comfortable living simply by writing Koranic texts on a chalkboard, then washing off and selling the muddy liquid, at exorbitant prices, as "good fetish," an example of lucrative synergy between the Muslim and pagan religions. It was impossible, in this part of the world, to say where animism ended and Islam began.

Upon their arrival in Kano, Clapperton and Lander had been formally welcomed by the governor of the town, the same Hajji Hat Salah who had given Clapperton such a chilly reception on his first expedition two years earlier. This time, if possible, he was even less cordial. The political dynamic in West Africa had changed dramatically.

Initially Clapperton was housed in his old quarters, next door to the hajji's "mansion," and his social calendar was overbooked with visits from the solemn Arab merchants with whom he got along so well before. At first, these men were open and friendly. They appeared to believe that Clapperton had come to put an end to the great war—a conflict that had ruined their trade and made transport of merchandise prohibitively dangerous. But when they found that Hajji Hat Salah no longer paid much attention to the Englishmen, the candor of the merchants dissolved into thinly veiled suspicion.

Kano's gossip was full of war and rumors of war. The two explorers tried to learn the underlying causes of the conflict between Sultan Bello and Sheikh El Kanemi, the better to undertake their own planning. These efforts quickly backfired, as no one in Kano seemed comfortable discussing such matters with white men. Clapperton had talked openly of going on to Kukawa, El Kanemi's royal capital, after he ended his talks with Sultan Bello in Sokoto. This aroused Hajji Hat Salah's mistrust, the more so since the war seemed to be going against the caliphate. The Fulani hierarchy in Kano worried that Clapperton might be in league with El Kanemi. They even speculated that he had been sent to Kano as a spy. Clapperton and Lander were soon confined within the city walls.

As he had often demonstrated, Clapperton lacked the qualities of a diplomat. He was prone to say exactly what was on his mind and just what he thought about anything. His opinions were an open book. He now expressed the dangerous view that if Sultan Bello was getting the worst of the struggle, it was no less than he deserved. After all, El Kanemi, with thousands of his people dying of starvation, had appealed to his powerful neighbor to send food. Sultan Bello responded by returning El Kanemi's ambassadors impaled on spears, taunting, "If you want food, come and fight for it." In Clapperton's view, El Kanemi had been rightly enraged by this tactless and brutal response. Affronted, El Kanemi gathered his army and advanced into Bello's empire, maintaining strict discipline among his troops. For once, the army of Bornu, which Dixon Denham had described as "nothing but a rabble," was grimly efficient, wiping out Fulani villages one after another. Thousands were slaughtered.

When the better-defended walled towns resisted, El Kanemi destroyed them with a diabolical weapon he had invented himself, one far more effective than the cannons Hillman renovated for him: his warriors caught vultures (not a difficult task when the birds were gorged), and wedged pieces of cloth into their claws. The rags were soaked in oil and set aflame, and the terrified birds were thrown into the air near the town walls. When their feathers began to burn, the vultures came crashing out of the sky, landing on the thatched huts within the town, setting them alight. Conflagration spread from hut to hut, creating urban infernos. In the ensuing panic, Bornu soldiers swept through untended gates, annihilating every living thing.

Only once in this deadly advance on Kano was El Kanemi seriously opposed. An ally of Bello, his cousin Jacoba, made a stand some miles from the great commercial capital, sending word to the hajji that he needed reinforcements immediately. The Kano troops hesitated too long behind the mighty walls of their city, and Jacoba's army was defeated. Compounding this disaster, Hajji Hat Salah at the last moment did scramble out with a strong force that might have turned the tide had he used it earlier. Instead, his army was mauled by El Kanemi's, though most of the Fulani soldiers managed to get back into Kano and slam the gates shut. The walls and ditches of the commercial capital of his kingdom were all that now stood between Sultan Bello and defeat.

While all this was going on, Clapperton took advantage of the chaos in Kano to sneak out of town. Feeling better now, he thought he could make it to Sokoto quickly—if he traveled alone. He ordered Lander to stay behind with their servant, a young man named Pasco. Lander's presence, Clapperton believed, would also serve to mollify the hajji when he discovered Clapperton's escape. In a sense, Lander would serve as a hostage, guaranteeing Clapperton's return. In any case, Lander had become ill himself in Kano and was so weakened by dysentery that the most he could do was guard the baggage. Clapperton had long ago stopped making the effort to dress as a naval officer—by this time, he said, he looked more like a London beggar. No one noticed as he passed through the gates.

Clapperton had reached the village of Zaria when El Kanemi's troops attacked Kano. Kano to Zaria was a brief march along a well-defined road, and news traveled fast. It became clear to Clapperton that this new outbreak of violence was not just one more of the perpetual skirmishes that had plagued the region since his first trip. He stopped in Zaria long enough to send a messenger back to Kano to learn Lander's fate. Hearing that his partner was safe, Clapperton again turned to Sokoto.

He was riding an exhausted camel during one of the worst tropical storms he had ever seen. The route was vaguely familiar, for he had traveled from Kano to Sokoto before, but conditions were dreadful, obscuring old landmarks. Rain showered down like sheets of pebbles; rivers of mud made the track impassable. Those travelers he encountered feared itinerant soldiers, who were always prone to highway robbery when strangers on the road had something worth stealing. But the hospitality of the local villagers never failed completely. A hut and some food was made available. In the mornings, Clapperton was often the first to awake, poorly rested, and he would watch whatever village he found himself in unwrinkle from sleep, listening to the soft slap of bare feet passing on mud streets. Constantly sick himself, he was awed by the robust health of the Fulani.

He found tame ostriches in each village to scare away the "evil eye," but there were wild birds, too—ibis, storks, and cranes. Clapperton noted vast Fulani herds of great horned cattle, all a brilliant white, carefully tended. Local wars were of no concern to these nomadic herdsmen. They wandered long distances, from lands we know today as Senegal all the way to the Congo estuary, guarding their cattle with tenacity and devotion.

At the high-walled town of Koki, Clapperton had an attack of "ague," but he tried to keep moving. The weather got worse. The roads, made of the beaten red laterite so common in West Africa and which is as hard as brick in the dry season, disappeared under the flood of tropical cloud-bursts. His starved camel sank to its stomach in orange mud. At Jaza, where he took a day or two to rest, desperately sick, much of the land surrounding the town had simply disappeared under swampy water.

While convalescing at Jaza, he met Sultan Bello's *gadado,* or prime minister, sent out from Sokoto to escort him to the royal court. The *gadado,* an easygoing man, was appalled at Clapperton's failing health. He tried to persuade him to go back to Kano until the rains passed. Though this advice was sensible, Clapperton was long past accepting it. In a country where there are ten bright days for every pair of rainy ones, Clapperton insisted on slogging on.

That night, part of his journal was stolen, perhaps taken for its power as *ju-ju,* or possibly "borrowed" by one of the *gadado's* minions to see if Clapperton was indeed an enemy scout, or simply to prevent the explorer from taking geographical and logistical information out of the district. Nothing was going right; the theft added to Clapperton's growing sense of ill omen. He rewrote as much of his journal as he could, but the original was never recovered. He went on to Sokoto with the *gadado* under armed escort. The weather cleared; the country approaching Sokoto was wild savanna, teeming with game, mainly elephant.

Clapperton reached Sokoto on October 20, 1826, where he was escorted to the same house he occupied on his first visit. He was cordially received by Sultan Bello, whom he found reading an Arabic translation of Euclid's *Elements.* "Bello's appearance was very little altered from what it was when I saw him last," wrote Clapperton, "except that he had got a little lustier [i.e., full of vitality], and dressed somewhat better." But Clapperton discovered that while Bello's outward demeanor had not changed, his interest in English explorers had decreased markedly. Though Bello received his English visitor kindly enough, it was with a reserve the exhausted Clapperton found impossible to penetrate. The African leader's mind was clearly on other matters. King George IV of England and the bizarre activities of his white emissary had receded into the backdrop of Bello's concerns. He asked if the English king was well, but no more.

Though worn out by his trip, Clapperton still clung to the hope of opening a trade route to the coast, building a shipyard for the caliphate, and persuading Bello to give up slavery in return for trade—especially imports of weapons—with England. The sultan had previously welcomed Clapperton's mission precisely because it seemed to him an efficient way to obtain munitions. In Clapperton's absence, Arab advisers had apparently convinced Bello that British explorers were on a mission of conquest, and that Clapperton particularly was the representative of a great power that would eventually seize his country and dispossess him. The bogey of India was constantly held up to him as an example of the disingenuous intentions of white people. Bello correctly (and presciently) understood that the explorers were the thin end of the wedge, the vanguard of the scramble for colonization that was, in fact, about to begin.

Bello was also preoccupied with the ongoing conflict with his arch-enemy, El Kanemi, and Clapperton found it next to impossible to get him to concentrate on anything but the prosecution of the war. Like Hajji Hat Salah, Sultan Bello was annoyed and provoked by Clapperton's planned visit to El Kanemi at Kukawa. Clapperton had presents for El Kanemi that Bello speculated might assist military efforts. Perhaps he had heard of Hillman's cannon, or the Congreve rockets. Bello opined that Clapperton might even give the Bornu leader information about the caliphate's military strength and plans. He bluntly advised Clapperton that his proposed journey beyond the caliphate's borders represented interference in the internal affairs of his country, as well as a provocation in a local conflict in which the English had no legitimate role. Clapperton was unable to convince him otherwise. Relations between the two men soured, and their meetings became less frequent and less cordial.

Ominously, Clapperton recorded that Bello harangued him that "when I was here two years ago, the Sheikh of Bornu had written to him, advising him to put me to death; as, if the English should meet with too great encouragement, they would come into Sudan, one after another, until they got strong enough to seize the country, and dispossess him, as they had done in India, which they had wrested from the hands of the Mahometans."

Clapperton said he could not believe that the sheikh of Bornu (El Kanemi), who had shown him such warm hospitality in Kukawa two years earlier, had ever written such a letter. When he demanded to see it, Bello said he had lent it to one of his ministers. Of course it was never produced. Discussions reached an impasse and days went by with no progress. By mid-December, six weeks after his arrival in Sokoto, Clapperton was sick again and spending much of his day in bed. In a final effort to convince Bello of his friendly intentions, Clapperton paid him a visit at a country retreat the sultan maintained outside town. This time Bello, who had left the city to amuse himself with cronies and concubines and temporarily to forget his troubles, lost his temper. He told Clapperton flatly that he would not let him continue to Bornu. "He was desired to say that I was a spy," Clapperton wrote, "and that he would not allow me to go beyond Sokoto; hinting, at the same time, that it would be better I should die, as the English had taken possession of India by first going there by ones and twos, until we got strong enough to seize upon the whole country."

Though Bello's position appeared to leave no room for negotiation, Clapperton continued to meet with him in increasingly chilly meetings back in the city, the distrust between the two men growing deeper. Though Clapperton was never imprisoned, after a time Bello no longer admitted him to audiences and showed only too palpably that the earlier friendship between them was over.

Though all of Clapperton's Arab merchant friends paid calls, he began to fear that they, too, were plotting his downfall. They knew, or he suspected they knew, that any success he might achieve as a commercial ambassador would mark the end of their days as wealthy merchants. Clapperton, after all, might well be the harbinger of the end of the slave trade, and slaves had long been their principal source of revenue.

In the meantime Lander, still in Kano, got a letter from Clapperton dated November 7, 1826, informing him that the sultan did not want him to go to Bornu. In words that applied as much to himself as to his servant, he advised Lander to keep his spirits up whatever their difficulties. "Think of your friends in England," he wrote, "and fancy yourself in their little circle; never permit hope to sink so far within you as to say to yourself, 'I shall never see my country again.'"

Lander was puzzled next by a message from Sokoto stating that Clapperton was ill and needed him, and that he should come right away—and be sure to bring all their baggage. Though suspicious at first, he decided to go to his friend's side. In fact, the summons had come from Bello, who wanted to see what goodies Clapperton was concealing in his equipage for El Kanemi. En route to Sokoto, Lander was given another letter from Clapperton dated December 18. "Their cursed Bornu war has overturned all my plans and intentions," Clapperton wrote, "and set the minds of the people generally against me, as it is pretty well understood by both rich and poor that I have presents for their archenemy the Sheikh."

Lander reached Sokoto on December 23, surprising Clapperton, who thought he was still safely in Kano. Outraged at the deception, Clapperton confided to his journal "that my business with the sultan is now finished, and I would have no more to say." Two days later, Christmas Day, Clapperton wrote: "I gave my servant Richard one Sovereign out of six I have left, as a Christmas gift; for he is well deserving, and has never once shown a want of courage or enterprise unworthy of an Englishman." It was becoming clear that in his race with Laing, he had come to a dead end and would have to regroup. It would be hard enough now to escape Sokoto, much less reach Lake Chad and find the Niger. But Clapperton was not a man easily thwarted.

Meanwhile, his conflict with Bello came to a boil. The sultan insisted on seeing George IV's letter to the sheikh of Bornu. Against his better judgment, Clapperton showed him the tin case in which the letter was kept, under royal seal, but refused to open it, saying: "To give up this letter is more than my head is worth." Bello said he would open it himself and send a letter of apology to London.

"The King of England would never so much as look at such a letter from you," Clapperton replied, "after his subjects had received such vile treatment." Clapperton was so high-handed with the sultan, known throughout his kingdom as "the Beloved of God," that one of Bello's courtiers remarked: "With truth, do you hear how that man talks before the Prince of the Faithful?" Bello was a ruler who put humans to slaughter as casually as an English farmer might order a chicken's neck wrung for dinner, yet Clapperton refused to yield, perhaps suspecting, rightly, that fear of British retaliation would temper his conduct.

In the end, Bello snatched the tin box, opened it, and had the letter translated. It did, in fact, mention various gifts entrusted to the explorer for El Kanemi. Bello, inquisitive and suspicious now about what

Clapperton's baggage contained, gave orders to have it confiscated. To accomplish this, the next day he sent his *gadado* to Clapperton's hut to seize the presents. Clapperton lay ill on his mat, but rose to protest that "they were acting like robbers towards me, in defiance of all good faith; that no people in the world would act the same, and they had far better have my head cut off than done such an act; but I supposed they would do that also when they had taken everything from me."

The *gadado* warned him that he risked execution if he continued to resist. "If I lose my head," Lander reported Clapperton replying, "it will be for no other crime than that of speaking for the just rights of my king and country; I repeat, you are a nation of scoundrels and robbers."

The confiscation of his baggage marked the end of any hope of rapprochement with Bello. It was the last straw in the privations and humiliations Clapperton had endured. Overwrought, frustrated, and probably half out of his mind, he now appeared to surrender what little natural caution he possessed. He went off to hunt game for several days. Away from camp, exhausted, he lay down on the ground and fell asleep in the open air, just as he had near the coast, with such dire consequences. When he woke up he had "caught a chill," in the language of his age, which soon developed into yet another bout of grave illness (probably malaria). His already undermined constitution could not take this additional strain.

For the next two months the explorers were prisoners in their beehive hut. Clapperton slid steeply into an overpowering depression compounding his physical distress. Lander, in turn, became sick also, in part from seeing that Clapperton had lost all incentive to try and get better. Something inside both men had cracked.

"On the 12th March," wrote Lander, "my dear, kind Master was again attacked by dysentery." Lander, alone and still ill himself, did what he could. Clapperton was wasting away. Lander dragged Clapperton's cot out into the open air in an effort to provide some relief from the oppressive heat—109 degrees in the shade was the normal midday temperature, according to his meticulous notes—and spent hours hovering over him with an improvised fan. But nothing seemed to revive his patient.

A ray of hope appeared with the return of Pasco, their servant, whose promiscuous behavior with Kano women had been so reckless that Lander had been forced to fire him months earlier. Pasco, now penitent, wanted his job back. He took over the chores of the meager household, cooking, washing, and bringing supplies from the market.

Lander was glad to have Pasco back; his loneliness and helplessness had become unbearable. It was a grim picture. Of the confident and happy party assembled on the deck of HMS *Brazen* on the expedition's arrival off the West African coast, only Clapperton and Lander were left. The Cornishman's tune on heading to shore, "Over the Hills and Far Away," had proved only too prophetic. Help could not reach them now. The leader of the team was clearly not long for this world. Only Lander, a servant whose name was not even known to Earl Bathurst, would be left.

The demoralized and distracted Sultan Bello offered no help. Worse, now that there was no chance Clapperton could deliver message or gifts to El Kanemi, the fate of two insignificant white men ceased to concern Bello. The African king had lost some of his confidence as a war leader.* At that moment El Kanemi was still at the gates of Kano and the whole of the Hausaland was in a state of chaos and terror.

In a significant act of the military acumen for which he was so famous, at the last minute El Kanemi pulled back his troops—he had made his point: that the Fulani could be defeated. Their aura of invincibility was badly tarnished, and Sultan Bello had been punished for murdering El Kanemi's embassy. The sheikh circulated the rumor that he was retreating to Kukawa, having accomplished his goal.

Clapperton's political impotence, coupled with unabating illness, had taken its toll. He had returned to these two warring African empires with a keen sense of optimism, only to find an opéra-bouffe world of shortsighted inefficiency, violence, bitter jealousies, limited goals, and an overall lack of cohesion. Even the hope of a safe return to England must now have seemed problematic.

Despite these reverses, Clapperton's journal is more interesting at this time than anywhere else in its pages. He continued to take copious notes on the people, races, places, customs—a remarkable social barometer of this new land. He recorded an oral history of Bello's father, Othman Dan Fodio, who had been more astute a military leader than the

---

* In part because he was haunted by the memory of his father, Othman Dan Fodio, whose reputation as a warrior had grown to mythic proportions after his death. The shadow of his memory darkened Bello's reign.

son. Clapperton surmised that Bello's vacillation in prosecuting his war with El Kanemi had its origin in his memory of Othman Dan Fodio, the illustrious father whose reputation dogged him.

Then came news of yet another skirmish with El Kanemi, one in which Bello's forces had won at least a fleeting victory. While pursuing him, Bello's forces had seized all his baggage, camels, and tents, 209 horses, and a number of slaves. Bello summoned Clapperton (for the first time in weeks) to revel in showing him the sheikh's copper water jug, which had three sword cuts in it. He danced a little jig, brandishing the jug in triumph, as though it were El Kanemi's head. The victory put Bello in an ebullient mood. He became outwardly friendly once more and sought out Clapperton, no longer overtly treating him as a spy. He asked Clapperton whether he ate pork, and the explorer replied that it was better than dog, which he had seen sold in the open market at Tripoli.

"The sultan said, it was strange what people would eat," wrote Clapperton. "In the districts of Umburm, belonging to Jacoba [Bello's cousin], they eat human flesh. . . . I said I did not think any people existed on the face of the earth that eat their own kind as food. . . . [T]he sultan said he had seen them eat human flesh, they said it was better than any other; that the heart and breasts of a woman were the best part of her body."

Clapperton's health improved with Bello's disposition. He went hunting daily. Dressed in a flowing robe and a white muslin turban, with a beard that had grown to patriarchal length, he was again treated with civility and respect. In the evening, he and Lander smoked cigars, their only remaining luxury (brandy bottles were long empty), read aloud, and laughed at stale jokes they both knew by heart. They thought of home and wondered whether Bello would ever let them leave Sokoto. Lander was discouraged by their detention, and wrote that "like the beautiful apple said to grow on the borders of the Red Sea, our hopes wore a fair and promising outside, but produced only bitter ashes."

In early March 1827, news arrived that the reverses of Sheikh El Kanemi had been only temporary. His troops had regrouped and laid siege to Kano once more. It was rumored he was about to march on Sokoto itself. Bello considered the threat so exigent that he evacuated the city to the low hill country nearby, taking Clapperton and Lander with him to ensure they would have no contact with the enemy. The intended attack never materialized. Bello and the explorers returned to Sokoto on March 10, to furnacelike heat of 110 degrees, further weakening Clapperton, who was again suffering from dysentery. This time, he was too weak to keep his journal.

His last entry, dated March 11, begins badly: "Nothing worth noting down." He then writes of the sultan's decision to let them leave Sokoto. But Clapperton was in no condition to leave, and he knew it. He had nightmares and complained of a burning in his stomach. Lander treated him with laudanum, Seidlitz powders, and Epsom salts.* Clapperton deduced he was doomed, and told Lander so: "Richard, I shall shortly be no more, I feel myself dying." Lander reassured him: "God forbid my dear master, you will live many years yet." He lingered on another month, hollow-eyed and skeletal. He gave his last instructions, which Lander reported in a letter that shows great stress in its absence of all punctuation:

What my master said to me at Sakatoo April 1827 Richard i am going to die i cannot help shedding tears as he had behaved like a father to me since i had been with him we went into the hut he was then laying in a shade outside he said Richard come here my dear boy its the will of God it cant be helped bear yourself up under all troubles like a man and an english man do not be affraid and no one will hurt you i do not fear that sir its for the loss of you who has been a father to me since when i have ben with you my dear boy i will tell you what to do take great care of my journals and when you arrive in London go to my agents and tell them to send directly for my uncul and tell him it was my wish that he would go with

---

* These were primitive medications of the era. Seidlitz salts were effervescing salts consisting of two powders stored in separate bottles, one with forty grains of sodium bicarbonate mixed with two drams of Rochelle salt (potassium sodium tartrate), and the other with thirty-five grains of tartaric acid per dose. When mixed together in water, they fizz impressively. Consumed while effervescing, they are a mild cathartic. Laudanum was a tincture of opium (usually dissolved in fortified wine, such as sherry) used as a painkiller, though it was rarely efficient because it also caused vomiting before the narcotic could be absorbed. Epsom salts, named for Epsom, England, were a bitter white crystalline salt consisting of magnesium sulfate, also having cathartic qualities when dissolved in water. These harsh chemicals, administered to a man near death, would tend to hasten it, though Lander, of course, could not have known this.

me to the colonoal office and delever the journals that they might not say their were anything missing my little money my close and everything i have belongs to you Bello will lend you money to buy cammels and provisions and send you home over the desert with the gaffic [*coffle,* or caravan] and when you arrive at Tripoli Mr Warrington will give you what money you want and send you home the first opportunity. . . . [W]rit down the names of the towns you go throw and all purticulars and if you get safe home with the journals i have no doubt of your being well rewarded for your truble.

A day or two later, Clapperton seemed to rally, feeling so much better that he talked of getting up and making a further effort to patch matters with Bello. He ate some food. The cramped beehive hut, for the first time in two months, momentarily radiated optimism.

But it was only the last bright flicker. The following morning Lander heard his master call "Richard" in a low voice, and turning quickly, saw the dying man sit up—an act he had not had the strength to do for days—and look around wildly. Lander went to the cot and took his pulse, which was rapid. Then, with no further movement, he lost consciousness. On April 13, 1827, Lander heard the death rattle in Clapperton's throat. He cradled him as he took his last breath.

A pathetic funeral service followed. Lander asked Bello for permission to bury his leader, and the sultan grudgingly put a court official and four slaves at his disposal. Clapperton's body was planted on the back of a camel and draped with the Union Jack. Lander headed the procession out of Sokoto. "We travelled," he wrote, "almost unobserved and at a solemn pace and halted near Jungavie, a village built on rising ground five miles southeast of the city." No one listened as Lander read the Church of England burial service, his voice drowned out by the slaves who stood near the grave shrieking, not from grief, but rather about how the gratuity for their services should be divided.

Hired as a servant, Lander now found himself alone in the African interior, commander of an expedition of one, surrounded by enemies and exhausted by illness. He too had malaria, and lay on his mat at Sokoto alternately sweating and shivering for two weeks after Clapperton's death. Bello's men searched the hut for weapons. They made it clear Lander was unwelcome and should leave expeditiously. Clapperton was dead, and Richard Lander's position must have seemed to him a nightmare. What hope did he have? What possible chance could there be for a safe return to England? He wrote, despairingly,

> One hundred and fifteen days journey from the sea coast, surrounded by a selfish and barbarous race of strangers, my only friend and protector and last hope mouldering in his grave, and myself suffering dreadfully from fever, I felt as if I stood alone in the world and wished, ardently wished, I had been enjoying the same deep undisturbed cold sleep as my master, and in the same grave.

This, it turned out, was far too bleak a view. Lander, as he would now demonstrate, had a knack for dealing with people at a personal level with all the warmth that Clapperton lacked. He made allies at Bello's court. He was a "commonsense" sort of person and he was good at making the right decisions on gut instinct. Lander's "last hope" was not, in fact, Hugh Clapperton, but his own fierce determination to live.

Intent at first on carrying out Clapperton's last wishes and returning via the northern route to Tripoli, he got permission from Bello to depart Sokoto with an escort. When he reached Kano, he was too poor to buy the camels and equipment he needed to cross the desert, so he decided to return the way he had come, to the coast and Badagri. He had already traveled this route, and he was glad not to have to join unfriendly Arabs for the long desert crossing. Also, he had caught from Clapperton the urge to discover, to be an explorer in his own right, and wanted, if the chance arose, to follow the Niger to the ocean in a canoe.

Crossing Yoruba country with Pasco, Lander survived the trials that were by now familiar to Niger explorers: he nearly drowned crossing a river; he was speared by a Yoruba warrior; he had to give presents wherever he went; and he was nearly murdered by the comically evil eunuch Ebo, King Mansoleh's adviser, who had harassed the explorers on the trip out.

Lander was resourceful. When asked for a charm to cure infertility, rather than ridicule the patient, he offered cinnamon oil, a scent unknown to the locals, which impressed them deeply. He was happy to dispense magical potions and written charms, writing out scraps of English ballads against a variety of ailments. One good turn deserving another, the emir of Zaria offered Lander a young female slave for a wife, and he "accepted her with gratitude, as I knew she would be serviceable to me on my journey." She washed his feet, bathed his temples with lime juice, and fanned him to sleep.

Lander reached Badagri on November 21, 1827, seven months after Clapperton's death. Gazing at the bay, fringed with palms and cocoa trees and the whitecaps on the great Atlantic Ocean beyond, he was sure his troubles were over. He had run the gauntlet of the African interior and was now only a ship's journey from England. In fact, the most dire threat to his life was still ahead.

Badagri in 1827 was a hellish place, a festering market for slaves run by thugs of a peculiarly brutal stripe, many of them Portuguese gangsters from Brazil. Since the English policed local waters, the slavers were afraid that Lander's presence portended a raid from the Blockade Squadron. A trio of bandits went to the king of Badagri and told him that Lander was a spy. If he wasn't stopped, they warned, he would return with an army. The gullible chief summoned Lander to a ritual "fetish hut." Surrounded by hundreds of overexcited, spear-brandishing locals, the chief told Lander: "You are accused, white man, of designs against our kingdom, and are therefore desired to drink the contents of this vessel, which if the reports be true, will surely destroy you; whereas, if they be without foundation, you need not fear, Christian; the fetish will do you no injury, for the fetish will do that which is right."

Lander was presented a wooden bowl of clear liquid, probably a potion, he later speculated, made from an extract of the poisonous bark of the redwater tree,* and told to drink it. From the expression on the king's face, he saw there was no alternative. "I took the bowl in my trembling hands," he wrote, "and gazed for a moment at the sable countenances of my judges; but not a single look of compassion shone upon them; a dead

---

* This tree (*Erythrophleum guineense*) is quite prevalent up and down the modern coast, where it is called "sasswood," "ordeal tree," "truthwood," or "doom bark." It is a large spreading tree valued for its shade. The boiled bark yields a red decoction containing a poisonous alkaloid, erythrophleine, which has properties similar to strychnine. In a bizarre irony, the tree's wood, which is very hard and useful for carving, is nontoxic and makes elegant salad bowls, which are as strong as cast iron.

silence prevailed in the gloomy sanctuary of skulls; every eye was intently fixed upon me; and seeing no possibility of escape, I offered up a prayer to the Throne of Mercy—the God of Christians—and hastily swallowed the fetish, dashing the poison chalice to the ground."

Lander got to his hut as fast as he could, where he forced himself to vomit the poison, evidently getting it all out in time. Since the fetish was often fatal, in the hours that followed, his accusers were amazed to see him still walking. The chief concluded that he must be under divine protection. Convinced now of his error, he befriended Lander, warning him never to go out alone or unarmed, for the Portuguese slavers would murder him at the first opportunity.

With this trial behind him, Lander waited for a ship. He took ethnographic notes, appalled at the human sacrifices prevalent here. Prisoners of war were taken to the "fetish tree" and given flasks of rum to drink as they were bludgeoned to death with sledgehammers and picks. "The head is severed from the trunk with an axe," he wrote, "and the smoking blood gurgles into a calabash. While this is in hand, other wretches furnished with knives cut and mangle the body in order to extract the heart entire from the breast, which being done, although it be yet warm and quivering with life, it is presented to the king . . . and his majesty and suite make an incision in it with their teeth, and partaking of the foamy blood, the heart is . . . affixed to the point of a tall spear and . . . paraded through town."

IN FEBRUARY 1828 the captain of the English brig *Maria,* hearing that an Englishman was stranded at Badagri, came to rescue Lander. The *Maria* took him to the island of Fernando Po, where the tired traveler was told a veteran explorer from an earlier mission to West Africa wanted to speak to him. This was none other than Dixon Denham, now resplendent in the feathered hat and gold-trimmed coat of His Majesty's governor of Sierra Leone.* Denham heard from Lander that his old nemesis and mission partner Hugh Clapperton had died in Sokoto. Ever punctilious, Governor Denham "expressed infinite concern to hear of the fate of his coadjutor in the previous expedition," Lander wrote.

---

*A post he would keep only months. He died May 8, 1828, at Freetown, of "coastal fever" (probably malaria), another victim of African disease.

Lander, who had left home in 1825 a servant, returned to England three years later a hero, but one of peculiar appearance. He wrote that "on arriving in London, I was met in the streets by a Jew, who ran forth and cordially embraced me, asking how I had left our Hebrew brethren in Jerusalem. The fellow, by my beard and singular appearance, had taken it into his head that I belonged to his own fraternity, and was just returning from visiting the Holy City."

Richard Lemon Lander would go on to edit and publish, in 1830, what remained of Hugh Clapperton's journals and records, guaranteeing Clapperton's posthumous reputation as one of Britain's great African explorers. That year, with his brother John, Lander returned to Africa and traced the course of the lower Niger to its delta, thus solving at last the question that had dogged Sir Joseph Banks so many years earlier. Published in 1832 in London, their joint account made both men celebrities. Lander had located the mouth of the river Englishmen had sought for more than half a century, and it was in a place—the Oil Rivers—England's sailors had known well for decades. The course of the great river Niger* could finally be traced, from origin to mouth.

Thoroughly seduced by Africa, Richard Lander made a third trip there organized by Macgregor Laird in 1832, a commercial venture. That journey proved fatal. He survived Clapperton by seven years, killed by angry Africans in 1834, at twenty-nine still a young man.

HISTORY HAS NOT BEEN KIND to Hugh Clapperton, never according him the fame Sir Richard Burton would later earn for his travels in East Africa (and for the gripping and wonderfully literate books he wrote), nor that granted to Henry Morton Stanley, who crossed the continent from ocean to ocean. Hugh Clapperton's fragmentary contribution to the world's increasing store of geographical knowledge earned him little credit, and no respect. There was not much romance in his expeditions, and less in his writing. He lacks the grace of Livingstone, the literary virtuosity of Burton, the personable qualities of Speke, the self-promoting (but always readable) compulsions of Stanley. Though lacking Stanley's

---

*At 2,950 miles in length, it is the world's fourteenth longest stream, a tad longer than the Missouri.

flair, in other ways he most resembles that explorer: tough, indomitable, irascible, certain of the rightness of his own causes, never willing to concede defeat. But he was not a gifted storyteller and he did not live to tell the tale of his second expedition in a book. But for Lander, and the account of his first trip Barrow insisted Denham include in Denham's own narrative, he might be remembered only in footnotes. ·

Too many men died under Clapperton's command, and England seemed, temporarily, to have tired of the exploits of explorers in Africa, where men went mainly, it seemed, to die, discomfiting those who had sent them. Public interest in Africa would take thirty years to rekindle.

Sadly, Clapperton went to his grave without having achieved any of his official goals. He did not find Timbuktu or the Niger's mouth, nor did he reach an agreement with Sultan Bello to end slavery. His journal, retrieved by Lander, is for the most part dry and colorless, though long and detailed. Clapperton, wrote Lander, was "never highly elated . . . nor deeply depressed," and one result of this stolid disposition was flat writing. Denham, who had published his florid and self-serving account of their first expedition, won all the attention and glory. This was unfair, for through his qualities of courage and leadership, and the way he stuck to his instructions at whatever cost (and in so many other respects), Clapperton was a far better explorer, and without question the better man.

Chapter Seventeen

THE CITY OF LEGEND

IN THE LAST DAYS of travel before Timbuktu itself came into view, Laing was under constant pressure from Mohammed bin Mokhtar, the late Sheikh Mokhtar's son, to turn back. "This is not the time to visit the city," Sidi Mohammed said. "The Fulani of Massina are about to seize the whole river." In fact, it was no time for any foreigner to linger at the southern edge of the Sahara. Death was in the air.

As Sidi Mohammed later reported to Warrington, all efforts to persuade Laing to turn back failed, though he was still a sick man and his superiors could not have held it against him had he simply made straight for the coast. But that was not going to happen; Sidi Mohammed did not understand what Timbuktu meant to Alexander Gordon Laing.

Laing must have looked at his own footprints in the red murrum soil at the edge of the desert, not far from where the land became fertile, and realized that no Englishman had ever stood within 300 miles of where he now stood, not for centuries, anyway, and certainly not in recorded history. To turn back now? He was so close.

And yet, to risk death again, to risk never seeing his wife, his beloved

Emma. To risk entering a city where he might be executed on the spot. A reconnaissance without the possibility of retreat, without the well-trained reinforcements he had commanded in doing battle with the Ashanti. At this moment, Laing must have recognized he had reached the most critical stage of his journey. He had to pass through the last gate. Was he strong enough, was he clear-sighted enough, to meet this final challenge? Had he assessed correctly what lay ahead?

A trip across the Sahara he had estimated would take, at most, a few weeks had in fact taken 399 days—he had counted every one—fifty-seven weeks of loneliness, suffering, privation, and bloodshed, fourteen months of solitude, without the companionship of a native of his own land, without the woman he loved—the wife he had abandoned just four days into their marriage. More than a year of solitary travel, including a horrific attack that had shattered his bones, crippled him, and nearly bled him dry.

Laing was at the edge of the Great Desert. It was his destiny, he had written, to be the first explorer to reach Timbuktu. Now, the reddening and diminishing sand, the hint of moisture that came from the south, the smell of black Africa in the air, told him his victory was near. He would become the first European to visit Timbuktu, the first white man to see the city since a Plantagenet sat on the English throne. Nothing would stop him. No terrors, no *hamada* devils, no Fulani warriors. . . . He had been promised this prize, he was certain of it.

Excepting the possibility of his death, what lay ahead was fulfillment. Fame, riches, the personal thanks of his king, the recognition that was his due, he felt, but that previously, in a profoundly painful and personal sense, had never come. If life had denied him position in an aristocracy of birth, he would now show he was worthy of membership in the aristocracy of merit, courage, intellect, and strength—an aristocracy of greater privilege than any duchy or earldom could imbue. He must have slept soundly that last night in the desert, a man convinced of his purpose.

ON SUNDAY, August 13, 1826, more than a year after he kissed Emma good-bye and eight months to the day before Hugh Clapperton's death, Alexander Gordon Laing saw the high walls of the lost city. Scorning his Muslim disguise, he threw it off and "as a Christian envoy of the King of

*A sketch of Timbuktu by René Caillié made two years after Laing
became the first European in several centuries to enter the "fabled lost city of
Central Africa." Caillié recorded that he was as profoundly disappointed by what
he found there as Laing had been.*

England" boldly entered a place reputed to be as fanatically anti-Christian as Mecca itself.

He had found Timbuktu, the great caravan terminal, the city that touched both desert and river, the mysterious trading metropolis built on gold, jewels, and ivory. He was the first Briton, and the first modern European, to set foot in this, the last truly remote population center on earth.

Laing presented himself to Timbuktu's governor, Othman bin Boubakr, who received him courteously and installed him in a little mud house (later restored, and which exists to this day). There he could rest and escape the sun. He was free to wander about the town; he even rode out, after nightfall, to Kabara, the port district of the city on the Niger. His military rank, coupled with his dignified bearing, so impressed the townspeople that they christened him "El Rais"—the Chief.

The city center, about seven miles from the port, indicated that the Niger had shifted over the centuries, as all large-volume rivers do on flat land. At one time there had been a canal linking river and town, but silt had made it unusable. Timbuktu's golden age had unquestionably ended long ago; the city was no longer a bustling center of culture and commerce.

Laing was surely disappointed to discover in Timbuktu not even the palest shadow of the city abounding in wealth and architectural wonders that he—and all Europe—had imagined. The metropolis was quite obviously caught in a spiral of decay and war. The urban center, a sprawling river settlement, was little more than a collection of discontinuous mud villages scattered over acres of mud flats. A thousand years old, it had a look of irreversible decrepitude. Unprepossessing even from a distance, up close Timbuktu was dirty and falling apart, stinking horribly of unwashed people and sick animals. Potholes riddled streets that were thick with windblown garbage. The air reeked of dung and the pungent odor of stale urine. Rotting waste and the detritus of recent riots blocked every alley. Sand blew across scrawny acacia trees, hobbled camels, and domed huts. Inertia gripped everyone and everything.

Though disgusted by the squalor, Laing found a retreat in the most important building in town, the Sankore Mosque, where the collection of Arabic manuscripts kept him in thrall for days. The building was raised by Mansa Musa after his performance of the hajj in 1324. Though five centuries old, it retained an uncluttered, well-kept interior—eerily quiet and rather dark, the coolest place in the city. Long strips of straw matting, padded with a thick layer of sand, carpeted the hallways and rooms. Nothing but Islamic script decorated the walls.*

Next door, a pyramid-like building had been the site of a university in the sixteenth century, when Timbuktu was still a center of Islamic scholarship. Mali's Muslim rulers had built 180 Koranic schools during Timbuktu's heyday, and black Africa's greatest Islamic university had been situated there. By 1450, Timbuktu's population had swelled to 100,000, including 25,000 Muslim scholars from as far away as Cairo. At the time of Laing's visit, fewer than 12,000 people inhabited the city, a calamitous reduction in population.

And yet Timbuktu remained, as it does today, the home of some of the southern Sahara's most appealing peoples. In encampments along the

*Islam proscribes images of any kind in a mosque.

banks of the river, Tuareg women swathed in black, with indigo dye staining their faces and hands, sat cross-legged on the sand grinding millet in
mortars and pestles. Baby goats and children frolicked nearby. At night,
wet skins were stretched across the mortars and tied firmly, transforming
them into drums. The women formed a circle in the sand, and a concert
would begin. Younger women accompanied the drumming and singing
with miniature one-stringed guitars. Tall, stately Tuareg men swept around
the camps in flowing, brilliant robes, heads wrapped in yards of fabric.
The men's faces were veiled, nothing visible but their eyes—inquisitive,
but also piercing and hostile. Laing was the first white man they had seen,
an object of great curiosity and fear. Men squatted on the ground to trade
among themselves. They bartered with leather boxes, knives of all sizes
and styles, colorful leather camel bags, and jewelery—simple yet dramatic
pieces of silver inlaid with ebony and gold.

Laing had arrived at Timbuktu during a period of political upheaval
that made his stay there even more dangerous than it would have been
in peaceful times. Over the centuries, blacks, Berbers, and Arabs fought
each other for control of Timbuktu and its trade routes. This troubled
history had reached a terminal phase when Laing arrived. While he was
crossing the desert, a Fulani zealot and henchman of Sultan Bello, Seku
Hamadu, had declared war on the Tuareg who controlled Timbuktu,
determined to take it from them. Most of the Tuareg had fled just days
before Laing strode through the city gates, but Seku Hamadu had not
yet occupied the city with his troops. Timbuktu had thus devolved into
a no-man's-land under the nominal control of Sheikh Othman, the city
governor, who took his orders from whichever faction appeared to him
most powerful at the moment.

In this anarchic political environment, Laing's movements about the
city, coupled with the probing questions he asked, created difficulties
for him. His high profile in the town and his inquisitive nature created
suspicion in Othman's mind that Laing had come to spy, though it was
not clear for whom.

Back in his clay house, Laing had time to reflect, keep up his journal,
and write letters. The discovery of Timbuktu was only a stepping-stone
to the discovery of the termination of the Niger, his other important goal,
especially now that Timbuktu had, in a sense, failed him.

For at least five centuries, Timbuktu had been known by name in western Europe, and for the greater part of that time, men had dreamed of a city of dazzling opulence, an African El Dorado. Now Laing saw the reality. He despaired at having to announce to a disbelieving world, in the book he hoped would make him famous, that Timbuktu was little more than a poor collection of mud shanties with no wealth, much less gold. The salt caravans had practically disappeared. Timbuktu had fallen into fatal decline.

The enduring vision of Timbuktu as a city paved with gold had been fostered, indeed nourished, by rumor and lack of hard evidence. Realizing now that Timbuktu could not live up to popular expectations, Laing was careful not to reveal his disappointment in the letters he sent home lest these revelations precede him to London and diminish the value of his planned book. Though he recognized that Timbuktu would be less exciting to write about than what he had hoped to find, he was by no means indifferent to his accomplishment, nor unaware of the public esteem that would attach to the discovery of what he liked to call, and still believed to be, the "far-famed capital of Central Africa." Laing knew, no matter its current state, that the discovery of Africa's most important lost city was bound to be a milestone in the history of geographical exploration.

The mythical quality of the planet's last great lost city—a real *city*, not merely a mythical Shangri-la or El Dorado—which had survived in hiding from Europe since the fourteenth century, died on the day Laing walked through its gates. Timbuktu would never again be the place in Africa "where the map of this world ends."

LAING STAYED IN TIMBUKTU for thirty-five days, gathering research, studying Arab manuscripts, copying city records, and talking to scholars. Then news arrived that interrupted his studies and forced his departure. In Sokoto, Sultan Bello, though agreeable to traffic with England by way of Tripoli and the Sahara, was dead against the notion of a thoroughfare open to the coast. He wrote to his satrap Seku Hamadu that Europeans were to be prevented from visiting any Muslim lands of the Sudan. Alarmed, Seku Hamadu wrote the following to the governor of Timbuktu:

*To the Governor Othman ben Al Khaid Abu Bakr, and those who are
his brothers in office:*

*To give you to know, that having heard that a Christian traveller
desires to visit our country, but not knowing whether he is arrived or
not (at Timbuctoo), you are to endeavour to prevent his entry, if not
already come, and if he is come, endeavour to send him away, and take
from him all hope of returning into our dominions. For I have just
received a letter from Bello Danfoda [Sultan Bello was the son of the
great military ruler Othman Dan Fodio], full of wholesome advice, by
which I am instructed to prevent Europeans from visiting the Musul-
man country of Soudan. This was caused by a letter he received from
Egypt, in which the abuses and corruptions the Christians have committed in that country are mentioned, as well as in Andalusia and
other countries in former times.*

These orders reached Sheikh Othman only after Laing had been officially
welcomed. Seku Hamadu's comment that Bello's change of heart occurred
as a result of "a letter he received from Egypt" was likely a cover story, for
it is improbable that events in Egypt and Spain were of much immediate
concern to Sultan Bello, who was safely insulated by vast distance from
such places. Unease about interference with the slave trade and his other
monopolies was likely the real reason for getting rid of Laing.

Sultan Bello's knowledge of conditions in far lands should come
as no surprise. Clapperton would document it, and before European
penetration of the interior of Africa revolutionized the pattern of African
trade, commercial intercourse extending from Egypt on the one hand
to Fez on the other, and from Tripoli to the coast of Guinea, was traditional in the northern half of the continent, reaching certainly as far as
Timbuktu. Consequently (and ironically), Saharan people were far better informed in Laing's day about events in remote countries than they
afterward became.

Othman personally had no objection to Laing—indeed, there is every
indication that he liked him—but he had many masters and dared not
disobey any of them, including the powerful Fulani warrior Mohammed Bello. He therefore warned Laing that if he did not leave at once,
Fulani warriors would likely be tasked to kill him. The message was clear.

Laing got his things together, taking time to send a final dispatch back to Tripoli:

Timbuctoo, Sept. 21st, 1826

My dear Consul,

A very short epistle must serve to apprise you, as well as my Dearest Emma, of my arrival at & departure from the great Capital of Central Africa, the former of which events took place on the 13th Ulto, and the latter will take place (Please God) at an early hour to morrow morning. I have abandoned all thought of retracing my steps to Tripoli, & came here with an intention of proceeding to Jenne by water, but this intention has been utterly upset, and my situation in Timbuctoo rendered exceedingly unsafe by the unfriendly disposition of the Foolahs of Massina,* who have this year upset the dominion of the Tuaric & made themselves patrons of Timbuctoo, & whose Sultan has expressed his hostility towards me in no unequivocal terms, in a letter which Al Kaidi Boubokar the Sheik of this town received from him a few days after my arrival. He has now got intelligence of my being in Timbuctoo & as a party of Foolahs are hourly expected Al Kaidi Boubokar, who is an excellent good man, & who trembles for my safety, has strongly urged my immediate departure, and I am sorry to say that the notice has been so short, and I have so much to do previous to going away, that this is the only communication I shall for the present be able to make. My destination is Sego [Segou], whither I hope to arrive in fifteen days, but I regret to say that the road is a vile one and my perils are not yet at an end, but my trust is God Who has hitherto bore me up amidst the severest trials & protected me amid the numerous dangers to which I have been exposed. I have no time to give you my account of Timbuctoo, but shall briefly state that in every respect except in size (which does not exceed four miles in circumference) it has completely met my expectations. Kabra [Kabara] is only five miles distant, & is a

---

*Massina is a great pastoral plain in what is today Mali. Its center lies about 110 miles southwest of Timbuktu. In Laing's day, the people of Massina, being closer to the coast, were more likely to have had some knowledge of the presence of European traders in places like Guinea.

*neat town, situated on the very margin of the river. I have been busily
employed during my stay, searching the records in the town, which are
abundant, & in acquiring information of every kind, nor is it with any
common degree of satisfaction that I say, my perseverance has been
amply rewarded. I am now convinced that my hypothesis concerning
the termination of the Niger is correct [presumably, that it emptied into
the Bight of Benin].*

*May God bless you all; I shall write you fully from Sego, as also
My Lord Bathurst, & I rather apprehend that both letters will reach
you at one time, as none of the Ghadamis Merchants leave Timbuctoo
for two months to come.*

*Again, May God bless you all, My Dear Emma must excuse my
writing, I have begun a hundred letters to her, but have been unable
to get thro' one; she is ever uppermost in my thoughts, & I look forward
with delight to the hour of our meeting, which please God, is now at
no great distance.—*

Yours ever truly

A. Gordon Laing

When Warrington received this letter many months later, he scribbled
a note on it, saying "From Major Laing to Consul Warrington dated 21st
September at Timbuctoo, Being the First Letter ever written from that
place by any Christian."

It would have been out of character for Laing to do anything, or leave
any place, exactly on schedule; he typically changed his route at the last
minute. But his departure from Timbuktu was the exception. The next
day, Friday, September 22, at three o'clock in the afternoon, Laing left
with his freed slave Bongola and an unnamed Arab youth, passing out the
gates of Timbuktu for the last time. Sheikh Ahmadu El Abeyd, who had
agreed to accompany him and offer the protection of his caravan, either
started with the trio or caught up with them later, near a place called
Sahab (northwest from the city, and away from the river).

Laing was still a bit weak, but much improved from the state in which
he had arrived five weeks earlier. He was elated at having met his first
objective, the discovery of a city not visited by Europeans for centuries,

though he had found no streets paved with gold nor palace walls embedded with gems.

About his second objective, he was "at sixes and sevens." Lord Bathurst had explicitly ordered him to follow the Niger downriver from Kabara (Timbuktu's port), delineate its course through the African interior, and especially to discover its debouchment into the Atlantic. How was he to accomplish this?

In one matter, the discovery of Timbuktu, he never wavered, even in the depths of illness. He was convinced it was the will of God that he should discover Timbuktu, and he never doubted that he merited this special favor from heaven. "I shall do more than has ever been done before," he wrote in the only surviving letter from Africa to his parents, "and show myself to be what I have ever considered myself to be—a man of enterprise and of genius."

But whether he could or should pursue the course of the Niger to its mouth—that was a question that dogged his last weeks. There was reason to believe such a trip was not feasible, and might even be suicidal. First, the governor of the town had warned him repeatedly that he risked death merely by staying in the vicinity, ordering him to retrace his steps through the Sahara back to Tripoli. Second, not long after arriving at Timbuktu, he learned that Fulani warriors were in force upon the river in pirogues, both upstream and downstream of Kabara, which precluded his use of a canoe if he hoped to remain undetected.

Had he decided to follow the river in either direction, he would have had to do so on land, and at some distance from the banks so as not to be seen. It is possible that he abandoned the idea of water travel on the Niger as early as the time of his stay at In Salah, when he had been comically, but dangerously, mistaken for Mungo Park. In reporting that incident to Warrington, he speculated that travel on the Niger would be far too dangerous, given the rage that still lingered from Mungo Park's vicious attacks on indigenous peoples. He suggests that he had already renounced his intention of following the river to its mouth by canoe, aspiring to make the trek by land, following the riverbank in concealment.

After much mental torture and deliberation (though not a "team player," he always took his orders from Lord Bathurst seriously), Laing determined that his only wise course was to abandon the Niger quest and go upriver to Sansanding and Jenne. From there he could make his way to the territories of Africa he knew so well, the hinterland of Sierra Leone, the land of the Ashanti. There he could easily reach the Atlantic and return to Tripoli by ship. His statement that he was bound for Segou, 400 miles *upriver* from Timbuktu, is consistent with this hypothesis.

In Tripoli, meanwhile, the first vague reports of the Tuareg attack against Laing in the Tanezrouft Desert were making their way back to the English Garden, where they alarmed the British consul and his increasingly fragile daughter. But the Warringtons had heard unsettling reports from the desert before, and every member of the family had supreme confidence in Laing.

They continued writing letters to him, dispatching them month by month, week by week, courier by courier, into the vastness, the oblivion, the baleful tranquillity of an indifferent "Zahara."

Chapter Eighteen

———— ·•· ————

THE LONG SILENCE

I N SPITE OF THE MESSENGERS and caravans crisscrossing its infinite solitudes, the Sahara was slow to give up news of Laing's progress. This was puzzling, for as Consul Warrington knew, in the desert, no matter its vast extent and the tiny number of people who populated it, news traveled fast. Everyone seemed to know what everyone else was doing. The trading caravans carried the local gossip of all the places they visited, from the great cities on the brim of the Mediterranean to the smallest oases in the heart of the Tanezrouft.

In the early nineteenth century, nothing caused more of a stir than the passage of a European through the desert. The activities of men like Clapperton and Laing were a great source of talk, though usually, and inevitably, unreliable and distorted as it passed from mouth to mouth and ear to ear. Many of the caravans converged at Tripoli, so it was not long before disturbing rumors began to reach the ever-attentive British consul.

Sequested in the English Garden, Emma Warrington Laing waited anxiously. Tales of the Tuareg attack on her husband had come to the city, but Emma's family conspired to say nothing about them to her. The first hard news arrived on November 3, 1826, when Hamet, Laing's camel driver, presented himself at the British consulate. He told Warrington of Sheikh Babani's treachery and death, of the epidemic at the camp, and of the death of Sidi Mokhtar, the desert leader who gave Laing sanctuary after the Tuareg attack. He had left Major Laing, he said, "on the point of proceeding to Timbuktu under Sidi Mohammed's (Mokhtar's son) special protection."

Hamet produced a letter in Laing's handwriting. Laing stated he would be in Ghadames by November and hoped to be greeted by a courier from Tripoli with the latest news and "a little tea and sugar and some sort of tin teapot, also half a dozen pairs of stockings and about 400 dollars," requests that seemed reassuringly quotidian. The consul, who took the camel driver's deposition, told his wife. But neither could face Emma with Hamet's account, which had been unsparing in its detail about Laing's grisly wounds.

Instead, the consul sent a courier (Jacob, Clapperton's reliable old servant) to Ghadames, giving him a letter to Laing containing a redacted version of the details of the attack, with the entreaty that he confirm them. He hoped Laing, by now, would have made it that far back. Afraid that it was wrong to keep Emma in the dark, he let her read the archived consular copy of his own letter containing the less vivid version of the attack in the Tanezrouft. Despite Warrington's effort to hide the worst of the details, Emma was shattered. Having been kept in total ignorance of "all the dreadful, cruel reports," as she put it, she was utterly unprepared for this sudden revelation of the truth.

In her anguish, Emma accused her parents of sending Laing to his death. Why had they let her deceive herself with hopes of his quick return? They were speechless, overcome by her anger. Eventually the consul and his wife convinced her that Laing might have survived. Propped up on cushions in her bed at the country estate, she listened to her father and mother discussing arrangements for a second courier's journey to Ghadames, fondling the purchases—the tea, the sugar, the tin teapot, the stockings, some sweets, a bar of soap—she had selected with her own hands and now insisted be sent to him.

While waiting for the courier to depart, Emma wrote her last, memorable letter to her husband.

Tripoli, 10th November, 1826

Yesterday, my beloved Laing, I had the pleasure of closing my letters and delivering them to the Maraboot and Jacob, who are now on the road to meet my own adored husband. I now begin to feel some ray of comfort. The departure of these people shews me that there is some prospect of my again being restored to happiness which for many a long month has been a stranger to my bosom. I have, this moment, by the Consul's desire taken a duplicate of a letter, which he has already sent by the Maraboot, and by that letter I see that I have been kept in perfect ignorance of all the dreadful, cruel reports in circulation about you. I do not know whether so doing was cruelty or kindness. Why let me deceive myself with the hopes of your speedy return? The month I first expected you to return in passed away, and disappointed and sickened, I looked forward to the next, but to be disappointed again. At last the dreadful truth was revealed to me and without being at all prepared for it, the blow was most severe. I heard of your wounds, of your sickness—the chill of death appeared to pass over me, not a word, not a complaint could I utter, not a tear would fall from my eyes to relieve the agonising oppression of my heart. I spent the whole night in a state of stupefaction, not understanding anything I heard. The morning dawned, the first object that presented itself to my eyes was your dear picture which hung from my neck. At the sight, my recollection returned to me, and I wept over it almost heartbroken.

Oh, my beloved, dearest Laing, alas, alas, what have you been exposed to, what danger, what suffering. To have saved you one pang, I would with joy have shed every drop of blood that warms this heart. Had I been with you in that fearful moment, my arms would have encircled you, might for some time have shielded you from the swords of those Daemons, and, at last, we might have fallen, pierced by the same weapon, our souls might have taken their flight together to that land where sorrow can never come. My beloved Laing, sorrow has laid a heavy hand on your Emma's head, and so it has on yours. Alas, Laing, how cruel, how sad has been our fate. Are we destined to endure more misery, or will a kind Providence at length pity our unhappiness and restore us to each other? Will you, my own idolised husband, return

*to your Emma's fond arms, will you come and repose on her faithful
bosom? Will you restore happiness to her torn heart?*

*Never for a Moment, my beloved Laing, have you been absent
from my thoughts. You have always been present to my imagination,
waking and sleeping. You will find your Emma the same in heart and
soul, as when you last embraced her, entirely and forever devoted to
her Laing. God of Heaven protect you, dearer to me than life. May he
guide you in health and safety and may your own dear Emma be cold
in death ere she shall again hear tidings of any evil or unhappiness
having befallen her idolised husband.*

*Adieu, my dear beloved, May Heaven soon restore you to the arms
of your adoring, devoted wife,*

Emma Gordon Laing

Emma Laing's writing, like that of so many women of her era, was
prone to what a modern reading sees as melodrama. But her own sincerity,
and the effect of her words on her husband, cannot be doubted—she
nearly brought him back from the desert when, at Ghadames, he
unwrapped the ivory miniature and read how much she missed him. But
in ending this letter with such heartrending words, she indicates that
somewhere deep in her heart, perhaps she doubted she would ever see
her husband again.

The letter was never delivered, because Laing was not in Ghadames
to receive it. Some years later, all these documents found their way back
to Tripoli, where they were returned to the British consulate. Rather than
restore Emma's letter to his daughter, Warrington filed it in the consular
archives. Of the many letters she is known to have sent to Laing on his
long journey, it is the only original known to have survived.

Christmas of 1826, a year beyond the Christmas Laing had promised
he would be back in her arms, was a black time for Emma. In a tiny consular community prone to little cheer even in the best of times, rumors
of bad news circulated obscenely, their repetition the major pastime of
bored consuls and their hapless wives. Though the Warrington parents
conspired with their other children to shelter Emma as much as possible
from lurid speculation about Laing's fate, averted faces, whispering that

stopped at her approach, and looks of pity from her mother's friends, even if inadvertent, must have been daily trials for her.

Concern about Laing had been growing in Consul Warrington's mind from the day he learned of the Tuareg attack, and he took advantage of his frequent audiences at the Castle to pump Yusuf Bashaw (whose "desert grapevine" was unsurpassed) for news. By the first days of the new year Warrington was becoming visibly worried. He put increasing pressure on the bashaw and his foreign minister to find out what had happened to Major Laing. After all, the British government had paid Tripoli's ruler handsomely to assure Laing's safety, and Warrington believed that Karamanli's influence extended much farther than it really did. In Warrington's mind, all answers lay at the Castle.

In the early months of 1827, as rumors of Laing's death circulated among the elites of Tripoli, Emma, finding the labored optimism of her parents intolerable, turned for sympathy and understanding to Timoléon Rousseau, eldest son of the French consul, who had long sought to marry her, starting his courtship of her well before Laing's arrival in May 1825.

Emma was usually not permitted to leave home unchaperoned, but now an exception was made. Though Warrington despised Timoléon, he let him take his daughter on long walks in town. The English Garden, though beautiful, was a lonely place, and Warrington understood that Emma found relief by losing herself in the crowds and bustle of the old city, in the company of the only male friend close to her own age.

Nearly four months after his departure, at the end of February 1827, Warrington's courier returned from Ghadames "without news, except that the letters to Major Laing had been forwarded south." This was a blow to Warrington. He had hoped Jacob would find Laing in Ghadames and that they would return together. By now gossips in Tripoli spoke openly of Laing's "disappearance" and the mystery surrounding his fate.

It was Warrington's nature to believe in plots, in part because of his long service in Tripoli, where conspiracies were always in the air. The paucity of news about Laing and the failure of any of his letters, journals, or papers to materialize led Warrington to suspect that a conspiracy hatched by his archenemy, Baron Rousseau, with the complicity of the bashaw or his intermediaries, must be responsible for Laing's misfortunes. He began to imagine Yusuf Bashaw guilty of treachery, focusing his wrath mainly on one of the bashaw's principal aides, his Francophile foreign minister, Hassuna D'Ghies.

In March 1827, Warrington's pressure on Yusuf Bashaw began to yield results. The ruler provided him with a poor English translation of a letter (but not a copy of the original) from a certain Mohammed el Washy, probably a merchant, undated, but addressed from Ghadames.

> *To His Highness The Bashaw saluting &c:*
>
> *Respecting what you have written me, regarding the Christian & desiring me to send to Inquire about Him & to obtain certain news I prepared every thing to set off, & Provision I had sent on, & we intended to start in the morning, when there arrived some People in the Eveng. from Tuat, by which I received a Letter from my Friend, mentioning that the Christian was Dead after His arrival at Tombuctoo who came with the son of Sheikh Mocktar & after their arrival the Felata took Tombuctoo, & demanded that the Christian should be sent away, otherwise they would Plunder the Town.*
>
> *When the People of Tombuctoo found that the Felata were determined to have Him, they assisted Him to escape & gave Him a Man to conduct Him to Banbarra, the Felata hearing this followed Him on the road & Killed Him. This is the true news, & come from God.*

Just after this document arrived from Ghadames, the bashaw also forwarded a longer missive from Mohammed bin Mokhtar, who had helped conduct the injured Laing from his late father's camp in the desert to the gates of Timbuktu.

> Then it was that he [Laing] entreated us to send him with an escort to Timbuctoo, and to trust him to his fate. . . . [T]hen we gave him camels and confided him to one of our cousins, who accompanied him to Timbuctoo without the least disagreeable accident.
>
> About their arrival at Timbuctoo, came the letter of Hammed Ben Mohammed Labbou, a Tollany [probably Fulani], who possesses and resides upon the territory of Jeuni and that neighbourhood, in which he advises and commands to prevent the passage of Chris-

tians who come by sea to the interior of Soudan from Timbuctoo and from all places under their dominion. . . .

He adds that this hindrance is ordered by the Sovereign of the Faithful Sultan Mohammed Bello, who gives him to understand the intention of the Christians, and says that Soudan is feeble, and that the consequences of these visits of the Christians will be mischievous, and the cause of perpetual war.

Then at the arrival of this order, the chief persons of Timbuctoo were embarrassed between obedience to the order of their new Sovereign, and the consideration they had for our recommendation. In order to reconcile the two interests, they permitted him to remain at Timbuctoo about a month, without allowing him to pass by water, until he met with the enemy of God and his prophet, Hamed Ben Abayd Ben Rachal El Barbuchy, who persuaded him that he was able to conduct him to Arawan, from thence in order to embark at Sansandyng, and thence to continue his road to the great ocean.

They departed from Timbuctoo together. When they reached almost half way, this guide ordered his negroes to seize the traveller in a cowardly manner, and to put him to a cruel death. . . . After this shocking action he searched his baggage. Every thing of a useless nature, as papers, letters, and books, were torn and thrown to the wind, for fear they should contain some magic, and the articles of value were retained. This is the faithful history of the circumstances. He who adds to or takes from these particulars does not declare the truth.

Warrington was aghast. Who was Hamed Ben Abayd Ben Rachal El Barbuchy? This was a name unknown in Tripoli. And how could anyone expect him to believe that one Muslim would denounce another powerful Muslim as "the enemy of God and his prophet"? Surely, too, it was perfectly improbable that a Muslim sheikh writing to the Muslim ruler of Tripoli would privately mourn the death of a Christian? The letter had to be a piece of showmanship intended for English eyes, Warrington believed. The death of a Christian was usually a cause for rejoicing. Warrington was not sure what or whom to believe. Dutiful consul that he was, he sent copies of both letters to the Colonial Office under the following cover letter to Earl Bathurst:

> *Tripoli, 31st March, 1827*
>
> *My Lord,*
> *I have the honor to refer your Lordship to [attached letters] being copies of two letters His Highness's Minister brought to me this morning. In the evening arrived my Dragoman & Jacob (Clapperton's late servant) who placed in my hands [more letters] evidently being meant as justification for having quitted their Post.*
> *It is indeed My Lord sad news, & although not confirmed to the full extent I do fear it is but too true—but I pray to God Almighty that it may prove otherwise . . .*

Warrington doubted the sheikh had written to the bashaw quite as the letter alleged. Indeed, everyone in Tripoli's consular community knew that the bashaw, at this period, was fearful he would be indicted as an accessory to Laing's death by the British government, and that he tried hard to appear well disposed toward Laing. But there was someone else at court who was *not* fond of Laing, or anyone English, and this man now found himself the target of Warrington's ire.

The British consul, distrusting the letters and angered beyond endurance by the delays in receiving Laing's dispatches and obtaining reliable news about him, demanded a special audience with Yusuf Bashaw, which was granted on April 20, 1827. On entering the throne room, "it must have been immediately apparent from his demeanour that Colonel Warrington meant business," according to a memorandum of the meeting written by his vice-consul, Giacomo Rossoni.* "The Bashaw's impassive countenance, schooled as it was by race, training and tradition, betrayed no emotion, but his hand, as it stroked his beard, had the tremor that in

---

* Rossoni was an Italian who served as British vice-consul at Benghazi. A number of Warrington's deputies over the years were third-country nationals hired in Tripoli to assist him in his ministerial duties. Rossoni was undoubtedly the most skilled of these, a man with contacts all over the Mediterranean who provided the British government with invaluable intelligence Warrington could never have gathered alone. Warrington liked him and often invited him to stay at Tripoli, a happy reprieve from his dreadfully hot and isolated post.

a man of another faith might have denoted alcoholism [the bashaw had a well-known fondness for brandy]. When the Bashaw began to prevaricate, the Consul abandoned diplomatic language and attacked Hassuna directly."

Hassuna D'Ghies, the bashaw's foreign minister, was the son of Mohammed D'Ghies, once Tripolitania's prime minister. In 1818 Hassuna, still a young man, had been sent to Europe by his parents to complete his education, and he stayed in France for several years, learning to speak French fluently. He earned unwelcome notoriety in Marseilles for his "extravagance and folly," becoming an early-day Arab playboy, "offering the ladies perfumes and shawls," according to the French newspaper *Le Sémaphore de Marseille*.

From Marseilles he went to London, steeped in debt, escorted by "women and creditors." His preoccupation with money problems combined with his affinity for the French may have motivated Hassuna, according to Warrington's hypothesis, to hinder Laing and other British explorers from penetrating into the interior. British influence, as he well knew, could eclipse the French in their efforts to colonize Africa and possibly presage the demise of the slave trade, an important source of his personal wealth. Upon his return to Tripoli (in November 1825), Hassuna was named minister for foreign affairs by Yusuf Bashaw. Hassuna had family ties with the Karamanlis, as well as wide-ranging business interests in Tripoli and Ghadames.

Consul Warrington had been wary of Hassuna from the day of his appointment. Hassuna did little to conceal his preference for all things French to Britain and the British. Moreover, his post gave him access to incoming documents, including letters or dispatches Laing might have sent home with any merchant doing business with the Castle, or any minor functionary of the bashaw's government. Warrington also knew that Hassuna was heavily in debt and needed money urgently—he owed 60,000 francs to the French consul alone.

That April day in the Castle, Warrington was livid. He suspected that Hassuna had intercepted official communications from Laing to His Britannic Majesty's government. "From Laing's remarks in the few despatches which had been received from him, it was obvious that other despatches had not arrived," Rossoni recounted. Where were they? What explanation could Hassuna give for the delay in delivering Laing's letters and dispatches?

At first, Hassuna was evasive, but Warrington was in no mood to put up with half-truths. He pressed hard. "Hassuna's face assumed a yellowish, unhealthy tinge. Cornered, he muttered in Arabic, 'Well, it is no great matter after all.' The Bashaw, angered by his minister's loss of face, was stung out of his impassivity. He raved at Hassuna in the same language. 'No great matter, indeed! No great matter. . . .' The minister shrank away, appalled by the Intensity of his Master's Rage, as His Highness added that he would appoint another to be his Intermediary with the British Consul."

The bashaw was in an unenviable position. European explorers had died before, but never with such alarming consequences. It is entirely possible that he did not have the slightest idea what had happened to Laing or his papers, and he probably could not begin to understand the tremendous importance his quixotic British consul attached to them.

While Britain's energetic activity to suppress the slave trade in the 1820s was far from effective, the diplomatic and military operations undertaken on behalf of this effort led Whitehall to much greater involvement in African affairs. Lord Bathurst was especially interested in acquiring new domains for his king to serve as bases for suppressing the "traffick" and for stimulating replacement commerce. He succeeded brilliantly—adding Sierra Leone in 1808; the Gambia in 1816; and the Gold Coast in 1821 to the burgeoning British Empire.

British naval squadrons touring the coast of Africa, stopping and inspecting suspected slavers of other nations and forcing African tribal chiefs to sign antislavery treaties, while they did not halt the expansion of the slave trade, helped Britain attain a commanding position along the west coast. This contributed to the expansion of England's commercial and colonial territory.

The importance attached to the work of African explorers in London and Paris cannot be overstated. Africa was the last continent to be carved up into colonies, and by 1825 competition for territory was fierce. In the early 1800s, colonial possessions in Africa were few, limited to the littoral, with large sections of the coastline and all the interior kingdoms still untouched. By 1900 Africa would be divided into families of separate possessions under the administration of European nations (with hardly any exceptions—independent Morocco and Ethiopia come to mind). Competition from the French was particularly worrisome to the British, for France was the lone European nation that had established a beachhead in Islamic North Africa.

The journals, maps, notes, and drawings of explorers like Laing and Clapperton had tremendous value in furthering political and economic agendas in Africa. These documents were literally worth more than their weight in gold to Britain and France. Lives were willingly sacrificed for them. They were road maps to a part of the globe less known than the surface of the moon. The moon, at least, could be surveyed with telescopes.

WHEN WARRINGTON RETURNED to his consulate after his explosive visit with the bashaw, a visitor was announced. It was the disgraced minister, Hassuna, who began to babble apologies and excuses in English. "Hassuna came & cried like a child & actually supplicated my Forgiveness & Protection on his Knees," Warrington wrote later that day to Bathurst. "I told him it was my Religion to return Good for Evil, & however Shameful his conduct had been, that my influence should be exerted in his favor, altho' I could not transact Business with him any longer in Person."

Hassuna's agitation was great and his anguished beseeching continued. "The ravings were incoherent. Then to the unspeakable confusion of everyone present, Hassuna threw himself at the Consul's feet, imploring his Protection and Forgiveness," Rossoni reported. "Colonel Warrington recoiled. . . . At last, shaking with emotion, he choked 'Get up, Sidi Hassuna! If you must kneel, kneel to your God alone.' The trembling Wretch rose and, still babbling incoherently, made his way to the door."

Though he reported to Whitehall that he could not decipher Hassuna's wild talk, the episode increased Warrington's anxiety about Laing's fate, a sense of unease that was already intense following the evasive circumlocutions he had heard from the lips of Yusuf Bashaw. He had well-framed concerns: Laing's whereabouts and the state of his continued exploration, whether he was alive or dead, the fate of his journals—where were the detailed and truthful answers to these questions?

Warrington pressured the bashaw to use all his powers to gather more information about Laing. He blamed the delay on the bashaw's well-known tendency to procrastinate even under the best of circumstances, and on a growing presentiment of what he began to call in his dispatches "some Foul and Underhand Work."

The Colonial Office shared the consul's apprehension. To give force to Warrington's protests at the Castle, and to provide incentive for the bashaw to produce Laing's papers, if he had them, Lord Bathurst directed three British frigates to call seriatim at Tripoli on "courtesy visits." All were well armed.

While efforts to obtain authentic news of Laing met little success, the curiosity of Europe's major newspapers made his fate a topic of international interest. In Paris, where there was fierce Anglo-French rivalry to send the first explorer to Timbuktu (and, indeed, to control all of West Africa), public discussion of Laing's expedition was as intense as in London. Then, to everyone's surprise, on May 2, 1827, Laing's death was stated as a fact on the authority of extracts from a letter published in the Paris daily, *L'Etoile*.

The letter was written from Sukhara-Ley, Tripoli, on April 5. Its opening words were painfully blunt: *"Le major Laing dont on avait annoncé la fin tragique, a réellement péri victime de sa courageuse persévérance, après pu néamoins visiter la fameuse ville de Tombuctou. Le pacha de Tripoli a communiqué cet avis d'après une lettre que . . . son vassal lui a écrite. . . ."*

The report went on to detail significant facts that, to British observers, raised more alarms. First, Sukhara was the name of the country house in the *menshia* occupied at the time by Baron Rousseau, the French consul at Tripoli. It was therefore assumed that the letter must have some real foundation, since Rousseau was a man of some stature,[†] with excel-

---

* "Major Laing, whose tragic death now appears beyond any doubt, apparently fell victim to his own courageous determination to visit the famous city of Timbuktu, an effort in which he apparently succeeded. The bashaw of Tripoli made public this news after having received a letter confirming it from one of his vassals." In light of subsequent events, it is notable that the French paper acknowledged that Laing had succeeded in reaching Timbuktu. France would later claim Caillié got there first.

† Joseph-Louis Rousseau was born in Paris in 1780, the son of Jean-François-Xavier Rousseau, French consul general at Baghdad, a distant relation of the more famous Jean-Jacques Rousseau, the philosopher.

lent contacts, and that the information had been supplied to Rousseau by a third party, most likely his friend Hassuna D'Ghies, whose position as foreign minister enabled him to get information from the interior more quickly than anyone.

Second, Warrington had yet received no official confirmation of Laing's death. How could a Paris newspaper confirm as fact what was only rumor in the British consulate? Third, the letter carried a strange and seemingly unnecessary emphasis on the improbability of recovering Laing's papers. How could anyone know this, the British queried, unless that person already knew where the papers were?

Warrington's steely and accusing gaze now shifted from Hassuna to the French consul, Joseph-Louis, Baron Rousseau.

ROUSSEAU WAS not only an expert in Middle East affairs, he was an avid writer on the subject. At one time, according to gossip making the consular rounds in Tripoli, he had expropriated the work of another French consul, one Monsieur de Coruncy, on the subject of an obscure biblical sect (the Rechabites), claiming it as his own. Warrington's deputy, Giacomo Rossoni, who had reliable sources on both sides of the Mediterranean, also believed that Rousseau had purloined not only the text but the drawings and plans of a young Frenchman who had written a history of Syria, where the young man had been employed for several years as a surveyor. Baron Rousseau had published this work on Syria under his own name, Rossoni claimed, "thus defrauding the author of merit and money alike."

Warrington surmised that Rousseau would have found Laing's papers a tempting target, both from a personal point of view and to appear to deny the British the prize of reaching Timbuktu first. As soon as he read the account in *L'Etoile,* Warrington demanded another audience at the Castle. At this meeting, Hassuna, who had been restored as foreign minister, denied any connection to the French newspaper article and "expressed his disbelief in its veracity."

Warrington hypothesized that Laing's journals, far from disappearing, had been stolen from the explorer's equipage and sent by secret messenger to Tripoli, where Hassuna D'Ghies had passed them on to his friend Baron Rousseau, probably to help defray his crippling debts. This scenario was not far-fetched. Clapperton's journal had been stolen in Jaza, and the doings of foreign explorers were of enough interest that their papers could (and often did) attract the attention of opportunistic thieves.

The consul's concerns were honed by the absence of additional information. His exaggerated sense of the extent of the bashaw's influence, which he believed actually did stretch to Timbuktu, had led him to suspect either that the bashaw knew what had transpired and was deliberately concealing it, or that he could easily find it out if he wanted to. Incensed at the unbroken silence, Warrington turned the chance visit of any British naval vessel to Tripoli into an opportunity to put pressure on the bashaw. As the bashaw likely did not have the slightest idea what had happened to Laing, and the naval pressure produced no results, Warrington began to attribute increasingly sinister motives to the infuriating silence.

A year passed. The strain in the Warrington household was becoming intolerable. Compounding Warrington's anguish, Emma, in despair, rekindled Timoléon Rousseau's interest in her, resuming their long trysts in the English Garden and at Sukhara, which she often visited without escort. The French consul's son had proposed to her months before Laing's arrival in 1825, and his intense passion for her had never ceased, even after her marriage. Though Warrington loathed Timoléon, he did not have the heart to refuse his daughter permission to see the one person whose company seemed to give her some comfort. Emma and Timoléon spent long afternoons together. It is likely, too, that Emma, certain now that Laing was dead, hinted to her father that a marriage to the baron's son would not be unwelcome.

On March 3, 1828, the French consul buttonholed Warrington a second time with a proposal that they unite their families by the marriage of their children. Warrington explosively lost his temper and, in a rage, demanded that Rousseau get out of his house, nearly coming to blows with him. Emma's distress was not reason enough for her father to become party to what he took to be the criminal acts of a duplicitous French fop. What is more, he had no incentive to forestall the scandal that was about to erupt.

Hoping to make his second refusal of Timoléon less painful, Warrington suggested that Emma "look with favor" upon Thomas Wood, his new vice-consul at Benghazi and a man he had long admired. Her feelings, apparently, were not consulted.

On April 22, 1828, HMS *Eros* sailed into Tripoli from Malta, her captain carrying a letter to the bashaw from Lord Bathurst. This document, sharply worded, was personally delivered by Warrington, according to his vice-consul "with a strong remonstrance to the effect that unless satisfactory news of Major Laing and Captain Clapperton [who was by now himself long overdue] were given, and proper measures taken for their safe conduct to Tripoli, if alive, and the preservation of their papers and property, if dead, he should, within four days, strike his flag." This would effectively sever diplomatic relations between the two nations at a time when the bashaw was deeply apprehensive about French intentions in North Africa.

At the eleventh hour on the appointed day, a reply came from the Castle admitting for the first time that Laing was dead, adding that the bashaw had already sent messengers across the Sahara to ascertain the true facts and gather up missing details.

Four months later, on August 28, 1828, Sheikh Babani's nephew, Alkhadir, accompanied by Bongola, the freed slave, appeared at the English Garden. Alkhadir told his story, which ended with Laing's departure from Timbuktu, but Bongola claimed definitively that Laing had been murdered.

Blinded by tears, Hanmer Warrington listened while shuffling through the pair of letters Alkhadir had brought him. Though distracted and agitated, he was alert enough to notice that the letters had been opened and that the dispatches from Timbuktu, which Laing had said in earlier letters that he would give to Alkhadir, were missing.

Though he could not detain Alkhadir, Warrington kept Bongola at his estate in the *menshia* under unofficial house arrest. Consular archives show that Bongola was extensively questioned by Warrington on September 1, 1828 (nearly two years after Laing wrote his last letter). This is the transcript Warrington's clerk kept of the interrogation:

> "What is your name?"
> "Bongola."
> "Were you a servant to Major Laing?"
> "Yes," [replied Bongola, producing a document that read:]

Azoad, July 23, 1826

I promise to pay Bearer, Bongola, the sum of 6 Dollars per month from the 15 Dec. 1825 'till my return to Ghadames. . . . A. Gordon Laing.

"When did you enter the service of Major Laing?"

"From Tripoli, as I went with Babani, Major Laing's conductor."

"Were you with Major Laing at the first attack?"

"Yes, and wounded," [Bongola replied, showing his head.]

"Did you remain with Major Laing at Mokhtar's camp?"

"Yes."

"Did you accompany Major Laing to Timbuctu?" [Warrington asked.]

"Yes," [replied Bongola.]

"How was Major Laing received by the natives of Timbuctoo?"

"He was received well."

"How long did he remain in Timbuctoo?"

"About two months."

"Did you leave Timbuctoo with Major Laing?

"Yes."

"Was Major Laing obliged to leave Timbuctu?"

"Major Laing wished to go."

"Who went with you?"

"A *koffila* of Arabs."

"In which direction did you go?"

"The sun was on my right cheek."

"Did you know where you were going?"

"To Sansanding."

"Did you see any water, and did you proceed without molestation?"

"We saw no water, we passed unmolested during the day, but on the night of the third day, the Arabs of the country attacked and killed my master."

"Was the attack on the *koffila* or only against your Master?"

"I do not know."

"Was any one killed besides your master?"

"I was wounded but cannot say if any were killed."

"Were you sleeping alongside your Master?"

"Yes."

"How many wounds had your master?"

"I cannot say, but all with swords, and in the morning I saw that his head had been cut off."

"Did the person who had charge of your master commit the murder?"

"The sheikh who was the person who accompanied my master killed him, being assisted by his black servants by many cuts of the sword."

"What did the sheikh then do?"

"He went on to his country. An Arab took me back to Timbuctoo."

So Laing's fate had been determined at last. Now the recovery of his papers became more compelling than ever, the more so when, in October 1828, the French explorer René Caillié returned to Toulon professing to have visited Timbuktu. Many Frenchmen, not to say Englishmen, doubted Caillié's claim.*

For the present, with Laing certainly dead and his papers, notes, maps, drawings, and other materials lost, the French explorer might be proved right, and the French people might wrongly get the honor due to Great Britain and her dead son.

While this predicament vexed Lord Bathurst, it was intolerable to the vitriolic Warrington, nearly to the point of driving him insane. *Where were Laing's papers?* They had to be found! Laing's property, especially his papers, belonged *to England.* Consul Warrington was determined to find them.

---

* Much later, when he published his book, Caillié acknowledged he heard talk of Laing when he reached Timbuktu, and that he never doubted that the Englishman had preceded him there.

Chapter Nineteen

---◆---

THE LOST PAPERS

W HILE THE LAING CONTROVERSY SIMMERED, René
Caillié, an impoverished and unknown Frenchman, reached
Timbuktu and returned safely to Europe. From childhood
Caillié "had always had an *idée fixe* about Timbuktu." He was the son of a
poor man sentenced to twelve years' imprisonment for stealing six francs.
His mother died when he was eleven. At the age of sixteen, Caillié sailed
for Saint-Louis as an officer's servant. Before he was twenty he had twice
visited Senegal. In 1824 he began to prepare for his journey to Timbuktu
by learning to speak Arabic and studying Islam, memorizing long passages
from the Koran.

Posing as an Arab traveling to Egypt, he left the coast of West Africa
in April 1827. His difficult journey was interrupted by five months of illness, and it took him seven months to negotiate the terrain. He entered
Timbuktu on April 20, 1828 (616 days after Laing's arrival). He stayed for
two weeks (less time even than Laing), then crossed the Sahara, reaching
Tangier on September 7, where he lay hidden in the French vice-consul's
house until he could be smuggled safely aboard a French ship. He, rather

*René Caillié, the man who returned
to tell the story of Timbuktu,
as he appeared in the frontispiece
of his 1830 book* Travels
through Central Africa to
Timbuctoo.

than Laing, won the award of 10,000 francs offered by the French Société Géographique for the rediscovery of Timbuktu.

Though Laing had been there first, he had failed to return alive, thus forfeiting the prize.

These developments, on top of everything else, made 1828 a miserable year for His Britannic Majesty's consul general at Tripoli. Warrington passed his days waiting and watching, while devoting his nights to consoling his widowed and grieving daughter. With the interrogation of Bongola on September 1, any lingering hope for Laing's safe return had died. Though he trusted Bongola no more than any other black man (which is to say not at all), the evidence of the freed slave did not seem to have been fabricated, and it could bear no other interpretation.

Laing was truly dead, murdered, so much appeared to be fact. But knowing Laing's fate offered no relief, no sense of closure, because his journals were still missing. Though it must have pained him to think it, Warrington understood that Laing's papers were far more important, from the standpoint of the British Lion, than the explorer himself. It was the consul's duty now, as his heart grieved for his son-in-law, to do everything in his power to retrieve them, and he devoted himself to the job with all his stupendous vigor.

If the journals of the articulate and observant Scot could be recovered, their author's fame as a great explorer would be unassailable and his country's honor saved. But where was Warrington to begin? He returned again and again to the testimony of Bongola. Bongola was the only eyewitness, not only to Laing's death but to what had happened to his belongings. Warrington reviewed the transcript tirelessly in his office.

"What property had your master when he was killed?"

"Two camels. One carried the provisions the other carried my master and his bags."

"Where were your master's papers?"

"I was so stunned with the wound I never thought of the papers."

"Were the papers brought back to Timbuctoo?"

"I dont know—they were in a skin of portfolios."

Why Laing's attackers spared Bongola could possibly be explained by the fact that he was a slave and therefore of no importance (though he had monetary value as a chattel). His story, perhaps revamped to exonerate himself of cowardice or negligence, was that he had been wounded in the attack and was so stunned that he did not see what happened to Laing's papers and other property.

Warrington later had the chance to reexamine Alkhadir (Babani's nephew), but all he gleaned from this was that Laing was almost certainly dead and that among Laing's papers were three large notebooks, one with red and two with speckled bands. Laing had left several blank notebooks of the speckled-band variety at the English Garden, and when Warrington produced one and asked whether it resembled the others, Bongola and Alkhadir both replied that it was identical.

As soon as Bongola was free to wander about Tripoli, Hassuna D'Ghies got hold of him through a servant and offered to house and clothe him. Warrington, when he learned of this, was upset. He summoned Bongola back to the British consulate, but he was "fobbed off by Hassuna's servants with evasive replies," according to Rossoni, his vice-consul. When Warrington insisted on seeing Bongola again to continue interviewing him, the bashaw forced Hassuna to give him up, but it was obvious the freed slave "feared for his life."

Moreover, he now told an utterly different story—so different that Warrington concluded Bongola had been threatened, perhaps terrorized, by Hassuna. Bongola now claimed that he had not personally witnessed Laing's death and had no idea what had become of his papers. Warrington hastily arranged Bongola's passage on a British warship bound for Malta, accompanied by one of his trusted servants, charged with keeping an eye on him.

Safe in British-controlled Malta, Bongola recanted his second statement, claiming that Hassuna had taken personal possession of Laing's papers, and told him that if he, Bongola, breathed one word of this, Hassuna would burn him alive (not an idle threat in a country where this was not an uncommon fate for unruly slaves). Bongola could not explain how the documents had made their way back to Tripoli, but there was now little doubt in Warrington's mind that Laing's papers had reached the coast in July or August 1827, a year earlier, and were delivered to Baron Rousseau.

Other evidence seemed to confirm this. Abram Curriel, who had been Rousseau's servant for eight months, claimed that toward the end of September 1827 Rousseau had had a conversation with Hassuna D'Ghies in the gallery of the French consulate. (This edifice in Tripoli, like the British consulate, had a large central atrium three stories high, with interior galleries on the upper floors giving access to it, allowing for circulation of air in that era before motorized fans. Unlike Warrington, Rousseau often used his consulate as his residence, though he, too, had a country house in the *menshia*.) According to Curriel, Rousseau said, "Do not be afraid of anything when I give you my word." But Hassuna seemed not much reassured by this pledge, and after some whispered arguing, Hassuna left the consulate.

That night Rousseau went to Hassuna's house, accompanied by Curriel and a French guard. Hassuna was in bed, but was roused by his staff. Curriel heard Rousseau say to Hassuna: "On my word and honor, no one shall hear anything of it." But Hassuna still was not comfortable. The next day, Curriel heard Rousseau give orders to his son, Timoléon (who sometimes served as his secretary), to draft an official demarche to the bashaw about Hassuna's personal debts to him. At that moment a letter came from Hassuna. Rousseau opened it, and immediately countermanded his order to Timoléon.

That evening Baron Rousseau again visited Hassuna. This time their conversation was friendly, and the next morning Hassuna again called at the French consulate. He rushed upstairs and went into the open gallery. From another floor, across the atrium, Curriel saw Hassuna and Rousseau sitting together on a sofa. He claimed to have observed Hassuna take three packages of papers from his robes, each about fourteen inches long and six inches thick.

"I hope no one will find out about these," Hassuna said. Rousseau swore no one would. He also pledged to Hassuna that the financial claims against him would be "arranged." As soon as Hassuna left, Rousseau called all his servants together and ordered that if anyone called at the consulate, they were to say he was indisposed. For the next two days Rousseau shut himself up in his office, presumably studying documents.

Though Curriel's tale seems almost too pat, when Warrington heard it, Rousseau's guilt seemed beyond doubt to him.

By late October 1828, two years after Laing penned his last known letter, Warrington was committing his own poisonous thoughts to paper. In an official consular dispatch to Robert W. Hay, Bathurst's permanent undersecretary of state at the Colonial Office, he wrote:

> You are aware of the Miserable Intrigue carried on here, and I have cause to suspect the French Consul may have purloined the papers of Major Laing. . . . If His Majesty attaches any importance to the papers, and is pleased to demand their production, we shall obtain them, I am fully certain. We know Mr. Rousseau to be a man replete in intrigue and what could be easier than with the connivance of the Minister [Hassuna D'Ghies] to intercept the papers. . . .

The oblique reference to King George was a clever way of raising the stakes of the contretemps with the bashaw and Rousseau. Warrington hoped to get a reply that would make the matter an issue of personal interest to his sovereign, thus increasing the pressure he could put on Yusuf Karamánli, who was very likely still bewildered by the importance Warrington attached to Laing's papers. By now through rumor, counter-rumor, accusation, and denial, the entire consular corps in Tripoli was drawn into the fracas. Warrington was supported by the Dutch consul, de Breughel, the Spanish consul, Joseph Gómez Herrador, and the whole British community. Rousseau and Hassuna D'Ghies, on the other hand, had a supporter in Charles D. Coxe, the recently arrived American consul, who, with the memory of the British capture and burning of the White House still fresh in his mind, loathed all things British.

Even if he was beginning to understand the international importance attaching to Laing and his papers, the bashaw was slow to help Warrington. He liked playing the British against the French, the only way, he thought, to keep either from making inroads in his own little corner of Africa.

Another painful year went by. Though Timoléon was still her constant companion in Tripoli, on April 14, 1829, Emma acceded obediently to her father's wishes and married his vice-consul in Benghazi, Thomas Wood, bowing to the parental authority that surely tormented her as much as her bereavement did.

In May 1829, Warrington reported to the Colonial Office that Hassuna D'Ghies was expecting not only a copy of the *History of Tomboucto* but also the arrival from Tuat of its author, one Sidi Ali Baba D'Arowan. Could this book, Warrington mused, be one that Laing had obtained in Timbuktu? He reminded Hay that Laing had written: "I have been busily employed during my stay, searching the records in the town, which are abundant, & in acquiring information of every kind, nor is it with any common degree of satisfaction that I say, my perseverance has been amply rewarded."

From this simple statement, Warrington took a leap: "We are surely justified," he concluded in his letter to Hay, "in believing that Laing was in possession of the *History of Tomboucto.*" Though not borne out by evidence or facts, it was but a quick step from this assertion to the inference that whoever possessed the *History of Tomboucto* also possessed Laing's journals. Moreover, circumstances pointed to the book having been in Rousseau's possession as far back as the previous July (while Laing's death was still debated in French and British newspapers). At the time, the baron had written to the *Bulletin de la Société Géographique* that he had obtained an Arabic volume on the history of Timbuktu. This suggested to Warrington that Rousseau had known far more than he had let on, and that he was now laying the groundwork for purloining Laing's work for dishonorable French ends.

Warrington was unwavering in his belief that foul play was involved, that Laing's journals had reached Tripoli, and that it was only a matter of pressuring Yusuf Bashaw to produce them. He decided, in June 1829, to do something more drastic than he had ever done before. "Driven beyond endurance," according to his vice-consul, Rossoni, Warrington struck his consular flag. He refused to communicate further with the Castle, effectively breaking diplomatic relations between England and Tripolitania.* He made arrangements for the Dutch consul to carry on all official business for the British with the bashaw. Warrington himself left town, retiring to his country villa in the *menshia*.

This development truly dismayed Yusuf Bashaw Karamanli. From his agents in Cairo, he had learned that the French were planning to invade Algeria (which they did, in 1830), and were proposing to the ruler of Egypt, Muhammad Ali Pasha, that he occupy the bashaw's throne. Loss of Great Britain's support at this critical time might be fatal to his dynasty. He sent Warrington a note declaring that he would rather "sacrifice his son . . . than go to war with England."

Meanwhile, Baron Rousseau was growing tired of what he construed to be British slander. On June 17, he wrote a furious letter to Warrington saying that he had learned "by the public voice" that Warrington had named him "more than once in the affair" of Laing's papers, and that Warrington had alleged a conspiracy between himself and foreign minister Hassuna D'Ghies. He demanded an explanation, and he ended: "Have the goodness to answer me in Italian; for I repeat what I have so often told you: I have no one about me who knows enough English to translate to me your letters; whilst amongst those employed in the British consulate several are to be found [he probably meant Rossoni] who talk and write fluently the first of those languages and even the French."

Warrington replied the same day that he did not feel called upon, in his official capacity, to "give the slightest information or to accede to the Baron's request," as probably that might defeat his goal, namely, the recovery of the journal and manuscripts belonging to the missing English explorer. "Permit me to say," he concluded caustically, "that I shall still assume the privilege of writing in my native language."

The situation was now ripe for the sort of conspiracy that came so naturally to Tripoli's steamy climate. Warrington regularly met in secret at the English Garden with messengers carrying news to and from Tripoli, some inspired by the Castle and repeated in the bazaars; it was one of many ways he kept his finger on the pulse of the country. It seemed to

---

* Warrington took this decision without instructions from Whitehall, a singularly bold (though possibly career-ending) move.

him that the bashaw, at last, had discovered the truth about Laing's murder and would be forced to reveal it. By now, Warrington had concluded that both Laing's death and the theft of his journal had been plotted in Tripoli, with the dire possibility that the bashaw himself had served as an accessory to Rousseau and Hassuna D'Ghies.

Supporting this hypothesis, on July 27 a sheikh "came to the English Garden and told Warrington that 'the Pacha [the bashaw] had given orders to the Head of a Tribe of Arabs to murder Major Laing on his road from Tripoli to Ghedamis'—that 'Alkhedir brought the papers down to Tripoli, and gave them to H. D'Ghies'—that 'they would not let Alkhedir deliver them to the Consul'—and that 'he learned all this from a Relation of Alkhedir who slept in his tents when the papers were brought down.'" Warrington faithfully recorded these tales, and forwarded them to London.

On August 5, 1829, nearly three years after Laing's death, Dr. John Dickson,* surgeon, Royal Navy, who was medical adviser to the bashaw, paid the ruler his customary annual visit to examine him. According to a report filed by Warrington, "after desiring Dr. Dickson to be seated, His Highness said: 'What I am going to say to you, you must consider as confidential and not to be repeated elsewhere.' Dr. Dickson agreed and His Highness continued: 'In two or three days the people of Ghadames, who are expected, will be down. If they declare that the papers of Major Laing were given to Sidi Hassuna and the French Consul, will the English Consul or Government have anything further to demand of me?'"

Dr. Dickson replied that he believed that if the papers were found and accounted for satisfactorily, that would make an end of "the differences existing between His Highness and the British Government, and he had no doubt that the flag would be immediately hoisted." But he added, in an interesting twist, "I cannot credit that the French Consul has done what Your Highness imputes to him with regard to the papers."

"By Allah, he has done it!" rejoined the bashaw. "And you will see it as I now tell you when these people come from Ghadames."

Dickson, perhaps just as the bashaw intended, immediately carried this news to Warrington.

---

*Not to be confused with Dr. Thomas Dickson, the Scottish surgeon who accompanied Clapperton.

This was indeed a sensational development. If true, it meant that the bashaw had turned against Rousseau and Hassuna D'Ghies, and that the way was now open for a rapprochement between the British consul and the Karamanlis, the possible recovery of Laing's papers, and the public humiliation of the French—a jolly prospect indeed. Warrington's hatred of Rousseau was far too rancorous for him to fail to embrace Dickson's story. He did not consider what, with hindsight, seems far more likely: that the bashaw was just up to his old trick, playing France against England while he stood aside, so that attention shifted from him. He had a favorite saying at the Castle: "When elephants choose to dance, it is the wise man who gets out of the way."

The bashaw hinted to Dr. Dickson that Hassuna might well seek asylum in the French or American consulate. In this, he was right. Hassuna persuaded Coxe to apply for a license to grant him the protection of the United States government. On the night of August 8, Hassuna was smuggled on board an American corvette dressed as an American sailor. The vessel sailed the next morning. When he learned of this, Warrington dashed off a note to Robert Hay: "I am apprehensive Mr. Rousseau will fly to America also, as soon as he hears his Infamous Villainy is detected."

The bashaw was silent when Warrington asked why he had not arrested Hassuna before he could escape. The plain implication, in Warrington's mind, was "that His Highness was too deeply involved." Yet Yusuf Bashaw was prepared to throw a bone England's way: Hassuna's brother, Mohammed D'Ghies, was soon arrested. After a stretch in the Castle's dungeons, Mohammed made a confession declaring that Laing's papers were brought to Tripoli and given to Hassuna, who then sold them to Rousseau.

To Warrington, this seemed conclusive proof of the collusion of Rousseau and Hassuna D'Ghies in the theft of the journals. The bashaw, sick of the whole affair and skittish about British hostility and the possibility of English warships in his harbor, decided to settle it the only way a Karamanli understood. With a well-armed vessel of His Britannic Majesty's Royal Navy anchored not a thousand yards from his throne room, he threw Hassuna and Mohammed D'Ghies to the wolves.

The bashaw sent for Warrington, the Dutch consul, de Breughel, and Warrington's vice-consul, Giacomo Rossoni. Summoning Mohammed D'Ghies, the elder brother of Hassuna and himself a former cabinet minister, Yusuf Bashaw drew his scimitar and in a melodramatic scene threatened the old man with decapitation on the spot if he did not confess to Hassuna's guilt. Thus threatened, Mohammed, who was aware that his brother was safe with the Americans, confessed to the crime. The bashaw could now sheathe his sword and wash his hands of the whole matter. Which he did.

The consuls drew up a document stating: "We, the Undersigned, declare that when, in the presence of His Highness, this 12th day of August 1829, His Highness said: 'Now I think that Hassuna D'Ghies and the French consul were the cause of the murder of Major Laing.'"

The next week, the bashaw made the document public. He recited Mohammed's confession and stated as fact that in exchange for Laing's papers the French consul had allowed 40 percent to be deducted from a large financial claim he had on Hassuna.

Vindicated, Warrington rehoisted the Union Jack and sent the warship back to Malta. Though there was little reason to accept Mohammed's confession as the truth, Warrington declared himself satisfied. The bashaw hailed Great Britain from the Castle with a thirty-three-gun salute. Normal diplomatic relations between Tripolitania and Great Britain resumed.

With Mohammed's confession in hand, Warrington took the logical next step, addressing a formal demand to the French consul in September for the restitution of Laing's journals. The Dutch consul, together with the Danish and Swedish and Sardinian consuls, paid a visit to Rousseau with Warrington's letter. Baron Rousseau replied that he was amazed that Warrington could accuse him of "receiving" Laing's papers. He denied having them, adding that he intended to prosecute Warrington before a French court for slandering him.

The consuls returned to the French consulate to confront Mohammed, who felt safer with Rousseau than in his own palatial villa, with his confession, which was written in Arabic. Mohammed now alleged that neither the writing nor the signature was his. With the consuls still present, he called for pen and paper and wrote a letter to the bashaw's son, Ali Bey, which he asserted would exonerate him, but which he refused to show to the assembled diplomats.

The next day, the consuls called on the bashaw *en banc* and announced to him that Mohammed now maintained his confession to be a forgery.

The bashaw, experienced practioner of political magic, speedily produced a letter that his son Ali Bey had momentarily received from Mohammed D'Ghies. In it, Mohammed claimed that when Baron Rousseau gave him sanctuary, he had made him promise to deny his confession as the price for his safety. Mohammed had been afraid, apparently, to make this assertion while in the French consul's house, and so resorted to the contrivance of a letter to the Castle to reveal "the truth."

Another day passed, and the already convoluted story took another bizarre twist. The consuls, now enlarged by the representatives of Spain, The Two Sicilies, Tuscany, and Portugal, paid a third visit to the bashaw, who laid before them yet another document signed by Mohammed D'Ghies, which read: "I hereby attest that the papers brought down by the people of Ghadames to my brother were those of the Major [Laing] and that he (my brother) told me he gave them to the French Consul." The bashaw then ordered the flag of the French consulate hauled down by his palace guard, thus breaking diplomatic relations with France.

Baron Rousseau, lurking behind the walls of his consulate, soon had a copy of the bashaw's declaration concerning Laing's murder. He was now entangled in a web of misunderstanding and intrigue from which it would be well-nigh impossible to extricate himself. Hassuna D'Ghies, his alleged coconspirator, was long gone, having fled the country (to Paris) with all the appearance of guilt. Though Rousseau was still the accredited French consular representative in Tripoli and entitled to all the courtesies and protection of his office, he had lived too long among Oriental potentates to feel secure. Reports of a French plan for the conquest of Algiers left Rousseau intensely anxious. The bashaw in his present mood might do anything to please the British. Consular immunity might provide little protection.

Warrington and the bashaw now addressed a protest to the American consul, Charles Coxe, for his intervention in granting protection to Hassuna, thereby allowing him to dodge Karamanli justice. Warrington wanted Coxe declared persona non grata, but wiser heads at the Castle prevailed. Consul Coxe said publicly only that he would not submit to the British consul's "dictation."*

---

*He later realized he had been duped and apologized to Warrington. "I have been most perfectly deceived and treacherously imposed upon in the matter of Hassuna," he wrote.

Further fueling the crisis, Mohammed D'Ghies was now also granted French asylum, since he had taken refuge with Rousseau. Mohammed's allegiences, it now seemed, might have been to the French all along, and his letter to the bashaw's son merely a ruse to throw the consular committee off the scent.

The French consul, at this point, received the following note from Warrington:

Sir,

I shall not disgrace my pen by addressing such a Convicted Villain, and with Infamy will I brand your name to the extremity of this World. I will, however, Glory in giving you Satisfaction, and, please God, sending you before a Tribunal where Treachery and Falsehood will avail you Nought, and where you will answer for your Unparalleled Iniquity.

As Rousseau instantly apprehended, this was nothing less than a challenge to a duel—Warrington was planning to publicly shoot him! The frazzled baron now grasped that he had only one option remaining if he valued his life. He stole away to the American consulate under cover of night, and the obliging Coxe smuggled him aboard an American merchant ship bound for France.

He had not yet played his last card. Before Baron Rousseau left Tripoli, he cleverly obtained a statement from Mohammed D'Ghies that his most recent confession had been extracted at gunpoint, a statement he left with Coxe, who made it public. As soon as Rousseau sailed, Mohammed denied the truth of this document also, and reaffirmed his previous confession. (Mohammed, it seems, while not steadfast as a witness, was certainly smart enough to produce whatever answer his current interlocutor wanted to hear, and to leave even his few adherents confused.)

The bashaw's hypothesis of Laing's murder had, weeks earlier, been forwarded to London by Warrington, where it prompted the British government to request that the Quai d'Orsay, seat of the French foreign ministry, undertake an investigation into the allegations against Baron Rousseau.

For France, Rousseau's exoneration became a matter of national honor. *L'affaire Laing* was now on the front page of every French newspaper. Jules, Prince de Polignac, the last French prime minister of the Restoration period, appointed a commission of inquiry chaired by one Baron Monnier, a distinguished Orientalist and diplomat. The Monnier Commission briskly concluded that the charges against Baron Rousseau lacked any foundation, and that it was improbable that Laing's journals had ever passed into the hands of Hassuna D'Ghies. Baron Monnier personally pronounced Rousseau innocent of all the charges on December 31, 1829.

Few in Europe accepted the verdict. On both sides of the Channel a consensus developed that Hassuna D'Ghies had stolen the Laing papers. In France, few doubted the culpability of D'Ghies; his long and disreputable history of gambling, womanizing, and defaulting on debts in Paris and Marseilles was well documented. Many Frenchmen were disposed to think him guilty of any crime attributed to him. There was also little confidence in Rousseau's integrity. In England, inevitably, most people dissented from the findings of the French commission.

The *British Quarterly Review* summed up most British and some French opinion when it wrote:

> Our conclusion, we must confess, is very different as regards both these persons [Hassuna and Rousseau]. So far from its being improbable, we think that it is morally certain that Hassuna D'Ghies, by fraud and perfidy, did obtain possession of Major Laing's papers. . . . But, admitting Hassuna to be guilty, what object, it may be asked, could make Baron Rousseau so anxious about getting possession of Major Laing's journals? The ambition of publishing the contents of the said papers in his own name. It seems he had already been dabbling in oriental literature, chiefly Arabic, and has been charged, with what truth we know not, of appropriating the labours of a young man in Syria, to himself.

AN ENGLISH EDITION of Caillié's two-volume work, *Travels through Central Africa to Timbuctoo; and across the Great Desert, to Morocco, performed in the years 1824–1828,* was published in London in 1830, the same year the original appeared in Paris. It was prefaced by an interchange between Edme-François Jomard, considered in France "the Very Incarnation of Geography," and Sir John Barrow, acknowledged in England as the nation's most eminent living geographer. They carried on a debate about Caillié and Laing, "beneath the graceful and pompous phrases of which a nasty under-current is evident."

The trouble, as far as the British were concerned, had little to do with geography or science. It was that Caillié was French, and that Laing, the Scot, had been robbed of his laurels. An English commentator wrote:

> A Frenchman, be it noted, not a German, or an Italian or a Dutchman, or a man of any other Christian nationality, *but a Frenchman!* The coincidence seemed so strange that he was at once denounced as an impostor. Thus many said he had been shipwrecked on the Barbary Coast and invented the whole yarn. Others, while admitting that he might have gone into the interior, denied his having been to Timbuktu. All attacked him for having disavowed Christ and travelled as a Musulman . . .

Warrington was naturally wary of René Caillié. The French vice-consul in Tangier who had sheltered Caillié was a man named Delaporte. And were not Hassuna D'Ghies and Delaporte "old and sworn friends?" According to the grapevine in Tripoli, they were. The consul "considered himself justified in forming his suspicions . . . and those suspicions would not be removed until M. Rousseau delivered the papers and gave a clear, circumstantial account of the fraud."

Warrington's views hardened. Laing had been murdered, he believed, and when the murder was reported, Rousseau—whose appetite for literary fame had been sharpened by information embodied in the letters Hassuna had expropriated during the course of Laing's journey—made every effort to seize Laing's other records. Warrington, in the end, seemed to believe that all of Tripoli was in on the conspiracy.

Meanwhile, encouraged by the findings of the Monnier Commission, which he interpreted as a vindication, D'Ghies went to London, where he presented himself to the Colonial Office as the innocent victim of the malevolent British consul in Tripoli, whose evil influence over the bashaw forced him to flee his own country. He produced "A Statement to the Right Honourable Lord Goodrich,* Secretary of His Britannic Majesty for the Colonies Concerning the Expedition of the late Major Laing to Tumbuctoo and the affairs of Tripoli By the Shereef Mahommed Hassuna D'Ghies late Minister of the Pacha of Tripoli." With its supporting documents, this formidable statement covered 227 pages in handwritten foolscap. It was a rambling indictment of Warrington, the bashaw, and the *Quarterly Review.* Hassuna accused Warrington of corruption and tyranny, a man "who had imagined the accusation about Major Laing in order to ruin Hassuna."

Hassuna, despite his anti-British sympathies, had a small coterie of friends in London. Backed by the more influential of these, he hoped to discredit Warrington and persuade the British government to use its influence to restore him to favor with the bashaw. Lord Goderich asked Major James Fraser to visit Tripoli to depose Warrington, who was expected to rebut Hassuna's charges.

Fraser, who had known Warrington for years, found that the consul had aged considerably. He now suffered from slight deafness, "always most apparent when his feelings are most excited." He is "irregular in his habits of business," said Fraser, "indiscreet in his communications, regardless of money to a degree that is painful to witness and cannot be justified by his circumstances, impetuous, even violent, where his feelings are excited or his duty concerned, yet provokingly indolent where they are not, and is on all occasions . . . incapable of small arrangements."

This was a polite way of saying that the consul was finally cracking up under the strain. But Fraser found it impossible "not to sympathize with the man so shamefully calumniated" and persuaded him to answer Hassuna's accusations. The consul was so frazzled that he could not reply coherently. He merely appended notes in the margins of Hassuna's diatribe.

"False, false, false," wrote Warrington.

"The more I see of the affair of Laing's papers," Major Fraser reported to the Colonial Office, "the more I am convinced of the Bashaw's hav-

---

* He meant Frederick John Robinson, Viscount Goderich, who succeeded Bathurst as secretary of state for war and the colonies in 1830. He later became First Earl of Ripon. His more famous son, also Lord Ripon, was viceroy of India and is remembered by Americans for resolving the "Alabama claims" arising out of the Civil War. Ripon Falls in Uganda is named for him.

ing . . . to conceal his own participation in this black business, and the warmer is my feeling towards poor Mr. Warrington." A month later, he said that he found no difficulty in believing that "some monstrous villainy had been committed or that Hassuna was implicated in it."

Warrington's actions in Tripoli frequently caused his masters in Downing Street uneasy moments, and as the years passed, the consul's blunders were the source of increasing official displeasure. There were many in London who privately wanted him sacked. One of these, who had befriended Hassuna D'Ghies and taken up his case in London, publicly called for Warrington to be removed from his post.

Yet firing Warrington would have been difficult, even for Viscount Goderich, a seasoned politician who had already served as prime minister and chancellor of the exchequer. The consul, in so many ways the incarnation of John Bull, had many supporters, in government and in the press. He was viewed as a patriot, defending England. Under these circumstances, and with rumored friends in Buckingham Palace, no one in Whitehall was prepared to criticize Consul Warrington too loudly, much less recall him.

After dragging on for another two years, the matter of Warrington's behavior was summed up by Goderich:

> I am by no means prepared to say our Consul of Tripoli may not, from excess of zeal, for the service of the government, and from a very natural eagerness in the pursuit of those persons who have been the cause of his Son-In-Law's death, and of the abstraction of his papers, have possibly adopted some erroneous conclusions and have occasionally acted with precipitation, although I must state, that after attentive perusal of the various papers which I have received from Mr. D'Ghies, I am wholly unable to discover what is the actual offence of which the Consul is asserted to be guilty. . . .

The quarrel between Britain, France, and Tripoli over Laing's vanished papers marked the beginning of the end for the Regency of Tripolitania and of the Karamanli dynasty. Indeed, by then the bashaw was foundering in a sea of other troubles. The traffic in Christian slaves, rich prizes from piracy at sea, large annual subsidies drawn from maritime powers for the security of their commerce—all these had slowly and inexorably dried up. Without these sources of revenue, the bashaw, addicted to an extravagant lifestyle, was probably doomed even before the Laing scandal.

Old, infirm, and growing daily more beset by controversies he could not truly fathom, he let control of his kingdom slip from his fingers. Already isolated in his palace, Yusuf Bashaw closeted himself with his harem, drinking brandy with three voracious and formidable concubines who squandered his money on jewels, alcohol, and their own numberless dependents. The country began to revert to the anarchy that had preceded Karamanli rule.

Meanwhile, the French took matters in Tripoli into their own hands. In August 1830 a French squadron consisting of a battleship, two large frigates, two corvettes, a brig, and a schooner appeared off Tripoli's Castle and threatened war if the bashaw refused to sign a treaty of peace. The squadron's advent was a direct result of *l'affaire Laing,* for French prestige had been sullied.

The treaty's first article was unambiguous: "His Excellency the Bashaw, Dey of Tripoli," it began, "will transmit to the Rear-Admiral commanding the French Squadron a letter signed by himself and addressed to H.M. the Emperor of France in which he will beg His Majesty to accept humble excuses in the circumstances which forced the [French] Consul General to quit his post."

In fact, the bashaw was told privately that he was expected to exonerate Baron Rousseau completely and absolutely. The Monnier report had cleared Rousseau of any crimes concerning Laing's papers and now France demanded reparation. The admiral's orders were not to negotiate, but to impose the following conditions:

> *First.* A public retraction of the accusations made by the bashaw against Rousseau, and a personal apology by either a son or nephew of the bashaw to Rousseau, on his return to Tripoli.
>
> *Second.* The immediate payment of the large sum of money owed, for a long period, by the bashaw to French creditors.
>
> *Third.* Complete abolition of piracy and the making of so-called Christian prisoners-of-war.
>
> *Fourth.* No increase under any pretext of the Bashaw's navy.

The bashaw was now "an elderly corpulent man," according to a contemporary observer, "who seemed very uneasy . . . being . . . disordered by a bad boil or carbuncle. He was growing tired of playing one Great Power against Another. Moreover, the French had only recently taken Algiers, and the Squadron looked very large by daylight."

Faced with the stalwart naval force in his harbor, the bashaw saw no alternative but to accept the crippling and humiliating French conditions. On August 11, he signed a new treaty. France was to be paid 800,000 francs, part of which was to be set aside for restitution to French creditors. Tripoli was also to accord once more to France her previous place as "most favoured nation" in precedence, a question that for over a hundred years had agitated French and British consuls.*

The fleet had barely cleared the horizon when an infuriated Warrington demanded an audience. He indignantly petitioned for the immediate retraction of Tripoli's acquiesence to French demands. This, the bashaw glumly told him, was impossible. Warrington, without informing London, struck his flag a second time, again severing diplomatic relations. He retired to the English Garden to sulk.

Yusuf Bashaw realized that he was now in deep trouble. He could not raise the large indemnity required by the French while his economy was in such a parlous state, not to mention the drain on his purse of perpetual tribal skirmishes in his hinterlands. News of the French capture and occupation of Algiers aroused fears of a Franco-Egyptian conspiracy to take over Tripolitania, especially if the British, his only ally, deserted him.

Fortunately for the bashaw, Warrington received a scathing rebuke from London for striking his flag without official orders. In November 1830, he resumed diplomatic relations, grudgingly and with a sour face. He presented the bashaw with a bill for immediate payment of 200,000 francs owed to British creditors. Warrington saw no reason why French

---

* In fact, then and now, almost every nation accords to any country with which it maintains diplomatic or consular relations "most favored nation" status, and the phrase carries little substance. The order of precedence of ambassadors and consuls is determined solely by the date of their arrival at post, not the *chaleur* (or *froideur*) of their relations with the host government. Warrington's decades of service at Tripoli had made him dean of the consular corps (and therefore the highest-ranking consul) many years earlier. He would retain that rank until his recall in 1846.

rather than British lenders should be paid first. Sadly, the old bashaw began to divest himself of the only assets remaining to him—his diamonds, his wives' jewelry, his precious stable of horses. A clique of his ministers even tried to persuade him to levy an additional tax on Tripoli's Jews, always the most vulnerable of the city's three main constituencies because they were neither Muslim nor protected by foreign warships.*

The row with the French was the last blow for the Karamanli dynasty, which had ruled Tripoli for 125 years. In 1835, Yusuf Karamanli was overthrown and Tripoli once again fell under direct Turkish rule. Stripped of his titles and his possessions, abandoned by his harem, the old man was repudiated by his own family and died in 1838, half starved and in rags, in a dank hovel a stone's throw from his former palace.

WITH THE PASSAGE OF YEARS, as other events attracted attention, the English public lost interest in Alexander Gordon Laing. But the British consul in Tripoli remembered. And he was grieved to realize that his son-in-law was forgotten.

"Let John Bull not forget the situation of poor Laing," he wrote years after Laing's disappearance, "whose every vein was letting blood in the cause for the benefit of mankind, and in forwarding what had been entrusted to him by his countrymen. His poor, poor bones lay whitening on the burning sands of Central Africa and none so poor to do him reverence."

---

*Modern readers, inured to daily accounts of Muslim-Jewish violence in the Middle East, should remember that Jews made up something like a quarter to a third of Tripoli's population during Yusuf Bashaw's long reign. They were an indispensable presence in the political, economic, and social fabric of the city. Though always vulnerable because of their religion and occasionally persecuted, many of Yusuf Bashaw's financial and political advisers were prominent Jews. The beleaguered ruler, usually so opaque to financial concerns, was far too astute politically to alienate his Jewish citizens at a time when he desperately needed good credit (which only they could provide—Muslim banks were nonexistent, and European banking had not then extended its reach beyond Malta). The idea of a special tax on Jews was a nonstarter and quickly fizzled. It was never implemented.

Chapter Twenty

———•◆•———

THE MYSTERY SOLVED

WHAT REALLY HAPPENED to Alexander Gordon Laing? It would take nearly a century for the full story to be revealed. Since Bongola's account was the only eyewitness report to survive, great weight has attached to his testimony. But how accurate was Bongola?

At the time of his examination by Warrington, Bongola was certainly fearful of how the bashaw and his foreign minister, Hassuna D'Ghies, might react. The evidence he gave about Laing was thus suspect in the mind of Consul Warrington.

If, in fact, the bashaw, Rousseau, and D'Ghies were not implicated in Laing's death but knew that Warrington suspected otherwise, their only interest would have been to make sure that Bongola told the truth. Under these circumstances, it is probable that he did so, though in several minor respects his story conflicted with other contemporary reports. Although these were not firsthand recitals, they called for a more critical review of Bongola's declaration. Every statement he made in his interrogation by Warrington was checked and confirmed. The only discrepancy adduced concerned the length of time he claimed Laing spent in Timbuktu—two months, an overstatement that cannot in fairness be held against a witness to whom chronological time meant very little.

There the matter of Alexander Gordon Laing's death and his lost papers rested for almost one hundred years. Although many hypotheses were advanced that the Laing journals reached Tripoli in 1827, no hard evidence ever surfaced either to confirm or to contradict the Monnier Commission's judgment that Baron Rousseau was not involved in Laing's death or the theft of his notes.

From time to time, relics of Laing were reportedly discovered in the wilderness. Caillié, less than two years after Laing's disappearance, wrote that "a Moor of Tafilet, who belonged to [my] caravan, had for his share of the spoil a sextant, which I was informed might be found in the country. As for the Major's papers and journals, they were scattered among the inhabitants of the desert. During my stay at Gourland, a village of Tafilet, I saw a copper compass of English manufacture. Nobody could tell me whence this instrument had come, and I concluded that it had belonged to Laing."

The two references to Tafilet are an indication that Sheikh El Abeyd's caravan was bound for Morocco. This is substantiated by Laing's report from Timbuktu that he had encountered Moroccan merchants there. In 1880, the Austrian explorer Oskar Lenz asserted that a sheikh of Arawan had a number of Laing's possessions, including "numerous bottles of medicine, clothes and underwear, written books and 45 Spanish Duros[*] in money."

Decades passed, and France emerged as the dominant colonial power in West Africa. In 1910, General François J. Clozel, the lieutenant governor of Haut-Sénégal-Niger, became intrigued by the Laing mystery. Hoping to prove incontrovertibly that his fellow Frenchman Caillié had been first to reach Timbuktu, Clozel ordered a new inquiry into Laing's death. He reckoned that some evidence of Laing's journey might be found, and that his journals, if they existed, could be retrieved. By this time, Timbuktu had become more accessible, part of the larger French sphere of

---

[*]Another term for a dollar. Spanish dollars, or "pieces of eight," were also known interchangeably in documents of this period as *pesos, duros, duros fuertes, thalers, dollars, and piastres,* and served as a kind of universal currency.

influence. A French army officer stationed in Algeria, Alexandre Bonnel de Mézières, was tasked with carrying out the investigation. Bonnel de Mézières was delighted with the assignment, for he was an amateur student of African history and had long been fascinated by the Laing story and the secrets that still shrouded it.

Bonnel de Mézières scoured the mosques and libraries of Timbuktu for evidence that Laing had been there, discovering among other things the mud house where Laing had resided. He found an eighty-two-year-old Timbuktu scholar, Mohammed Ould Mokhtar, who claimed to be the nephew of Sheikh Ahmadu El Abeyd, the Arab widely believed to have escorted Laing from Timbuktu and to have murdered him. Mohammed Ould Mokhtar told Bonnel de Mézières that his uncle had openly boasted of killing Laing. He enjoyed recounting to his extended family the bloody details of how he had, quite properly in his mind, slaughtered the infidel Christian.

According to this man, Laing, accompanied by his two servants, departed Timbuktu and went ahead of El Abeyd, following the road to Arawan. About thirty miles from Timbuktu they came to a place called Sahab, where they rested in the tenuous shade of an acacia tree. Suddenly four horsemen appeared: El Abeyd, one Mohammed Faradji Ould Abdallah, and two others. El Abeyd rode up to Laing and called on him to renounce his faith and accept Islam. When Laing refused, El Abeyd ordered his men to kill the white man, but they hesitated. When the sheikh insisted, two of his slaves seized Laing's arms and El Abeyd himself plunged a spear into Laing's chest, instantly killing him. Faradji then decapitated him. They also killed an Arab boy in Laing's party. Bongola was not mentioned in the Arab's account.

Excepting his money, all Laing's possessions, including his papers, were burned, for Sheikh El Abeyd feared their alleged magical properties. He divided the cash with his three colleagues. "After that," El Abeyd allegedly told his nephew, according to Bonnel de Mézières's account, "we burned his cases, because he had come to poison the land, and we held our noses as we burned them." The bodies were left unburied at the foot of a tree.

Bonnel de Mézières was struck by the marked differences between the narrative he obtained from the aging descendant of Sheikh El Abeyd and

Bongola's sworn testimony before Consul Warrington eighty-three years earlier. Bongola had stated that the attack occurred at night, when he was sleeping at Laing's side. Mohammed Ould Mokhtar's account (at second hand, of course, and nearly a century after the event) described an attack by day when Laing was resting under a tree, a demand that he should renounce his faith, and upon his refusal, the plunging of a spear into his chest. Bonnel de Mézières also wondered why only the Arab boy had been murdered, while Bongola had clearly survived and returned to Tripoli.

Bonnel de Mézières reasoned that the notion of Laing's two servants suffering with their master from the thrusts and slashes of the attackers' swords was consistent with a night attack, but not with an assault in daylight, when, typically, the infidel white man would have been singled out. Servants and slaves, after all, were valuable property and their lives would not have been squandered. Moreover, a night attack, like the one staged by Laing's Tuareg escorts near Wadi Ahnet, was typical of the country.

Bonnel de Mézières found two Arab manuscripts describing Laing's death, dated the year 1242 (corresponding to 1826 in the Christian calendar). Taken to the spot where the murder reputedly occurred, Bonnel de Mézières recovered skeletal remains from a shallow grave at the base of an ancient tree, which he photographed. The bones, mainly pieces of skull and vertebrae, were taken to an army doctor, who identified them as belonging to a European adult and an adolescent of indeterminate race. Respectful of the human remains he had found, Bonnel de Mézières ordered a miniature coffin constructed to contain them. Later the skeletons were interred in the local European cemetery.

Sheikh Ahmadu El Abeyd had bragged, his nephew claimed, that he left Laing unburied to be devoured by vultures. A passing Tuareg may have seen the bodies and buried them under the tree, not realizing that one was a Christian. (The corpses of Christians were believed by Arabs to be "unclean" and were typically not buried because they would render the earth infertile.)

Based on this evidence, Bonnel de Mézières pieced together an account of Laing's final days.

On September 21, 1826, after being warned by Sheikh Othman that he was not safe in Timbuktu, Laing gathered his belongings. He took the time to send a final letter to Warrington, his last known written

The small wooden coffin in which Laing's remains were re-interred by Bonnel de Mézières in 1912, after he concluded his forensic investigations.

words. He described his difficulties and announced his intention to head west toward Segou and the Atlantic, apparently abandoning his quest for the source of the Niger. Ever the optimist, he said he hoped to get there in fifteen days.

The most direct route to Segou was along the river and its banks, but since that path was overrun with Fulani, Laing would detour north into the desert and then west. Not suspecting the trap that lay ahead, he accepted the offer of an apparently friendly sheikh named Ahmadu El Abeyd to take him part of the way.

The next day, September 22, Laing likely left Timbuktu under the protection of Sidi Ahmadu, along with the ever-faithful Bongola and an Arab boy (possibly the source of the unidentified second skeleton). A day or two out of the city, Sheikh El Abeyd may have begun to argue with Laing about religion, urging him to embrace Islam, or he may simply have felt that Laing was worth robbing, or he may have been acting at the behest of unknown third parties. Soon they reached Sahab, thirty miles into the desert north of Timbuktu. There, Sheikh El Abeyd, either in someone's pay or acting out of his own religious zealotry, turned on Laing and knocked him off his horse, commanding him to renounce Christianity and accept Islam.

Laing refused. El Abeyd commanded his servants to kill him. When the servants would not obey, they were ordered to hold Laing's arms so El Abeyd could do the job himself. El Abeyd thrust his sword into Laing's chest. Laing's body was then decapitated.

THE EVIDENCE COLLECTED by Bonnel de Mézières differs from Bongola's testimony, and both vary, in small ways, from other accounts of

Laing's death. But surely it cannot be a coincidence that two skeletons were exhumed from the tree at Sahab. They were likely those of Laing and the Arab boy. And while Bongola's testimony could not pinpoint where the murder took place, he did say that it occurred on the third day out. Sahab was about thirty miles from Timbuktu, and it is likely that Laing would have reached it three days into his journey, for he typically started out late on the first day of a new leg.

D'Ghies's confession and the bashaw's own admission of complicity proved, at least to Warrington, that Rousseau had somehow gotten wind of Laing's death before anyone else, and that he found an opportunity to steal Laing's journal. Bonnel de Mézières never did clear up that part of the mystery—indeed, the two Arabic accounts of Laing's death he cites specify that all of Laing's property and papers were burned. This is more probable than the elaborate conspiracy theory spun by the overwrought and sometimes overimaginative Warrington.

GIVEN THESE CIRCUMSTANCES, most observers have concluded that Bongola's testimony was accurate in all its important dimensions, and that Alexander Gordon Laing died at Sahab, probably at night, on Sunday, September 24, 1826.*

A FINAL REVELATION, the most compelling of all, awaited Bonnel de Mézières: in a casual aside, Mohammed Ould Mokhtar told him that Sheikh Ahmadu El Abeyd had kept a souvenir of Laing's death, a trophy. This was a "little gold rooster" that in 1910 was still in his family's possession. Bonnel de Mézières asked to see this artifact. It was apparent at once to his Western eyes that the object before him was not a rooster at all, but a small golden bird Emma Warrington Laing had given her husband on their wedding day eighty-five years before, to bring him good luck on his long journey. That removed all doubt from Bonnel de Mézières's mind that he had solved the enduring mystery of Laing's disappearance and death.

LAING'S FATE having been surmised by Warrington, there remained in the late 1820s the need to discover what had become of his journals.

---

* Three months short of his thirty-second birthday.

As far back as May, when he was recuperating from the ghastly Tuareg attacks, Laing had written that he intended to send his dispatches back to Tripoli from Timbuktu. These would certainly have included his journals, since he had received definitive instructions from Lord Bathurst to do so.[*] Their carrier, Laing wrote, would be Alkhadir, whom he had found to be "a remarkably fine young man." Yet in August 1828, at long last, Alkhadir turned up in Tripoli with Laing's letters but without his journals. This was the turning point in a quest that had been going on for some months and was to continue, with unabated wrangling between the British and the French, for several more years. It turned out to be a long and dreary chronicle that never reached closure, and from which none of the principal characters emerges with much credit.

Alkhadir denied having brought the journals with him from Timbuktu. This meant little to Warrington, who believed that Alkhadir, like Bongola, was under the spell of Hassuna D'Ghies. Warrington, we read in a consular dispatch, "did not fail to observe upon the extraordinary length of time that the letters, particularly that of the 10th May, had been upon the road, and also that Alkhadir was the bearer of it . . . and lastly his coming down without the dispatches, of which Major Laing in that letter expresses an intention of making him the bearer. . . . His suspicions of foul play were never lulled, and received strength from the pains taken to prevent his intercourse with Alkhadir, and the Negro [Bongola], both of whom were fed and clothed by H. D'Ghies but rarely came to the British consulate, tho' he expressed a wish to take the Negro into his service, both were examined by him and deposed to Major Laing's having papers with him, also to various particulars relating to the murder—and yet nothing that could throw a light upon the fate of the papers was elicited from either."

As it was generally believed that the report of Laing's death published in *L'Etoile* had originated with Baron Rousseau or Hassuna D'Ghies, Warrington inevitably suspected either or both of them of pilfering the journals. By October 1827 Warrington was convinced Rousseau had the journals and that "they would eventually come to light if the demand for

---

[*]It is astonishing that Bathurst did not insist that Laing and Clapperton send copies of their journals, or the documents themselves, back to London at periodic intervals to avert precisely this catastrophe.

their production were persevered in." In this, of course, and not for the first time, he was wrong.

IN THE DECADES of silence that followed Laing's disappearance, something like the story Bonnel de Mézières eventually reconstructed must also have formed in the unhappy mind of Hanmer Warrington. With the certainty of Laing's death and the departure of his longtime enemies Rousseau and Hassuna D'Ghies, Warrington fell into an angry lethargy, clinging to his post, the only thing that gave any meaning to his unhappy life. His neglected wife died. He outlasted even the change of the bashaw's regime, carrying out his consular duties until 1846, when his quixotic temper and erratic behavior finally led to his forced resignation. He was now sixty-nine, but age had not mellowed him. That year, he quarreled with a Neapolitan consul named Morelli over a box of cigars. The next time he saw Morelli in the street, Warrington began thwacking him over the head with his walking stick.

That was the last straw for the Foreign Office. King George IV had died in 1830, his brother, William IV, in 1837, and the scandal-hating Victoria had long since ascended the throne. The aging Warrington no longer had friends at court. A letter to Consul Warrington dated April 7, 1846, from Lord Wellington's foreign secretary, George Hamilton Gordon, Earl of Aberdeen, arrived in Tripoli not long after the affair of the cigars:

> I regret to perceive in the Despatches now under my consideration that your conduct towards the Chevalier Morelli, the Consul of a Friendly Power of Her Majesty's, has been and continues to be most unjustifiable *and incomprehensible.* Considering all the circumstances of these unbecoming altercations in which you have suffered your feelings to involve you, I regret to be compelled to observe that it appears to me that it would be no less for your own future comfort than for the benefit of Her Majesty's service that you should make up your mind to retire.

After thirty-two years, Warrington's consular career in Tripoli had come to its ignominious end. Granted a pension of 900 pounds sterling a year, he was soon bound for the Greek port of Patras to visit his son-in-law, Thomas Wood, who was serving there as British consul. But Warrington was not the type who could survive the reflective inactivity of a graceful retirement. He drank vastly and died a year later.

POOR EMMA WAS by then nearly twenty years in her grave. Emma's desolation over Laing's death, which was placed beyond all doubt when Bongola and Alkhadir arrived in Tripoli in August 1828, can only have been made more intense by learning from his last letters to her father that he had not written to her at all during the last weeks of his life. Whatever sympathy she may have received from her own family (for all his foibles, Hanmer Warrington was a doting father, and Emma was his favorite), she got none from her husband's. Warrington complained to Hay that when he wrote to Laing's parents telling them of their son's death, he got no reply. This seemed extraordinary to the consul after what he considered so desirable a marriage for the son. "I should apprehend," he wrote in one of his more pompous moods, "in respect of Ancient Pedigree or even Pecuniary Resources that His Family must have been the gainers." It did not occur to him that Emma's ancient pedigree, on one side, anyway, may not have impressed Laing's pious Scottish and schoolmarmish parents.

Emma was not to know her second husband, Thomas Wood, longer than her first. After their marriage in April 1829, the couple went to Italy, to Leghorn, where she was to recover from her grief and where, her new groom hoped, the balmy climate might restore her shattered health. On October 2, 1829, less than six months after her second marriage, she died at Pisa of consumption, and was buried in the English cemetery there. She was twenty-eight years old and had survived her first husband by less than four years. Wood later married another of the Warrington girls, Emma's older sister Jane, by whom he had four children.

Her father attributed Emma's broken health to anxiety over Laing. He cited to Hay the "Watchful Days and Sleepless Nights . . . and all the subsequent Tragical events" which brought "my adored Daughter to an Untimely Grave." He took a final swipe at his archenemy: "Thus has that Monster of Iniquity the Baron Rousseau sacrificed two victims to his Diabolical Intrigue—for to my last, shall I conscientiously believe he was concerned in that sad history. . . ."

Timoléon Rousseau, who continued to pursue Emma even after

Consul Warrington refused a second time to permit their marriage, fared no better than the woman he loved. He died March 6, 1829, five weeks before Emma married Thomas Wood, and only seven months before Emma herself passed away. He was thirty years old. His tombstone is preserved to this day in the French embassy in Libya. It is inscribed *"Alexandre Timoléon Rousseau, Mort à Tripoli, Victime d'un amour insensé,"** words that might well have served, too, as Emma's epitaph.

IN THE NEAR CENTURY that has elapsed since Bonnel de Mézières conducted his investigations, no trace of Laing's journals has ever been found.

---

* Alexandre Timoléon Rousseau died at Tripoli of a broken heart (more literally, "died of an unrequited [or foolish] love").

AFTERWORD AND
ACKNOWLEDGMENTS

———•—•———

THIS BOOK was in many ways inspired by *The Strong Brown God*, Pulitzer Prize–winner Sanche de Gramont's magisterial account of the long and colorful history of the Niger River. I read *The Strong Brown God* when it was first published in 1979, and again in the fall of 2001 on a long train trip from Los Angeles to Dallas. *The Strong Brown God* is to the Niger River what Alan Moorehead's *White Nile* is to the Nile—the classic and definitive account of the river's history for the general reader. It revived my interest in Laing and Clapperton and the strange story of the race to discover Timbuktu. I have drawn on it extensively in thinking about and writing this book, and my debt to it cannot be overstated.

When I first set foot in Africa, in March 1963 at Port Said, I was not especially glad to be there, though the tarry smells of the harbor and the promised mysteries of Egypt helped me to forget, temporarily, the smoldering resentment I felt toward my parents for dragging me so far from home. Just weeks before, they pulled me out of comfortably coed Swanson Junior High School in Arlington, Virginia, to attend a grim, all-male boarding school in Kenya. It was not lost on me, either, that while my own life was ruined, my father would be a happy man. He was leaving a routine job at the State Department for new and exciting duties at the tiny U.S. consulate general in Kenya Colony,[*] helping to prepare for the arrival of the first American ambassador to Kenya[†] later that year. I could hardly blame him—if only for the alteration in climate: any sane person would instantly exchange Nairobi for Washington. I accepted, grimly, that I would spend the next four or five years in exile in Africa, not to see my school friends again until I was ready for college—an eternity to a thirteen-year-old.[‡]

I disembarked the SS *La Bourdonnais*, the sedate liner run by the Messageries Maritimes that had carried us from Marseilles to Alexandria, so that I could make a quick side trip to Cairo to see the Pyramids and visit the famous Museum of Antiquities. My mother had been to Cairo many times in days when it was a more insular, happier place, and was determined to stay on board. My father wanted to see the Suez Canal. When I wrangled permission to travel to Cairo on my own, a British couple, friends of my parents, promised to keep an eye on me. A day or two later, we would rejoin the *La Bourdonnais* (which in the meantime would negotiate the canal) in Suez Bay at the northern terminus of the Red Sea, and continue our voyage to the Indian Ocean and Africa's eastern seaboard.

The great Egyptian Museum in Tahrir Square seemed to me to be larger than the Pentagon (it is not, though it has more than one hundred halls). Outside this edifice, in open-air bookstalls not unlike those lining the Quai de la Tournelle across the Seine from Notre Dame, were new and secondhand books on a great variety of subjects, and many were in English. I bought a half dozen for reading on board ship. One of these, with an abraded chocolate cloth cover, quite worn, was a 1926 edition of Arthur Percival Newton's classic *Travel and Travellers of the Middle Ages*. I paid twenty-five cents for it (a quarter, in U.S. coin, then very much in

---

[*] Kenya Colony and Protectorate became independent of Great Britain on December 12, 1963, about eight months after I arrived there, an occasion that will always be linked in my mind with the death of President Kennedy, the announcement of which devastated the tiny expatriate American community in Nairobi only three weeks before independence, on November 22.

[†] The late William Atwood, the wonderfully erudite and literate editor-in-chief of *Look* magazine, who later wrote of his experiences in newly independent Kenya with grim humor in *The Reds and the Blacks* (New York: Harper & Brothers, 1967).

[‡] Those five years in Kenya, from 1963 until I came home to go to college in late 1967, turned out to be among the happiest of my life.

demand in Cairo, no doubt to the consternation of Gamal Abdel Nasser). Though this book did not directly introduce me to that Scot who would be the first white man to enter Timbuktu, Professor Newton's essays on Africa seemed to me *at least* as gripping as any of those fictional tales of Henry Rider Haggard, who was (briefly) my favorite author. Two or three weeks later, with sweltering stops at Djibouti and Aden behind us, we had rounded the Horn of Africa and docked within sight of Fort Jesus in Mombasa, where most of the English passengers debarked. By then, I had read and reread Newton's essays, and it was inevitable that, in time, I would read everything I could get my hands on concerning the exploration of that continent I now reluctantly called "home."

A year or two later, still in Nairobi, I got a copy of Bovill's essays on Laing. By then I was roughly smitten by the romance of nineteenth-century exploration of the Sahara. With the endocrine intensity only a lonely and slightly nerdy teenager could have brought to it, I puzzled over Laing's complex relationship with his wife, staggered that he could abandon her in Tripoli. Why didn't he *take her with him?* The tales of Burton and Stanley, so much better known to me, were, by comparison, two-dimensional. Most African explorers, it seemed to me, were just aging Boy Scouts trekking leisurely across the savanna, shooting the occasional lion. Laing was different.

I would not have attempted my own account of Laing's travels (and travails) but for that adolescent introduction to the ineffable mysteries of the sandy wastes of North Africa, and those English men and women of a certain stripe held spellbound by them. As for Laing, I was hooked by the man, the woman, the Sahara, *and the story.*

I did not realize then, but understand today, what a Herculean task E. W. Bovill set himself when he decided to catalogue Laing's papers. Laing's journals, after all, were lost forever, probably burned by the blood-thirsty Sheikh El Abeyd, and Bovill, an amateur historian, must have doubted at the outset whether he could re-create all the important elements of the Timbuktu Mission merely from Laing's letters. But he did. He also saved me, in many instances, from the onerous task of deciphering Laing's handwriting. Though copperplate when he was healthy and happy, Laing's hand often degenerated into chickenscratch in the desert, and after his injuries in the Tanezrouft when he picked up his pen with his left hand—*well!* Always, I was grateful to Bovill.

E. W. Bovill,* likely best remembered for his two classics, *Caravans of the Old Sahara and The Golden Trade of the Moors,* was simply a fabulous historian, a gifted raconteur, and a crisp writer. After spending a year with Laing's papers in the early 1960s he chose to move on to matters he considered more important to the larger scheme of African history. So far as I know, he never wrote another word about Laing.

That is the story of the germination of this book. So I begin by thanking Mr. Bovill, a man I regret never having met.

After Bovill, I owe as much, perhaps more, to my brilliant agent, Christy Fletcher, assisted by her partner Emma Parry and their staff at Fletcher & Parry, who brought verve and grace and wit to the task of marketing the proposal for *The Race for Timbuktu.* In the end, she found the perfect home for it with Dan Halpern and Gheña Glijansky at Ecco, a most happy day for me.

I am grateful to my dear friend and personal editor Kate Gerard for her help in constructing the proposal. She also proofread my manuscript meticulously during the two years I wrote it, making scores of helpful suggestions, both grammatical and structural. She often reminded me that *stories* are what interest readers, not concatenations of facts, and she prodded me to evoke the drama that so captured me in reading Laing as a

---

* E(dward) W(illiam) Bovill (he never used his full name), born Christmas Day, 1892, was educated at Rugby School and at Trinity College, Cambridge. He served in the First World War with Britain's elite Tenth Royal Hussars and the West African Frontier Force, where he had his introduction to the continent that would hold him in thrall for the rest of his life. With the publication of *Caravans of the Old Sahara* in 1930, he launched a thirty-five-year career as a writer of nonfiction books about Africa as "an upholder of the ancient and honorable tradition of amateur scholarship," in the words of Robin Hallett, perhaps the most eminent historian of Africa of the last century, who edited a posthumous edition of one of Bovill's books. Though many of his readers assume Bovill was an academic, he was in fact a very successful City of London businessman, serving as a director of Jardine Matheson & Co. Ltd., the giant British importing and shipping conglomerate, from 1936 to 1945, and as chairman of R. C. Treat & Co. Ltd., Britain's principal manufacturer of fragrances and flavors, from 1942 to 1961. Active in the prestigious Hakluyt Society for many years, between 1962 and 1966, the year of his death, he researched and wrote the four-volume *Missions to the Niger,* which includes a volume on Laing, published for the Hakluyt Society by Cambridge University Press.

teenager. In the end, it was not a hard thing to do; Laing and Clapperton did much of the work for me.

My editor at Ecco, Gheña Glijansky, brought skill, tact, and enthusiasm to taming a manuscript that still had lumps in it. Though I was often distressed at how many little infelicities she found in sentences I had labored on for hours, she kindly fixed them, while managing to interlard her e-mailed notes to me with lots of "well done!" and "love this!" and sometimes just "Oy!" Gheña saw an early proposal for the project and speedily embraced Laing. Her affection for him, for Emma, Hugh Clapperton, and even for the odious Warrington, strongly informed her editing of my text. She also brought the patience and skill of a jeweler to her work, finding so many ways to improve words, sentences, and paragraphs. If any passages in this book now glow, that is Gheña's work, not mine. And if there are passages that still are ponderous, they remain so in spite of her many exhortations to me to improve them.

Very special thanks also to Amy Robbins for her meticulous copyediting, correction of grammatical faux pas, and many helpful suggestions; and to David Koral, senior production editor at HarperCollins, for his indispensable competence in preparing this book for the printer.

I want to express my appreciation also to Dan Halpern, publisher of Ecco, who took the risk of committing to *The Race for Timbuktu* while it was just a woolly idea. Without publishers like Dan, most books would very likely simply die before they were written. I hope this one merits the faith he showed in it, and in me.

I've been assisted in this project by librarians everywhere, especially by Joanna Corden, archivist of the Royal Society, London, for so kindly providing me with copies of index cards relating to the society's holdings for Major Laing; to Jane Shillaker in the Research and Editorial Services Department of the Public Record Office of the National Archives at Kew; to Matthew Bailey, librarian of the Picture Library, National Portrait Gallery, London; to Dr. Marion Wallace, curator of Africa Collections at the British Library, and Hedley Sutton, also of the BL; to Professor Roy Bridges, president of the Hakluyt Society, London, and Gillian Costain Batement, also of the Hakluyt Society; to my friend and frequent lunch partner at the Dallas Committee on Foreign Relations, Professor Larry D. Sall, Ph.D., Dean of Libraries, the University of Texas at Dallas (and all his helpful staff) for making the magnificent Eugene McDermott Library at UTD available to me, as well as all the vast library resources of the University of Texas System; and to Cynthia Mayo of the Dallas Public Library, Business and Technology Division, Dallas, Texas, and all the staff at the Renner/Frankford division of the DPL (who must rue their proximity to my house, and my constant predations).

I would be deeply remiss were I to fail to thank my friend, primary physician, and oncologist Charles K. Connor, M.D., whose healing gifts saw me through a long and challenging battle with Waldenström's macroglobulenemia* while I was writing this book. I am indebted also to Howard M. Kussman, M.D., and my ophthalmic surgeon, Kimberly S. Warren, M.D., and many other wonderful physicians and nurses at the North Texas Regional Cancer Center, Plano, Baylor University Hospital, Dallas, and the M. D. Anderson Cancer Center, Houston. I owe them more than I can say.

I am also grateful to the men and women of Africa who befriended me and shared their confidences and their continent with me, as a teenager and as an adult, in many happy years of residence in Kenya, Zaire, Gabon, and Congo, and shorter stays in pre-Gaddafi Libya, Niger, Mali, Algeria, Mauritania, Spanish Sahara, Senegal, Côte d'Ivoire, Guinea, Sierra Leone, Togo, Benin, and Nigeria, as well as Morocco, Tunisia, Egypt, Sudan, Djibouti, Ethiopia, Somalia, Equatorial Guinea, Cameroon, São Tomé and Príncipe, Namibia, Uganda, Angola, and Zanzibar, Tanganyika, and Rhodesia (as they were then known), and the Seychelles. Africans have suffered much. The face of Africa may not improve much in a year, or in five years, but Africa and Africans will bloom once more, for I believe (with the great abolitionist Theodore Parker) that while "the moral arc of the universe is long, it bends toward justice."

Finally, I must acknowledge my debt to Alexander Gordon Laing himself, the forgotten "African traveler." I was often jolted by the thought that we have only a fragment of his journal, which disappeared with him when he died. Like Bovill, I have relied mainly on his letters to reconstruct his journey across the Sahara. Were it not for his prolific letter writing, we would know only the barest outline of his story. He put so much in his letters, *but what marvelous treasures did he save just for those journals?* What have we missed? No doubt a great deal—wonderful things, facts that are

*A rare (but treatable!) blood cancer.

still untold, insights unshared. They will likely remain so. Sometimes I hope, against all logic, that portions of the missing journals lie hidden in some trunk, swaddled in darkness and dry air for almost two centuries now, just waiting for the lock to snap open, for the sunlight to stream in. . . .

Sir Thomas More's Dutch friend and intellectual sparring partner Desiderius Erasmus of Rotterdam said of More that he was *omnium horarum homo*,[*] an encomium rendered in English by Sir Robert Bolt (with more grace than accuracy) as "a man for all seasons." It strikes me that Alexander Gordon Laing was a man for *no* seasons, both in the literal sense that he never seemed fully alive until the thermometer hit triple digits, and more metaphorically (and profoundly) in that he lived in the bubble of his own mental world, the foil of men like Saint Thomas, whose gift was to be so attuned politically, socially, and emotionally to everything going on around him, with almost perfect pitch. Laing, the introverted Scot, was tone-deaf in so many ways, as Emma and most everyone dear to him learned—at their cost. But only such a man as Laing would have attempted the tasks he chose for himself. And Laing most emphatically *was*, in a way that the sedate and deliberate knight and martyr was not, *omnium horarum homo*—never sleeping, burning the candle at both ends with his own peculiar manic energy, always ready to meet the next challenge, always willing to throw himself into the breach, his soul dilated and pulled forward by that astonishing, that hypnotizing rose light of the Sahara. He was drawn to the wilderness hoping to find *Dieu sans les hommes*,[†] in Balzac's phrase—God unburdened by all those additions we humans add to him, and so often choke on—only to discover that he needed humanity after all.

I hope I have done right by him, poor Laing, and his long-suffering wife. I do hope they are together now at last, alone and beyond reach of murderous sheikhs, lovesick Frenchmen, and that egregious old reprobate, the colonel.

Frank Kryza
Dallas
May 2005

[*] "a man for all the hours"
[†] "*Dans le désert, voyez-vous, il y a tout, et il n'y a rien. . . . Dieu sans les hommes.*" (In the desert, you see, there is everything, and there is nothing. . . . God without men.)

NOTES

------◆◆◆------

IN HIS SHORT LIFETIME Alexander Gordon Laing published only one book, *Travels in the Timanee,* in 1825, about his earliest effort to locate the Niger. Tragically, Laing's principal journals documenting the Timbuktu Mission—hundreds of manuscript pages in his trademark bound notebooks—disappeared in 1826, and Laing himself did not survive to tell his story.

The last of Laing's letters to survive is dated September 21, 1826, three days before he died. Though some of Laing's dispatches certainly failed to reach their destinations, lost in transit, enough survive to make possible the telling of his entire story, not just in broad outline but in day-by-day detail. These materials have been available for years, catalogued by the great amateur Africanist E. W. Bovill in the late 1950s and early 1960s for the Hakluyt Society. Bovill reprinted all the important ones in 1964.*

The materials I used to tell Laing's story consist principally of the autograph letters of Alexander Gordon Laing, official and private, and the responses they generated from his correspondents in London and Tripoli. These primary materials are archived in two of the great British repositories of historical documents: the Public Record Office at Kew, Richmond, Surrey; and the archives of the Royal Society in London.

------

*These became widely available through Cambridge University Press. I was not surprised to find complete copies in each of Dallas's two main university libraries, in addition to my own working set.

Supplementing his private letters, Laing also sent back official reports to the Colonial Office. Some of this correspondence was later catalogued by the Foreign Office, but the great bulk of the files relating to the Timbuktu Mission were eventually recombined in the Public Record Office at Kew, where they can be found today. Though each collection is arranged by date, the complete chronology shifts from file to file—most of the letters Laing addressed to Warrington, for example, are separately catalogued from those to Bathurst. We know that Laing also wrote a number of letters to his family in Scotland, but I was able to find only one of them.

Laing was an avid drafter of memoranda. These were often no more than brief notes on scraps of paper, but sometimes they were long and careful studies to which he gave titles, such as his *Cursory Remarks on the Course and Termination of the Great River Niger* and his *Notes on Ghadames*, both of which were catalogued by Bovill and are reprinted in the Hakluyt Society collection of Laing materials.

Finally, two portions of excerpts from Laing's journal *did* survive. The first carries the story of the expedition as far as Ghadames. The second covers his journey up to his departure from In Salah. Both of these documents appear to be summaries of a more detailed private journal and to have been prepared and dispatched to London as a formal report to the Colonial Office on the progress of the mission. Laing had ample leisure in Ghadames and In Salah to "catch up" and issue such reports, above and beyond his private letters, which he often wrote daily. He probably edited and transcribed his primary journal at each of these desert oases, and sent redacted transcripts back to Warrington. If only he had followed this practice at later stops!

The Park, Hornemann, Lyon, Denham, Clapperton, Oudney, and Lander expeditions do not present the challenges of Laing's. Except for Park's second trip down the Niger, these journeys were well documented, often in independent narrations by more than one of the participants. Not so with Laing. Of course, Clapperton, too, died in Africa, as did Ritchie, Oudney, and Lander, but unlike poor Laing, these men were accompanied by faithful collaborators who carefully preserved their journals and notes. Laing traveled alone.

I AM NO SCHOLAR, and this is not a scholarly book.

To appeal to the general reader, I resisted burdening the text with citations. Beyond Laing's own writings, which formed the core of my research, I consulted other texts found in the bibliography, relying especially on the primary materials of Lyon, Oudney,* Denham, Clapperton, Lander, Caillié, and Bonnel de Mézières,

---

*Dr. Walter Oudney died on his mission, en route to Kano with Clapperton. His name will not be found in the bibliography because he did not survive to publish his own account. Denham attached Oudney's name to the *title* of his book (but shared credit as author only with Clapperton), and this only at the insistence of Sir John Barrow, who was appalled by Denham's predilection for taking credit for the work of others while making catty comments about them. In any case, Denham had already expropriated many of Oudney's most important observations.

supplemented by the formidable commentary and analysis of Bovill and Hallett, two of the greatest twentieth-century historians of Africa.[*]

Preceding the bibliography are notes for each chapter, pointing to sources for quotations and other materials. Unless otherwise indicated, when I have provided English translations of French source material, the translations are mine.

LAING'S ITINERARY IN HIS LAST TWO YEARS:

1825

May 3	Depart Malta
May 9	Arrive Tripoli
July 7	Depart Tripoli
September 13	Arrive Ghadames
November 3	Depart Ghadames
December 2	Arrive In Salah

1826

January 9	Depart In Salah
January 26	Enter Tanezrouft Desert
Early February	Recuperation at Wadi Ahnet
August 13	Arrive Timbuktu
September 22	Depart Timbuktu
September 24	Death (at Sahab)

In the notes below, complete citations for books referenced only by the author's last name will be found in the bibliography. The acronym PRO refers to the Public Record Office of the British National Archives; FO the Foreign Office; CO the Colonial Office; RS the Royal Society; and *Proceedings* to the *Proceedings of the Association for Promoting the Discovery of the Interior Parts of Africa*. The numbered citations following letters are their catalogue numbers, sometimes including the document number when I thought that important.

ONE / A SCOTSMAN AT TRIPOLI

Supplementing Laing's many letters from the city in the two months he stayed there, Miss Tully's *Letters written during a ten years' residence at the Court of Tripoli*, published in 1816, less than a decade before Laing's arrival, helped me set the scene in terms of geography, mood, and magical sense of the place. Miss Tully also

[*]Hallett, born in 1926, lived to see the new millennium. He died in February 2003.

provides detailed information about street names and the construction of the British consular buildings. Warrington's voluminous correspondence was also helpful, as were Ward and Furlong. Laing's first impressions of the city, including all direct quotations in this chapter and Chapter 3 (except those from correspondence), are taken from that portion of his journal which survived (PRO, CO 2/15, 188), a transcript of which he sent back to London from Ghadames. The day after Laing landed at Tripoli, Warrington wrote to Wilmot Horton (May 10, 1825) describing Laing's arrival (PRO, FO 76/19, 1191). Laing himself wrote several letters to Bathurst assessing the situation prior to departure, including a long letter (May 24, 1825) in which he describes his arrival (PRO, CO 2/15, 1455). On the same day, Laing wrote to his friend James Bandinel sketching the city and telling of his excitement at the prospect of his expedition (RS, 374[La] 78). The organization of Lord Bathurst's ministry and the complex reporting relationships of Robert Wilmot Horton, Robert William Hay, and Henry Goulbourn, all of whom also had reporting relationships with Warrington and Laing and corresponded frequently with them, are outlined in Young. Furlong helped me to see Tripoli as the vastly more important nineteenth-century diplomatic and geographic center it once was, as did Fisher.

TWO / THE AFRICAN ASSOCIATION

The founder of the African Association, Sir Joseph Banks, best remembered as the author of *A Journal of a Voyage Round the World in His Majesty's Ship Endeavour* (which has become, in effect, Captain James Cook's biography), was an obsessive keeper of records and notes, and the history of the African Association is thus a detailed one. The primary source for this chapter (and much of Chapter 4) is the *Proceedings* itself, along with Hallett (*Records*), which carries the story forward to 1831, with help from O'Brian. John Ledyard's association with our third president is recounted in Jefferson. Dearden provides the most detailed history of the Karamanli dynasty. Park is his own best biographer, with much additional helpful material in Lupton, especially as regards the fatal second expedition, during which Park's journals were stolen or lost. In terms of a broad understanding of the overarching British policy that dates from this period to the late nineteenth century, Hallett (*Africa*) has no peer.

THREE / A WEDDING IN THE ENGLISH GARDEN

Dearden provides a crisp biography of Warrington, as does Warrington himself, in a letter to Lord Bathurst dated March 14, 1826 (PRO, FO 76/20, 1255). The layout of the English Garden and Warrington's additions to consular properties (and details of their costs) are spelled out in a letter to Lord Bathurst dated February 7, 1820 (PRO, FO 76/14). Laing's adoring comments about Emma are recorded in a letter to James Bandinel dated June 7, 1825 (RS, 374[La] 81). Laing kept Lord Bathurst apprised of his preparations for departure from Tripoli in a series of painstakingly detailed letters, including one dated May 14, 1825 (PRO, CO 2/15, 1455). Warrington's frustration with the temporizing of the bashaw is also recounted in the previously cited letter to Wilmot Horton (PRO, FO 76/19, 1191). Laing complains to Bathurst of the *douceur* required by the bashaw in a letter dated from his camp "Tripoli in the West, May 24th, 1825" (PRO, CO 2/25, 1455). The complex interior geography of the Castle and all the exotic denizens therein is wonderfully laid out in Dearden. Warrington's bizarre and unctuous account of Laing's wedding to his daughter Emma, quoted in full in this chapter, is addressed to Lord Bathurst, July 14, 1825 (PRO, FO 76/19, 1725). My two biggest disappointments in writing this book were my inability to locate drawings or likenesses either of Hanmer Warrington or of his daughter Emma.

FOUR / WHITE MAN'S GRAVE

The early history of the exploration by Europeans of the Congo River basin is treated at length in Forbath and Anstey, and Tuckey provides his own riveting firsthand account.* The challenges and mysteries of Dr. Mungo Park's second (and fatal) expedition are detailed in Lupton, Hallett (*Records*), O'Brian, and de Gramont, from which I have pieced together this much shorter account. The abbreviated story of Hornemann's expedition is taken from Bovill (*Missions* 1), which contains the complete journal

FIVE / THE "AFRICAN TRAVELER"

The organization of nineteenth-century desert caravans has been described by many contemporary and modern authors, most compellingly and brilliantly by Maugham in his short but spellbinding first-person account. I have never been able to hear the words "*Nemchou Y'Allah!*" (Depart, by the grace of God!), without thinking of the Spanish "*Vaya con Dios!*" which is its practical equivalent. I consulted Fisher, Maugham, Moorhouse, and Bovill (*Golden Trade*), to flesh out Laing's own notes, which are sometimes short on things like housekeeping and logistics. The story of Laing's early life is adapted mainly from Bovill (*Missions* 1), with the help of Graham in grasping the grimmer qualities of life in the Scotland of Laing's childhood. Laing's letter of reprimand from Captain Ross is in the archives of the Royal Society (RS, 374[La] 64). Laing's effort at self-promotion is a two-page attachment to a letter to Lord Bathurst dated January 12, 1825 (PRO, CO 2/15, 209). General Turner's brutal censure of Laing is in a letter to Bathurst dated April 9, 1825 (also PRO,

---

*Though Tuckey got author's credit for his book, he died in the Congo estuary aboard the *Dorothy*, the ship he commanded, before returning to England, and could not actually have written it. The style betrays the gifted hand of secretary of the Admiralty Sir John Barrow, who almost certainly wrote Tuckey's account from his notes, and, characteristically, took no credit on the spine of the book for this parting tribute to his fallen friend.

CO 2/15). The episode of Laing's fall from grace with his regimental commanders is nicely detailed in Bovill (*Missions* 1). The story of Earl Bathurst's early years, and his relationship with Goulbourn and others at the Colonial Office, is adapted from Young and from Bathurst's short entry in the *Encyclopaedia Britannica*. Competing theories about the courses of the Niger and the Congo abounded in early nineteenth-century England. Anstey, Boahen, Curtin, Forbath, Hallett (*Africa*), Hatch, and Lloyd were helpful to me in articulating the British strategy for exploration and, later, colonization of Africa.

SIX / THE TRIPOLI ROUTE

The evolution of the strategy of the conquest of Central Africa via Tripoli is detailed in Smyth and in Bovill (*Missions* 1), and in the engaging biography of Barrow by Lloyd. Tripoli's importance in the early nineteenth century is documented in Ward, Furlong, Fisher, and Curtin. The story of the Cologhis in Tripoli, and of the Karamanli dynasty's origins and bloody rise to power, is told in Dearden, Fisher, and Clissold. Short biographical sketches of the consul are found in Dearden and Bovill (*Missions* 1). The broad overview of British policy presented in this chapter owes much to the always deeply insightful analysis of Hallett (*Africa* and *Penetration*). The story of Ritchie is told in Lyon, who accompanied him, and whose personal account of their harrowing expedition I found riveting. The physical characteristics, climate, and conditions of the Sahara are helpfully explored in Goudie, Gautier, and de Villiers.

SEVEN / HUGH CLAPPERTON

Though one could argue about who was the better explorer, there is no question that Hugh Clapperton's life and his two expeditions in Africa are much better documented in the literature of African exploration than those of Laing. The primary source for this chapter, and the three chapters that follow, is Denham (cowritten by Clapperton and Oudney), along with the account of his second expedition in Clapperton, and the account also in Lander, the devoted assistant who became his best friend. Also essential were Bovill (*Missions* 4), Bovill (*Missions* 2), and Bovill (*Missions* 3), all of which are devoted to the Oudney-Denham-Clapperton expedition to Bornu.

EIGHT / THE JOURNEY TO BORNU

Denham's splenetic outburst to Lord Bathurst is dated August 26, 1822 (PRO, CO 2/13). Robert Wilmot's* stern reply is dated September 9, 1822 (PRO, FO 8/8). Dr. Oudney's difficult position is outlined in a long letter to Wilmot dated September 17, 1822 (PRO, CO 2/13), and in many shorter complaints to Warrington. Most of the important events of this chapter are detailed in Bovill (*Missions* 2), who quotes

---

*Robert John Wilmot, Bathurst's undersecretary of state, adopted the surname "Horton" in 1822. "Wilmot," "Wilmot Horton," and "Horton" are thus all the same person.

verbatim the most important letters. The itinerary of the expedition, and some of the day-to-day events recounted, is from Denham.

NINE / UNDISCOVERED EMPIRES

Denham is the main source, along with correspondence, for the expedition's first weeks in Kukawa and the exploration of Lake Chad. His account of his partial circumnavigation of the great inland sea counts among his best writing. The contretemps concerning Denham's allegations of Clapperton's homosexuality begins with Oudney's July 14, 1823, letter to Warrington (PRO, FO 76/17) and is further detailed in Bovill (*Missions 3*), which contains transcripts of most of the relevant letters. Warrington's long letter to Wilmot Horton about the whole sordid episode is dated November 4, 1823 (PRO, FO 76/17). Denham is the only source for his (probably much exaggerated) participation in the slaving expedition with the warrior Barca Gana. In addition to the account of it in his book, he wrote about it in a 3,500-word letter to Warrington dated May 15, 1823 (also PRO, FO 76/17). Dr. Oudney's last letter before his death is dated December 10, 1823, and addressed to Robert Wilmot Horton (PRO, FO 76/18). Clapperton's moving account of Dr. Oudney's passing is in Denham.

TEN / THE RACE BEGINS

Clapperton's literary contributions in Denham, preserved by Barrow, provides the basis for my account of his trip to Kano and his long stay there, along with Bovill (*Missions 2*) and Bovill (*Missions 3*). Toole's appointment is detailed in a memorandum by Barrow written in September or October 1823 (PRO, CO 2/14). Further instructions to the expedition were transmitted to Oudney by Horton in a letter from Downing Street dated October 9, 1823 (PRO, FO 8/8). Bathurst's revised instructions to Denham, once Denham had apprised him of his arrival at El Kanemi's court, are contained in a letter dated October 9, 1823 (also PRO, FO 8/8). Denham related the Toole story to Warrington in a letter dated January 20, 1824 (PRO, FO 76/18). Tyrwhitt's suicidal decision to remain at Kukawa is related in a letter to Horton dated August 17, 1824 (PRO, CO 2/13).

ELEVEN / OVER THE RIM OF THE WORLD

Laing's icy acknowledgment of his receipt of Clapperton's letter of advice is recorded in a letter to Wilmot Horton dated August 3, 1825 (PRO, CO 2/15, 1986). Laing's early optimism, and his initial satisfaction with the conduct of Babani, is recorded in two letters to Warrington, both written on the same day: August 3, 1825 (PRO, CO 2/20, 144, 145), the second one ending with his hilariously disparaging remarks about Clapperton's advice. Laing had written about Jack le Bore, his Caribbean-born servant, years earlier in Laing. He thought well enough of him to take him back to London after the Ashanti campaign, and with him to Tripoli and

Timbuktu. Laing complains that Clapperton will "snatch the cup from my lips" in a letter to Bandinel dated August 3, 1825 (RS, 374[La] 91). The crossing to Ghadames is detailed in Laing's journal (PRO, CO 2/15, 188). I gained some personal sense of the vastness and moonlike sterility of the Hamada el Homra when I flew over it myself in 1966, and crossed portions of the Sahara in Mauritania, Mali, and Niger by air and by Land Rover in 1977, 1989, and 1993. It is still hard for me to imagine anyone crossing the Tanezrouft on foot.

TWELVE / CLAPPERTON CATCHES UP

Warrington peppered Laing with letters of encouragement and advice as he crossed the Sahara, ever recommending Clapperton to him and expressing the hope they would meet. "May you meet & return to Tripoli together, I sincerely hope. It will be to me a happy and joyful day," he writes on November 22, 1825 (RS, 374[La] 105). Such letters drove Laing to distraction. The letter from Warrington to Clapperton (also addressed to Denham) is dated February 9, 1825 (PRO, FO 76/19). Clapperton wrote a bland reply on February 10 (also PRO, FO 76/19), but significantly did nothing to respond to Warrington's request for information for Laing. I did not succeed in locating a copy of Clapperton's letter of advice to Laing, and we know of its contents only though Laing's sarcastic remarks about it. Lord Bathurst's delight with the Denham and Clapperton mission must have been based in part on Clapperton's bright assessment of it, in a letter to Wilmot Horton written at his London hotel on June 6, 1825 (PRO, CO 2/13), months before the world learned these details in Denham. The account of Clapperton's second mission to Africa is based largely on Clapperton and Lander, with much supportive material and analysis from Bovill (*Missions* 4). The quotation about the "unweary, unostentatious, and inglorious crusade . . ." is from Lecky.

THIRTEEN / THE IVORY MINIATURE

Laing's happy arrival at Ghadames is recorded in a letter to Warrington dated September 13, 1825, "8 o'clock PM" (PRO, FO 76/19, 2434). This letter is followed by at least a score more, as Laing was still energized and writing several thousand words daily (in his letters alone—no doubt he wrote much more in his private journal). Laing's tone changed markedly on September 17, 1825, in the letter he sent to the consul reporting the arrival of Emma's picture (PRO, CO 2/20). This letter arrived in Tripoli on November 17, 1825. Warrington's worried reply is dated November 22, 1825 (RS, 374[La] 105). By September 19, 1825, Laing was so upset about Emma that he offered to abandon his mission and come home, and he said so to his father-in-law in another long letter (also PRO, CO 2/20). By October 5, 1825, he had recovered sufficiently to write a 5,000-word letter to Warrington indicating that he would continue, though he caviled about how much he missed Emma (also PRO, CO 2/20). This letter arrived in Tripoli on January 5, 1826. The letter to Bandinel about the auspicious comet which "beckons me on" is dated October 20, 1825 (RS, 374[La] 103), by which time we can assume he had completely recovered his urge to find the lost city.

FOURTEEN / THE WIDOW ZUMA

The material in this chapter is taken from the firsthand accounts of the second Clapperton expedition, as recorded separately in Clapperton and Lander. Hallett (*Niger Journal*) provides much additional commentary and primary source material (mainly letters) not included in Clapperton's and Lander's published accounts.

FIFTEEN / TREACHERY IN THE TANEZROUFT

Laing was in an upbeat mood when he had rested at In Salah and started writing letters there, starting with one dated November 3, 1825, and addressed to Warrington (PRO, CO 2/20). A long stream followed, to Wilmot Horton, Lord Bathurst, Emma, and the last one to James Bandinel, dated January 9, 1826 (RS, 374[La] 113), written the day before he set out for the Tanezrouft. These two months of relative loquacity were followed by utter silence. Though Laing wrote to Wilmot Horton on January 26, 1826, in a letter he datelined "Desart of Tenezerof," that letter did not arrive in Tripoli until years after his death. As early as March 29, 1826, Warrington wrote to Hay (PRO, FO 76/20, 1258) about disturbing rumors of marauding bands beyond In Salah. Tripoli and London were in the dark about Laing's whereabouts after he departed In Salah. Laing's first account of his attack in the desert is to Warrington, dated May 10, 1826, written months after the event from the relative safety of Mokhtar's camp (PRO, CO 2/20, 211). It arrived at the consulate on November 3, 1826, nine months after Laing was injured. By July 1, 1826, Laing revealed to Warrington just how badly his condition had deteriorated (PRO, CO 2/20, 212), though acknowledging also his determination to persevere. He wrote again on July 10, 1826 (PRO, CO 2/20, 218), to announce that he would resume his search for the lost city the next day.

SIXTEEN / TROUBLES FOR CAPTAIN CLAPPERTON

This chapter picks up where we left off in Chapter 14, using the same sources, namely Clapperton, Lander, supplemented by commentary from Hallett (*Niger Journal*). The account of Clapperton's death from exhaustion and disease in Lander, written by the loyal friend who had once been his servant, is as moving as anything written by British explorers in the nineteenth century.

SEVENTEEN / THE CITY OF LEGEND

Hard information about Laing's journey after the near-fatal attack in the desert is thin, in part because terrible injuries limited his ability to write. This chapter is based mainly on three letters from Laing, along with Bovill's interpretation of them in light of other contemporaneous documents, and Warrington's long forensic study of Laing's disappearance and death. Laing describes the final leg of his journey to Timbuktu in a letter to Warrington dated simply "Monday" (PRO, CO 2/20), which arrived at the English Garden years later, on August 28, 1828. Though it cannot be dated precisely, its content suggests that it must have been written not long after an earlier important letter, also to Warrington, dated July 10, 1826 (also PRO, CO 2/20), which arrived in Tripoli on November 3, 1826. Finally, there is a third letter, the earliest of the three, which Laing also wrote in a state of deep depression after Mokhtar's camp had been ravaged by disease and he lost his faithful Jack le Bore, a devastating blow. It is dated July 1, 1826 (also PRO, CO 2/20), and landed in Tripoli also on November 3, 1826. Sidi Mohammed's letter to the bashaw describing Laing's arrival at Timbuktu was provided to Warrington by Hassuna D'Ghies (PRO, FO 76/33). Laing's only letter from Timbuktu, dated September 21, 1826 (after he had been there more than a month), is addressed to Warrington (PRO, CO 2/20) and was delivered by Alkhadir, along with the letter of May 10, 1826, referred to in Chapter 15. In his own visit two years later, Caillié pieced together his own version of Laing's earlier visit.

EIGHTEEN / THE LONG SILENCE

The autograph copy of Emma Warrington Laing's magnificent, heartbreaking letter to her husband, sent out into the Sahara to find her husband and later returned unopened to Tripoli, is dated November 10, 1826 (PRO, CO 2/20). The verbatim transcript of the report of Laing's death published in *L'Etoile* of May 2, 1827, is in Bovill (*Missions* 1). Yusuf Bashaw's copy of Mohammed el Washy's letter announcing Laing's death (PRO, FO 76/22 1315) was transmitted to Bathurst by Warrington as an appendix to a letter dated March 31, 1827 (also catalogued as PRO, FO 76/22, 1315). Warrington's analysis of the French position expounded in *L'Etoile* is in a long letter to Sir Frederick Hankey* dated August 2, 1827 (PRO, FO 76/22, 3511).

NINETEEN / THE LOST PAPERS

René Caillié tells his own story best, in Caillié. Warrington's transcript of his examination of Bongola is in the archives of the Royal Society (RS, 374[La] 131). Warrington's letter to Hay concerning the "Miserable Intrigue" is dated October 28, 1828 (PRO, FO 76/23, 3263). The story of Warrington's search for the lost papers is detailed in Bovill (*Missions* 1) and Dearden. Warrington's challenge to Rousseau to a duel is dated August 12, 1830 (PRO, CO 2/20, United Service Club Volume).

---

*Hankey was chief secretary to the government of Malta, and therefore, in effect, Warrington's purser.

Lord Goderich's tepid defense of Warrington is in a letter to Sir James Scarlett dated October 19, 1832 (PRO, FO 76/33).

TWENTY / THE MYSTERY SOLVED

Alexandre Bonnel de Mézières, the French army officer who disinterred Laing's bones eighty-five years after his death, included a half dozen "Kodaks" in his monograph (Bonnel de Mézières), none more heartrending than that of the tiny coffin, not much bigger than a hatbox, he built to rebury them. The analysis presented here is largely his, with support from Bovill (*Missions* 1), especially in the importance attached to Warrington's examination of the eyewitness Bongola as the foundation for a theory of Laing's death. Warrington wrote at length about his efforts to recover Laing's missing journals, mainly to R. W. Hay, Bathurst's deputy as permanent undersecretary of state for war and the colonies. Cited is his letter to Hay dated October 28, 1828 (PRO, FO 76/23, 3263). Warrington's August 12, 1830, "I shall not disgrace my pen" missive to Rousseau survives only as a copy he kept at the consulate (PRO, FO 76/26, 2799). Foreign secretary Lord Aberdeen's letter cashiering Warrington is dated April 7, 1846 (PRO, FO 76/33, 2867). Possibly because of debts, Warrington steered clear of England upon his recall and accepted an offer from his daughter Jane Wood to live with her at Patras, Greece, where her husband was British consul. The Woods were not burdened with him long. His son-in-law, Emma's second husband, raised this elaborate monument to him:

> *Sacred to the memory of Lieut. Colonel Hanmer Warrington*
> *who died at the British Consulate, Patras,*
> *on the 17th August 1847, aged 70.*
> *The life of this gallant officer was devoted*
> *to the service of his country,*
> *32 years of which he was employed,*
> *as H.M.'s Agent & Consul General at Tripoli.*
> *And long will his name be remembered in that land*
> *Where the slaves and the free were equally*
> *Objects of his protecting care.*
> *He was a kind and affectionate*
> *Husband and Father*
> *An unflinching friend and Noble Defender of the Rights of Man.*

SELECTED BIBLIOGRAPHY

Anstey, Roger. *Britain and the Congo in the Nineteenth Century.* Oxford: Clarendon Press, 1962.

Berenson, Mary. *A Vicarious Trip to the Barbary Coast.* London: Constable & Co., Ltd., 1938.

Boahen. A. Adu. *Britain, the Sahara, and the Western Sudan, 1788–1861.* Oxford: Clarendon Press, 1964.

Bonnel de Mézières, A. *Le Major A. Gordon Laing.* Paris: Emile Larose, Libraire-Editeur, 1912.

Bovill, E. W. *Caravans of the Old Sahara.* London: Oxford University Press, 1933.

———. *The Golden Trade of the Moors.* London: Oxford University Press, 1968.

———. *The Niger Explored.* London: Oxford University Press, 1968.

———. ed. *Missions to the Niger.* Vol. 1, *The Journal of Freidrich Hornemann's Travels from Cairo to Murzuk in the Years 1797–98; The Letters of Major Alexander Gordon Laing, 1824–26.* Cambridge: Cambridge University Press for the Hakluyt Society, 1964.

———, ed. *Missions to the Niger.* Vol. 2, *Major Denham's Narrative.* Cambridge: Cambridge University Press for the Hakluyt Society, 1966.

———, ed. *Missions to the Niger.* Vol. 3, *Major Denham's Narrative.* Cambridge: Cambridge University Press for the Hakluyt Society, 1966.

————, *Missions to the Niger*. Vol. 4, *Captain Clapperton's Narrative*. Cambridge: Cambridge University Press for the Hakluyt Society, 1966.

Caillié, René. *Travels through Central Africa to Timbuctoo; and across the Great Desert, to Morocco, performed in the years 1824–1828*. London: Henry Colburn, 1830; Frank Cass reprint, 1968.

Clapperton, Hugh. *Journal of a Second Expedition into the Interior of Africa*. London: John Murray, 1829; Frank Cass reprint, 1966.

Clissold, Stephen. *The Barbary Slaves*. New York: Barnes & Noble, 1977.

Curtin, Philip D. *The Image of Africa: British Ideas and Action, 1780–1850*. Madison: University of Wisconsin Press, 1964.

David, Saul. *Prince of Pleasure*. New York: Atlantic Monthly Press, 1998.

Davidson, Basil. *The Lost Cities of Africa*. Boston: Little, Brown, 1959.

Dearden, Seton. *A Nest of Corsairs: The Fighting Karamanlis of Tripoli*. London: John Murray, 1976.

Denham, Dixon, and Hugh Clapperton. *Narrative of Travels and Discoveries in Northern and Central Africa in the Years 1822, 1823, and 1824 by Major Denham, Captain Clapperton and the late Doctor Oudney*. London: John Murray, 1826; Darf Publishers reprint, 1985.

Durou, Jean-Marc. *Sahara: The Forbidding Sands*. New York: Harry M. Abrams, 2000.

Fisher, Sir Godfrey. *Barbary Legend: War, Trade and Piracy in North Africa, 1415–1830*. Oxford: Clarendon Press, 1957.

Forbath, Peter. *The River Congo*. New York: Harper & Row, 1977.

Forbes, Rosita. *The Secret of the Sahara: Kufara*. New York: George H. Doran Company, 1921.

Furlong, Charles Wellington. *The Gateway to the Sahara*. London: Chapman and Hall, 1909.

Gautier, E. F. *Sahara: The Great Desert*. New York: Octagon Press, 1970.

Gibb, Sir Hamilton A. R., ed. *The Travels of Ibn Battuta, A.D. 1325–1354*. Cambridge: published for the Hakluyt Society by Cambridge University Press, 1958, vol. 1; 1962, vol. 2.

Goudie, Andrew S. *The Search for Timbuktu*. Oxford: Clarendon Press, 1986.

————. *Great Warm Deserts of the World*. Oxford: Oxford University Press, 2002.

Graham, Henry Grey. *The Social Life of Scotland in the Eighteenth Century*. London: Adam & Charles Black, 1899; reprinted 1964.

Gramont, Sanche de. *The Strong Brown God*. Boston: Houghton Mifflin, 1976.

Hafsa. *Desert Winds*. New York: Century, 1927.

Hallett, Robin. *Africa to 1875: A Modern History*. Ann Arbor: University of Michigan Press, 1970.

————. *The Penetration of Africa; European Exploration in North and West Africa to 1815*. New York: Praeger, 1965.

————, ed. *The Niger Journal of Richard and John Lander.* London: Routledge and Kegan Paul, 1965.

————, ed. *Records of the African Association, 1788–1831.* London: Thomas Nelson and Sons Ltd, 1964.

Hanum, Princess Djavidan. *Harem Life.* New York: Dial Press, 1931.

Hatch, John. *The History of Britain in Africa.* New York: Praeger, 1969.

Herodotus. *The Histories.* Translated by George Rawlinson. New York: Alfred A. Knopf, 1997.

Hibbert, Christopher. *George IV, Regent and King, 1811–1830.* New York: Harper & Row, 1973.

Holmboe, Knud. *Desert Encounter.* New York: G. P. Putnam's Sons, 1937.

Jackson, James Grey. *An Account of Timbuctoo and Housa.* London: 1820; Elibron facsimile reprint, 2003.

Jefferson, Thomas. *Thomas Jefferson's European Travel Diaries.* Edited by J. M. Morris and P. Weene. New York: Stephanus Sons, 1987.

Kamm, Josephine. *Men Who Served Africa.* London: George G. Harrap, 1957.

Laing, Major A. G. *Travels in the Timanee.* London: John Murray, 1825; Elibron facsimile reprint, 2002.

Lander, Richard. *Records of Captain Clapperton's Last Expedition to Africa.* 2 vols. London: Frank Cass & Co., Ltd., 1967 (facsimile reprint of the 1830 edition).

Lecky, William E. H. *History of European Morals from Augustus to Charlemagne.* New York: G. Braziller, 1955.

Lister, R. P. *The Travels of Herodotus.* London: Gordon & Cremonesi, 1979.

Lloyd, Christopher. *Mr. Barrow of the Admiralty: A Life of Sir John Barrow, 1764–1848.* London: Collins, 1970.

Lupton, Kenneth. *Mungo Park the African Traveler.* New York: Oxford University Press, 1979.

Lyon, Captain G. F. *Travels in Northern Africa.* London: John Murray, 1821; Frank Cass reprint, 1966.

Maugham, Robin.* *The Slaves of Timbuktu.* New York: Harper & Brothers, 1961.

Moorehead, Alan. *The Blue Nile.* London: Hamish Hamilton, 1962.

————. *The White Nile.* London: Hamish Hamilton, 1960.

Moorhouse, Geoffrey. *The Fearful Void.* New York: J. B. Lippincott, 1974.

Newton, Arthur Percival. *Travel and Travellers of the Middle Ages.* New York: Alfred A. Knopf, 1926.

Norwich, John Julius. *Sahara.* New York: Weybright and Talley, 1968.

O'Brian, Patrick. *Joseph Banks: A Life.* Boston: David R. Godine, 1993.

* Robert Cecil Romer Maugham, Second Viscount Maugham of Hartfield, published his novels and nonfiction under the pen name "Robin Maugham." The nephew of W. Somerset Maugham, he died in 1981.

Park, Mungo. *Travels into the Interior of Africa*. London: Eland Books, 1983 (facsimile reprint of the first edition).

Penzer, N. M. *The Harem*. London: Spring Books, 1965 (reprint, with a new preface, of the 1936 edition published by George C. Harrap).

Piccioli, Angelo. *The Magic Gate of the Sahara*. Translated by Angus Davidson. London: Methuen & Co., Ltd., 1935.

Porch, Douglas. *The Conquest of the Sahara*. New York: Alfred A. Knopf, 1984.

Powell, E. Alexander. *In Barbary*. New York: Grosset & Dunlap, 1926.

Proceedings of the Association for Promoting the Discovery of the Interior Parts of Africa. London: printed for T. Cadell, in the Strand, 1791; Elibron fascimile reprint: 2004, Adamant Media Corporation.

Riley, Captain James. *Sufferings in Africa*. New York: Lyons Press, 1965 (reprint of 1817 edition).

Rodd, Lord Rennell. *People of the Veil*. Oosterhout, Netherlands: Anthropological Publications, 1970 (reprint of 1926 edition).

Saad, Elias N. *Social History of Timbuktu*. Cambridge: Cambridge University Press, 1983.

Scott, A. MacCallum. *Barbary*. New York: Dodd, Mead and Company, 1921.

Smyth, William Henry. *The Mediterranean*. London: J. W. Parker & Son, 1854 (the only copy available to me was on microfilm).

Tooley, R. V. *Collectors' Guide to Maps of the African Continent and Southern Africa*. London: Carta Press, 1969.

Trench, Richard. *Forbidden Sands*. London: John Murray, 1978.

Tuckey, J. K. *Narrative of an Expedition to Explore the River Zaire*. London: John Murray, 1818; Frank Cass reprint, 1967.

Tully, Richard. *Letters written during a ten years' residence at the Court of Tripoli*. 1816; reprinted with an introduction by Seton Dearden, London: Arthur Barker Ltd., 1957.

Villiers, Marq de, and Sheila Hirtle. *Sahara: A Natural History*. New York: Walker & Company, 2002.

Ward, Philip, *Tripoli: Portrait of a City*. New York: Oleander Press, 1969.

Ward, W. E. F. *The Royal Navy and the Slavers*. New York: Pantheon Books, 1969.

Welch, Galbraith. *The Unveiling of Timbuctoo*. New York: Morrow, 1939.

Wellard, James. *The Great Sahara*. New York: E. P. Dutton, 1965.

Williams, Harry. *Quest Beyond the Sahara*. London: Robert Hale, 1965.

Worger, William H., Nancy L. Clark, and Edward A. Alpers. *Africa and the West*. Phoenix, Ariz.: Oryx Press, 2001.

Young, D. M. *The Colonial Office in the Early Nineteenth Century*. London: Longmans, 1961.

ILLUSTRATION CREDITS

THE REPRODUCTIONS OF the large continental maps of Africa by Blaeu and Hall were made from originals in the author's collection. The maps of Tripoli Harbor and the "Tripoli Route" are reproduced courtesy of the British Library, London. The portraits of Alexander Gordon Laing, Lord Bathurst, Sir Joseph Banks, Hugh Clapperton, Richard Lander, Sir John Barrow, and Dixon Denham are in the collections of the National Portrait Gallery, London, and are reproduced here by permission. The portraits of Mungo Park and René Caillié appeared originally as steel engravings in the frontispieces of their respective books. The hand-drawn map of Laing's route from Tripoli to Ghadames, the drawing of the English Garden, and E. W. Bovill's map of Laing's journey from Tripoli to Timbuktu are reproduced with permission of the Hakluyt Society and Cambridge University Press. The photograph of "the Castle" appeared originally in Angelo Piccioli's 1935 *The Magic Gate of the Sahara*, published in London by Methuen and Company, and is reproduced here by permission. The reproductions of the steel engravings of Aney Mountain, Lake Chad, El Kanemi, Barca Gana, the Fulani lancer, the woman of Sokhna, and the city of Kano are taken from Dixon Denham's account of the Denham, Oudney, and Clapperton expedition, published by John Murray in 1825. The drawing of Timbuktu is from Caillié's 1830 book. The engravings of the slave caravan and the Tuareg warrior appeared originally in Lyon's 1825 account. The photograph of Laing's tiny coffin appeared originally in Bonnel de Mézières's 1912 monograph.

INDEX

————◆◆◆————

Entries in *italics* refer to captions